"David and Stephen have once again demonstrated the beauty and power of fraternal collaboration in their newest book, *Wild Things*. If I didn't know otherwise, I would assume these two guys were granddads, not young dads, when I consider the depth of wisdom and breadth of practical applications captured between the covers of this volume. How I wish I'd had this book when my son was younger, yet the same principles of loving well are applicable from generation to generation. If you want hope and not hype, buy this book. It is a joy to unequivocally endorse it, and I look forward to putting it in the hands of many dads, and moms as well."

—SCOTTY SMITH, founding pastor, Christ Community Church, Franklin, Tennessee

"As a pediatrician, I see parents every day wrestling with how to understand and guide their sons. If you're looking for practical parenting skills, these pages are filled with sound advice. The authors break down each stage of a boy's journey, and the book is filled with effective, simple tips that you can implement now. This is one of the best parenting resources I've seen."

— DR. LINDA BRADY, pediatrician, Nashville

"I loved this book! As a single mom for the past seven years, I couldn't wait to dive into Stephen and David's timely work. This mom of two wild things and two softer things needed their road map and driving instructions for the dangerous journey we are traveling. Bless you both for the wisdom you have given to me. May all our boys be nurtured and loved until they are the honorable men God intended for them to become."

— ANGELA THOMAS, speaker and best-selling author of *My Single Mom Life*

T0275193

"These two men are deep with an honesty that touches the heart without being sentimental. I am many years older, but not wiser; they simply offer truth that transforms my passions so that I walk away wanting to know God and amazed that he knows me."

— DAN B. ALLENDER, PH.D., professor of counseling at Mars Hill
Graduate School and the author of
How Children Raise Parents

"God has entrusted a unique and powerful gift to David Thomas to understand the complex language of a boy's heart and to help interpret it for those of us who love and lead boys. This is an important book about a very important subject."

— STEVEN CURTIS CHAPMAN AND MARY BETH CHAPMAN

"David Thomas is a godsend! I cannot express how valuable he has been to the life of my son. His compassion and love for children is overwhelming. I know that this book will impact parents and children like no other. This is a must-read for every parent."

— SARA EVANS, recording artist

WILD THINGS

the art of nurturing boys

STEPHEN JAMES and **DAVID THOMAS**

TYNDALE
MOMENTUM®

The Tyndale nonfiction imprint

Visit Tyndale online at tyndale.com.

Tyndale, Tyndale's quill logo, Tyndale Momentum, and the Tyndale Momentum logo are registered trademarks of Tyndale House Ministries. Tyndale Momentum is the nonfiction imprint of Tyndale House Publishers, Carol Stream, Illinois.

Wild Things: The Art of Nurturing Boys

Designed by Jessie McGrath

Edited by Dave Lindstedt

Published in association with the literary agency of Greg Daniel Literary Group, LLC, Nashville, TN.

For information about special discounts for bulk purchases, please contact Tyndale House Publishers at csresponse@tyndale.com, or call 1-855-277-9400.

Library of Congress Cataloging-in-Publication Data

James, Stephen.
    Wild things : the art of nurturing boys / Stephen James and David Thomas.
        p. cm.
    Includes bibliographical references.
    ISBN 978-1-4143-2227-8 (sc)
1. Parenting—Religious aspects—Christianity. 2. Parent and child—Religious aspects—Christianity. 3. Boys—Religious life. I. Thomas, David. II. Title.
    BV4529.J3545 2009
    248.8′45—dc22   2008037976

Printed in the United States of America

27   26   25   24
22   21   20   19   18

To all the boys and men who have allowed us to

travel with them on their dangerous journeys.

~

TABLE OF CONTENTS

"Wild Thing!"

*The night Max wore his wolf suit ...
his mother called him "WILD THING!"*

MAURICE SENDAK, *Where the Wild Things Are*

A friend of ours tells the story of the family dog he had growing up. His name was Midnight (the dog, not our friend), and he was a mutt of indeterminate ancestry from the local animal shelter. From what they could tell, he was part black Lab, part English sheepdog, and part collie. As you might imagine, Midnight was big, black, and shaggy.

As our friend tells it, he and his brother had been assigned the task of repainting the white picket fence that ran around their rather large front yard. It was the first week of summer break, and this chore seemed like unusually cruel punishment by the standards of an eleven-year-old boy and his thirteen-year-old brother, given that they hadn't done anything wrong.

Their parents had left for work that day with the expectation that the fence would be painted by supper. By late morning, the sun was beating down, and the boys were bored silly with only half the job done. Their frustration had turned into griping about the task at hand and discussing how they would spend the rest of the summer once the work was completed. Midnight, minding his own business, was curled up in the only shade he could find, under the porch.

Shortly before noon, our friend had what he thought was an entertaining idea. "You know what would be funny . . . ," he said.

Armed with their paintbrushes and a can of white paint, the brothers ambushed Midnight. Before the dog knew what had happened, he looked like Pepé Le Pew's big brother. "A giant skunk dog," our friend recalls. As the two brothers were admiring their handiwork, their father came home on his lunch hour to check on their progress. What he found was a half-painted fence, a frightened black (and now white-striped) dog running around the yard, and his sons rolling on the lawn in laughter. "There were," as our friend puts it, "great reparations to be paid."

The award-winning children's book *Where the Wild Things Are*, by Maurice Sendak, tells a similar story of a mischievous and imaginative young boy named Max, who one evening storms through his home in a wolf costume, "making mischief." In short order, he builds a tent with a blanket, lynches his teddy bear, chases the dog with a fork, and threatens to eat his mother. As punishment, Max is sent to bed without supper. But that's only the beginning of the story. Off in his room, Max creates a world in which he explores distant lands, encounters strange monsters, and becomes a king. Eventually, he returns home to where he is loved and a warm dinner awaits him.

The themes in Sendak's classic children's tale paint a great picture of the world of boys—how they are made, what they are made for, and what they need. Every boy faces a long and intricate journey on his way to becoming a man. This journey encompasses physical, emotional, and spiritual changes, and it takes place as much, or more, on the inside as it does on the outside. The journey is perilous, costly, and fraught with uncertainty.

The Treacherous Journey

Plato, the ancient Greek philosopher, writes, "Of all animals, the boy is the most unmanageable, inasmuch as he has the fountain of reason in him not yet regulated."[1]

Can we get an *amen*?

As a general rule, boys are more difficult to rear than girls. They are tougher to parent. They are tougher to teach. They are tougher to relate with. They are tougher to mentor and coach. The wise and witty journalist G. K. Chesterton said it this way: "Boyhood is a most complex and incomprehensible thing. Even when one has been through it, one does not understand what it was. A man can never quite understand a boy, even when he has been the boy."[2]

Though we may never fully understand boys, and it will never be our goal to try to tame them, we can do a better job of coming alongside them and helping them on their treacherous journey to becoming men.

That's why we've written this book. *Wild Things* illuminates the world of boys and the role of the adults in their lives. If you're a parent, educator, counselor, or mentor, it will give you important insights for guiding the boys you love on their journey toward manhood. Anyone involved in the life of a boy must take this calling seriously—if you care about boys and their future.

Wild Things is built on a few basic but very important ideas:

- All children are a divine gift. Boys are no exception.
- Boys bear a unique image of our wild, playful, and imaginative Creator.[3]
- How boys are nurtured directly affects who they will grow into as men.
- How boys are designed often requires a different approach from what we would take with girls, if they are to find their way and mature into noble men.
- Boys are (more than) a little squirrelly—but a whole lot of fun.

There is a lot that goes into the makeup of a boy: physiology, genetics, culture, emotions, spirituality, snips and snails and puppy dog tails, and so on. Boys are very complicated—much more complicated than we often give them credit for being. It would be impossible to exhaustively examine every possible aspect of boyhood, but in *Wild Things* we tackle as many as we can, and enough to give you some solid guidance in your role as parent, teacher, or mentor to boys. We've done our best to put together a comprehensive look at boys that will inform and prepare you to engage the boy(s) in your life with wisdom, love, and confidence.

Art and Nurture

We hope you've taken note of the subtitle for *Wild Things*—"The Art of Nurturing Boys." This isn't just a random phrase or something dreamed up by our publisher's marketing department.

Instead, it captures, in just a few words, the essence of our approach to working with boys. Though much of our experience comes in clinical settings as counselors—or in our own homes— we've learned that raising boys is more of an art than a science. Certainly, there are principles we can apply to the challenge of developing boys into men, but it takes a certain amount of finesse and creativity to do it well.

One of the ways this book may be a bit different from other books about boys is that we approach the material with teachers' hearts. We don't offer a black-and-white list of dos and don'ts for rearing boys; instead, we create a framework that will help you engage, guide, and walk with the boy you love throughout his life. Nurturing boys is far too complex to be boiled down to a bullet list of dos and don'ts. It's much more personal, individualized, and artistic.

That's why we prefer the term *nurture* over words such as *mold*, *shape*, or *sculpt*. *Nurture* means "to give tender care and protection to a child, . . . helping [him or her] to grow and develop; to encourage somebody or something to grow, develop, thrive, and be successful."[4] Nurturing is an important concept when we consider how to engage with boys, as opposed to "instructing" or "teaching"—which are important, too, but not enough. We know it's nitpicky, but concepts such as "molding," "shaping," or "sculpting" suggest that we actually have the ability to *make* boys turn out the way we want them to. That's arguable. And even if we could, is that what's best for them? That is why we think "nurturing" is a better mind-set. It first takes into account who a boy is created to be, and then looks secondarily at our role as influencers on that design. In the classic nature vs. nurture debate, we like to say, "It's our job to nurture the nature." Boys need us first to recognize who they are. Then they need the help of wise and committed adults in navigating their way from boyhood to manhood.

Three Perspectives

There are many ways to define what a boy is and what a boy needs. Thus, we have divided *Wild Things* into three parts, each one looking from a different perspective at what it means to nurture boys. Together, the three parts offer an integrated, holistic view.

Part 1, "The Way of a Boy," takes a largely developmental view of boys from conception to manhood. It provides a chronological and topographical road map of the journey a boy must take on his way to manhood. Part 2, "The Mind of a Boy," looks closely at male neurology and physiology. We touch on areas such as brain development, learning styles, and other key physiological issues that affect the life of a boy. Part 3, "The Heart of a Boy," addresses the emotional, spiritual, and moral development that a boy needs if he is to become a strong, wise, and good man.

Throughout the book, we have included sidebar articles with helpful tips, important reminders, and excellent resources for parents, educators, mentors, and coaches. We also provide a lot of real-life examples—both personal stories and stories about boys and men we have worked with in our counseling practices.[5]

Your Guides for the Journey

Unless you've already read our other books, you might be wondering who we are and why we're writing this book. For starters, we are both practicing counselors who have made the nurturing of boys a large part of our life's work. Though we have somewhat different training and areas of expertise, we share a common calling and a profound passion for boys and the men they become.

More importantly, we both have skin in the game—with five sons among the seven children between our two families. So this topic is deeply personal for us as well.

Through his clinical practice, individual therapy, group counseling, and summer camps at Daystar Counseling Ministries in Nashville, David has worked with thousands of boys and their families as they have struggled with the issues and challenges of boyhood.[6]

Stephen works as a private-practice psychotherapist, teaches classes on marriage and parenting, and has served as a pastor.

Much of the content of this book was developed from a class called Nurturing Boys that David regularly teaches. Over the past several years, he has helped hundreds of parents, mentors, and educators grapple with the difficult task of living with boys, guiding them during their formative years, and launching them into manhood.

If you are a parent or a grandparent, we thank you for caring enough (or maybe you're simply desperate enough) to better prepare yourself for what the boys in your life need. If you are a teacher or a youth worker, we applaud you for going the extra mile to continue to grow in your ability to do your job well.

Our combined experience confirms that boys are indeed a different breed. And if we as parents, teachers, and mentors are to serve boys well, we must engage with them—and with the challenge of nurturing them—with as much of our hearts and minds as possible. To do that, we must be willing, able, and prepared to venture into the far-off land that Maurice Sendak dubbed "where the wild things are."

Part 1

The Way of a Boy

"And now," cried Max, "let the wild rumpus start!"

MAURICE SENDAK, *Where the Wild Things Are*

One evening, I (Stephen) was giving my three-year-old twins a bath when I stepped out for a second to answer the phone. I was gone for less than a minute when I ran and got the phone. As I was hurrying back down the hall, I heard laughter and then a loud *thump!* When I raced into the bathroom, I was shocked by what I found: a seventy-pound mound of preschool flesh flopping on the tile floor like two mackerel on the deck of a fishing boat. Henry and Teddy were engaged in a no-holds-barred wrestling match. Water and bubbles were everywhere. Walls. Ceiling. Vanity. Mirrors. Light fixtures. Door. From where they lay, the boys looked up at me with delight in their eyes and squeals of joy.

"Daddy, watch!" one of them exclaimed. "We have big fun!"

In the brief moment that I was away retrieving the phone, my twins had created a SeaWorld–quality water park right there in the bathroom.

In *Where the Wild Things Are*, Maurice Sendak captures well the wildness and imagination of boys. Soon after being confirmed as king of the wild things, Max declares an edict to the beasts: "Let the wild rumpus start!" What ensues is a wild dance and frolic, including howling and swinging and prancing, reminiscent of a tribal war dance mixed with a punk-rock mosh pit. Sendak got it mostly right. All that was missing were the bathtub, water, and soapsuds.

What's Normal

For as long as we have been working with boys and parents of boys, we have been asked the question, "Is this normal?" hundreds, if not thousands, of times. Usually, what is behind the question is a deeper, scarier concern that parents have: "Is *my* son normal?" Most often, the answer is yes, and much of the parents' fears and concerns can be allayed by good information and education. But whenever boys are in the equation, you may have to broaden your definition of *normal*. (This is especially true for women.) Once you have a boy in your life, things you never dreamed of become normal.

With boys, you will find yourself saying things and hearing things that you never thought needed to be said or heard. Like the night my (Stephen's) wife had to insist to our two-year-old twins that "sixteen times is really enough washing to get your penis clean." Or the day one of my sons screamed from the bathroom, "Guys! Come see how big my poop is!" As a caregiver to boys, you will be blown away by how many thousands of times you will have to say things such as, "Please keep your feet to yourself" or "Don't lick the floor" or "Hey! Farting is for private."

Boys are quite their own creatures, yet there's much about the way they respond to their environment, themselves, and others that can be explained by the various stages of their development. Understanding how boys develop is foundational to our ability to care for our boys well, and it can diminish our worries and concerns as our boys pass through the different stages. (It also can help us sound really smart at PTA meetings.)

The progression of a boy from infant to twentysomething is much more fluid than solid, and far more gray than black-and-white. Even to say that the categories overlap would be too concrete. It's much more accurate to look at a boy's development as a spectrum (like a rainbow), with all the colors bleeding into and through the rest.

It's important to understand male development in these flexible and fluid terms, because what's present and needed in a boy's life at age two doesn't disappear by the time he's five or twelve; rather, it becomes part of a bigger whole. It's not uncommon to find toddler-typical behavior present in adolescents (or forty-year-old men, for that matter). Equally so, there are several identity-forming stages within the span of boyhood that are similar to one another.

What a boy needs at age three (boundaries, for example) doesn't go away as he gets older. It's just that he might need more of something else at age five (such as redirection) or ages nine or ten (involvement).

The older a boy gets, the more he needs from his caregivers. This perspective is different from that held by other, more traditional, views of child development that assume or suggest a boy needs less from his parents as he becomes a teenager and then a man. In actuality, the older a boy gets, the more complex and dynamic his needs become. His needs move from primarily physical (birth to age three) to increasingly more relational, emotional, and spiritual.

This is not to say there isn't a progression from one stage to the next, because there is. And it's our job as caregivers to help our boys move from one stage to the next. It's important to understand that what a boy gets, or doesn't get, at one stage of his development will directly affect how well he will transition to the next stage. The reason that so many men struggle relationally, emotionally, and spiritually is not a lack of intelligence or morality. It's the effects of having not reached key developmental milestones; of being rushed through one stage to another; or of simply skipping entire stages altogether. Here's how John Eldredge puts it in *The Way of the Wild Heart*:

> Each stage has its lessons to be learned, and each stage can be wounded, cut short, leaving the growing man with an undeveloped soul. Then we wonder why he folds suddenly when he is forty-five, like a tree we find toppled in the yard after a night of strong winds. We go over to have a look and find that its roots hadn't sunk down deep into the earth, or perhaps that it was rotten on the inside, weakened by disease or drought. Such are the insides of Unfinished Men.[1]

Sadly, this condition is not uncommon. Every man is unfinished in some form or fashion. To one degree or another, we are all boys in men's bodies, dressed up and disguised with costumes of masculinity—Harleys or pickup trucks or bank accounts or families or careers. For some men, the developmental deficits are more severe than for others. The danger is that we might become "self-made," which is really the worst kind of man we could become, because it tempts us to rely on our own paltry resources and inhibits us from trusting others and God.

What Eldredge refers to as "unfinished," psychologists call "developmental lags." We believe that these "lags" are better understood as developmental *short circuits*, in which some part of a boy's wiring gets overloaded and shuts down. Fortunately, most boys find a way to rewire or compensate for the deficits.

Often, these developmental short circuits (when they're not physiological in nature) are caused by some kind of significant emotional or relational shift. For example, I (David) see a number of boys in my counseling practice whose families are in a shift of some kind. The most common shift is that of parents' separating or divorcing (which on the scale of shifts is more like an earthquake). I've also worked with several boys who have lost a parent to death (which on the shift scale is like California, after the earthquake, falling into the ocean). These are two of the most significant shifts a boy can experience, and the impact can either slow down or halt his emotional development or cause him to skip right over a stage and assume more authority or responsibility than he is prepared to handle.

When seismic shifts occur in a boy's life, our job as caregivers is to jump-start his development and help him play catch-up for any time he has lost. We may need to help him go back and rewire the important things that he should have experienced or acquired during those "shifted" stages. For some boys, this is a slow and painful process; for others, the journey is not as lengthy or as difficult. A lot depends on factors such as the support of family members, community resources, the child's level of emotional resilience, the circumstances surrounding the transition, birth order, age, and so on.

A shift doesn't have to be as traumatic as divorce or death to have a significant impact. It can be uniquely significant to the individual boy. For some boys, a move from one neighborhood to another can be a huge transition. For other boys, moving from one state to another doesn't register as a blip on the radar screen. Losing a game can be as traumatic as losing a family pet, depending on the surrounding factors and the boy in question.

A lag in physical growth is another common factor that can affect a boy's progression through the stages of development. Dealing with growth lags often requires the assistance of a physical or occupational therapist as a part of a team of individuals caring for the boy. Early intervention is always best. We have encountered too many parents of adolescent boys who observed some kind of lag early in the boy's life but assumed it would work itself out and never sought help. The outcome could have looked different had early intervention been a part of the equation.

Developmental short circuits and lags can be temporary or permanent. But they should all be monitored closely. If you sense that a boy in your care has slowed down, halted, backtracked, or skipped a stage in his psychological or physical development, get him the appropriate help. You may want to talk with a professional—such as a pediatrician, an educational consultant, or a school guidance counselor—or consider a consultation with a family therapist who specializes in boys and adolescents.

In the next five chapters, we provide some categories for understanding how boys progress on their developmental journeys.

- The Explorer (ages 2–4)
- The Lover (ages 5–8)
- The Individual (ages 9–12)
- The Wanderer (ages 13–17)
- The Warrior (ages 18–22)

What we have outlined here is an amalgamation of many other developmental theories, views, and opinions. We've tried to lay things out and explain them in a way that will provide some clarity. We also hope to offer you some signposts for identifying your boy's progress on his journey to manhood—and maybe help you stay a little saner, to boot.

We have assigned age ranges to each stage of development, but these are only loose parameters. Maybe you should repeat that last clause out loud, so that you're certain to hear it: *These are only loose parameters.* Each boy will take the journey to manhood at his own pace. Some will seem to race through the stages. Others will take it in fits and starts. And a few will meander along like . . . well, like a boy in a toy store, with no intention of ever leaving. It's our job as parents, educators, coaches, mentors, youth workers, and counselors to help our boys along the way by knowing where they are and by giving them what they need.

We're all familiar with boys who seemed mature or exceptional at an early age (emotionally, intellectually, or physically) only to be "average" by the time they reached high school. In our counseling practices, we have worked with boys who developed slowly for several stages and then suddenly "caught up" with their peers. Likewise, we have seen boys reach a particular stage and slow down for a season, only to pick up steam again later. It is far more important for a boy to embrace each stage as fully as possible than to be forced to fit into a fixed age bracket.

To help you make the best use of the information and fully benefit from part 1, we have divided each chapter into four sections:

1. The Lay of the Land
2. Who He Is
3. What He Needs
4. Putting the Principles into Practice

In the first section of each chapter, "The Lay of the Land," we will give you an overview of the developmental stage and a general picture of what boys are like at that point on the journey. The second part, "Who He Is," will address some key characteristics and features of boys at that stage of development. The third section, "What He Needs," will specifically address what a boy at that stage requires from those responsible for guiding him on his journey toward manhood. The final portion of each chapter, "Putting the Principles into Practice," will give you some practical direction for how to constructively engage with your boy at each stage of his development.

CHAPTER 1

The Explorer

(ages 2–4)

From the ages of two to four, three of our sons attended preschool together. When they were in Ms. Becky's four-year-old class, Witt and Baker (David's boys), and Stephen's son Elijah invented a game that they acted out on the playground. They called it "Star Wars," but it had nothing to do with Luke Skywalker, Han Solo, or Darth Vader, because the boys hadn't yet seen the movie series. What it did entail was our three sons terrorizing the other children on the playground—in particular a little girl named Lea. They would taunt her and shoot lasers from their fingers at her until she'd had enough. Then she would chase them, and they would run and hide.

Humorist Garrison Keillor paints an accurate picture of this unique aspect of boys:

> Girls . . . were allowed to play in the house . . . and boys were sent outdoors. . . . Boys ran around in the yard with toy guns going *kksshh-kksshh*, fighting wars for made-up reasons and arguing about who was dead, while girls stayed inside and played with dolls, creating complex family groups and learning how to solve problems through negotiation and role-playing.[1]

We all recognize that boys and girls are not the same. But what is the basis for these striking differences?

The Lay of the Land

The journey of boyhood actually begins before birth. Even while in his mother's womb, a boy is remarkably different from a girl. And these differences will have a great impact on every aspect of his life.

Dr. George Lazarus, associate clinical professor of pediatrics at Columbia University, points out that the differences between boys and girls are evident even in the blastocyst stage—one of the earliest stages of development.[2] At the fetal stage, testosterone levels in boys reach adult intensity, which influences the development of the male brain.[3] As early as the eighth week of gestation, boys are bigger than girls. On average, full-term boys weigh 131 grams (4.6 ounces.) more than infant girls in the United States, and the disparity just expands from there. By the time boys are a year old, the 131-gram difference has ballooned to almost 800 grams (28.2 ounces).[4]

The differences aren't just physical. It's probably no surprise that, from birth, boys are more active and wakeful than girls. Girls, on the other hand, show a greater aptitude for communicating and are more sensitive to relationships, compared to boys. At birth, all babies born in hospitals are given an Apgar score. This tool, used to evaluate a newborn's well-being minutes after birth, consists of five components: respiratory effort, heart rate, reflex irritability, muscle tone, and color. In preterm infant girls, Apgar scores are significantly higher than those of boys.[5] This suggests that girls are more sensitive and responsive earlier than boys are.

One study involving two- to four-day-old babies showed that baby boys spent 50 percent less time than baby girls holding eye contact with an adult. It has also been discovered that infant girls cry less often than boys when unhappy and that girls tend to comfort themselves by sucking their thumbs.[6] Anne Moir and David Jessel report in their book *Brain Sex* that in tests between baby boys and baby girls, the girls were more easily comforted by soothing words and singing. It seems that girls are better than boys at recognizing the *emotion* of speech even before they can understand language.[7]

From birth, both baby boys and girls like to grunt and gurgle. The difference is that girls prefer interacting with people, whereas boys are equally happy to chatter away at nearby toys or abstract geometric designs. The male brain is wired for activity; the female brain is biased toward personal connections.[8]

Before my (David's) daughter was born, some friends hosted a baby shower for us, and we received numerous gifts—everything from a Baby Bjorn carrying pouch to a year's supply of diapers in every size. One of the items we received was a kit containing every item a family would ever need for baby proofing their home—cabinet fasteners, outlet plugs, doorknob protectors, etc. I remember looking at the kit and thinking, *I had no idea our home was so dangerous.*

I remember finding that kit somewhere in the basement about six months after my daughter came on the scene. I brought it upstairs and then managed to lose it somewhere in the laundry room. (But at least it was now upstairs.) I found the kit again just after my daughter turned one, and I vowed to baby proof our home, as any responsible parent would. My daughter had long been crawling, exploring, and finding her way around the house. By this point, she was walking (or something like it), and what was interesting was that every time she found an object on the floor, she would make her way over to my wife or me to proudly share her new discovery. We called it toddler show-and-tell. It never occurred to her to put one of Connie's ponytail holders up her nose or stick paper clips in her ears. She was content to explore the object and then hand it over to one of us.

She often opened the kitchen cabinets, but she never attempted to drink the antibacterial kitchen cleaner or stick her finger in an electrical outlet. Despite being encouraged in our childbirth education class to post the number for poison control on the fridge, we never quite got around to it. We never mapped out the quickest route to the emergency room, and my daughter has never required a trip there. Though I'm certified in CPR, I've never needed to remember the ratio of breaths to compressions. Parenting my daughter has been a relatively safe and peaceful journey.

Her brothers, on the other hand, are completely different beasts. I don't remember how many months old they were before they learned to climb out of their cribs; I just remember waking to the sound of a loud *thud* followed by screaming. I don't remember which of my twins first pulled the blinds off the wall; I just know I've replaced the brackets on several occasions. I've lost count of how many times they've broken the toilet seat by slamming it down or yanking it off the screws. (I kid you not.) One of my boys had been in preschool only for a short time before the school called to say that he had bashed his head open and would likely need stitches.

I've replaced doorknobs, mirrors, cabinet hardware, clocks,

lamps, stereos, televisions, picture frames, bath faucets, consoles, refrigerator doors, kitchen appliances, dishes, glassware, bath towels, couches, ottomans, and chairs, and I've had the walls repainted—all before they turned five.

Who He Is: The Explorer

About as soon as they can walk and talk with some proficiency, boys move into what we call the Explorer phase. It's a time when they show a greater interest than girls in exploring the edges of their worlds. A boy's greater muscle mass helps him explore and range farther afield than girls. And boys make fewer trips back to the reassurance of their mothers. One bit of research really illuminates the difference between preschool boys and girls. Scientists performed a test in which a barrier was placed across the room separating a young child from his or her mother. The girls tended to stand at the center of the barrier and cry for Mommy to come and get them. The boys moved to the edge of the obstacle to see if there was a way around it. And some boys even tried to knock it down and climb over it.[9]

For my (Stephen's) oldest son, Elijah, this difference was abundantly evident. When he was born, Elijah entered a highly emotional and sensitive culture. He was brought home to parents who are both counselors, and a very caring older sister. But from the time he could toddle, Elijah was more at home in the dirt than on the asphalt. If we were walking on the sidewalk, Elijah would veer off into the mulch or mud that paralleled the pathway. Watching him walk on flowers and climb over mounds of muck, Heather and I joked that Elijah would go "off road" whenever possible.

In the Explorer stage, a boy's ability to form images and ideas in his mind—especially of things he has never seen or experienced directly—is powerful and fascinating. As Explorers, boys live in their imaginations as much or more than they do in "reality." Unable yet to separate fantasy from reality, they live in a fairy-tale world.

To his mother's dismay, all Elijah wanted for his fourth birthday was a laser gun. (Hadn't we learned that boys shouldn't play with toy guns?) But after Elijah had demonstrated multiple ways to create guns out of ordinary objects (such as a piece of bread at lunch or a stick in the yard), we acquiesced, and on his birthday he got a Star Wars Imperial Blaster. By the time Eli turned five, his room was full of swords and shields, superhero comic books, a toy bow and arrows, spaceships, laser guns, cannons, and photon blasters. With little encouragement (and sometimes outright discouragement) from his parents, Elijah became caught up in the epic struggle between good and evil, and almost every aspect of his play reflected the hunger for adventure and exploration.

There are some key expressions of a boy in the Explorer stage that make this stage of development one of the most entertaining and challenging for parents. Explorers are simultaneously delightful and demanding. Their moods swing on a dime, and nothing compares to the joy that overcomes them when they make a new discovery. Boys who are in the Explorer stage are *active, aggressive, curious,* and *self-determined.* Let's take a closer look at each of these characteristics.

ACTIVE

Explorers are bundles of energy. Like little Energizer bunnies, they keep going and going and going. That cute little infant or toddler you once could hold for hours on end is now a squirmy, fidgety, active ball of motion. As parents and caregivers, we spend much of our time chasing Explorers around, up, down, over, and through.

When it comes to discipline, Explorers are often stubborn learners. There's good reason for this. The Explorer's brain secretes less serotonin than the brain of a similar-age girl. Among other things, serotonin works as an impulse-control agent and is responsible for inhibiting some of the aggressive effects of testosterone.

Afton, the son of one of my (David's) colleagues, is a classic Explorer. When he comes to the office, he climbs the chairs, the cabinets, the couches. During the holidays, he found the Christmas tree and attempted to scale it in an effort to pull off candy canes. One day, while his mom was returning a phone call, he made his way into the waiting room, scaled a chair onto an art table, and helped himself to a bucketful of permanent markers. Before he was corralled again, he painted some fascinating marks across his cheeks, forehead, and chin, like a miniature Apache war chief. When I saw what he had done, I bowed and saluted him like the great Native American chief he'd made himself out to be, and he smiled and laughed throughout the ritual, pleased with his efforts.

AGGRESSIVE

All the activity in an Explorer's life helps to fuel another common feature of this developmental stage: *aggression*. As strange as it sounds, boys in the Explorer stage demonstrate love and affection through wrestling, head butting, and sometimes even hitting. Now that's not to say they don't also hug, kiss, and cuddle, but it does show that aggression as a male form of intimacy starts early. (Ever see two grown men jump up and slam their chests into each other as a means of celebrating a touchdown? Classic residual Explorer behavior.)

The Explorer's aggression can be an emotional response and a means of communication. At times, by being aggressive, Explorers will signal to us that they are overstimulated. It's their way of telling the adults around them that the environment is simply too much to handle at a given moment—which is why tantrums are common with Explorers. Losing his grip can be an Explorer's way of saying, "I'm tired" or "I'm hungry."

CURIOUS

One of the more economical decisions made in my (David's) household started when my sons turned two. We began wrapping up old cell phones, calculators, and remote controls for them at Christmas and for their birthday. We tried the educational toy route, believe me. But regardless of what fantastic, cleverly designed gizmo we purchased and placed in front of them, my sons always found their way back to those common household objects. They would stare at the colored buttons, examining the various shapes and sizes, and then they'd punch away with force and delight. The exploration was considered a success if they could hit the side bar that changed the tone and volume of the ring.

Explorers are deeply curious. Investigation is the means through which they discover and engage the world around them. In the beginning of their development, boys are kinesthetic learners, meaning they need to touch and feel everything. In this phase, you'll hear things like "Let me see!" (which means "I want to hold it!") or the ever-popular "Why?" If you have ever walked with an Explorer through a store, then you have witnessed his need to touch, handle, and study every object he sees.

SELF-DETERMINED

Explorers are self-determined and desire to do things independent of other people. That's why parents at this stage hear so much of "Mine!" and "I can do it myself." Explorers need to be given an opportunity to do some tasks independently. If not, they will become more and more demanding.

Throughout this book, we will discuss a boy's hunger for purpose and power. When we afford him the opportunity to exercise power and control in certain areas that are safe (and minimal, in the big scheme of things), we honor a developmental and emotional need of his. When we deny him some opportunities and turn every exchange into a power play, we function in opposition to some of his basic needs.

Instead of telling Afton to stop climbing all the time, my colleague simply finds safe places within our office for him to exercise his need for being active as well as his desire for self-determination. She's a great mom, who understands that his need to be active, aggressive, curious, and self-determined are all part of his developmental journey.

What He Needs: Space and Structure

At his core, the Explorer has an energetic drive to understand how things work and how his world operates. Because Explorers are marked with specific characteristics (such as being active, aggressive, curious, and self-determined), they also come with a unique set of needs. Most of what an Explorer needs from his parents and his caregivers comes in the form of discipline, structure, and patience. For a boy to thrive as an Explorer, he requires *boundaries, open space, consistency*, and *understanding*.

BOUNDARIES

"Mine!" the three-and-a-half-year-old screamed. "Mine!" Arms flailing and feet stomping, he pushed and shoved his little sister. Then he fell to the floor, crying, in a full-blown tantrum.

Match an Explorer's activity level and aggression with his curiosity and determination, and you've got a lot on your hands. Because of where he is in his development, an Explorer is incapable of self-regulating. He needs help in setting limits. Perhaps the Explorer's number one need is that of boundaries.

Explorers will push their limits—they're explorers, after all—and this can be a trying part of dealing with boys at this age, but they do need boundaries. Boundaries help a boy feel safe and let him know what he can and cannot do. He depends on the external parameters that come from attentive, caring adults. It's in the context of these loving boundaries that a bond grows between a boy and his caregiver. This responsiveness from his caregiver helps the Explorer's brain develop the capacity for creating and maintaining healthy emotional relationships.

A common mistake that parents make with Explorers is to place unrealistic expectations on them to control their own behavior. Requiring high levels of self-control at this stage only sets up an Explorer for failure. This is *the one part* of the journey of boyhood where we need to expect less from boys and be pleasantly surprised when they self-regulate. We are not suggesting that you have no expectations, just realistic ones.

A common example of an unrealistic expectation is asking an Explorer to be quiet or still for an extended period of time. This is impossible for most Explorers. A more productive and reasonable way to set boundaries for an Explorer is to redirect his energy toward usefulness. For example, rather than say, "Stop hitting," say, "It's not okay to hit your sister, but it *is* okay for you to hit the tree with a bat." Here are a few more examples:

> "It's not okay to pound the coffee table with your Lincoln Logs, but it is okay for you to punch your pillow."

"I notice that you seem fidgety. Let's see how many times you can climb up and down the stairs in two minutes."
"You can't be that loud in the house, but you are free to go to the basement or the backyard and be as loud as you want."

Another unrealistic expectation for an Explorer is asking him to pick up his toys by himself. This is an impossible task for almost every boy at this stage. What an Explorer needs is for the adult to join him in the activity. One suggestion is to try making a game of it or turning it into a race against the clock. With an older Explorer, you can ask him to individually gather up one item—such as his blocks or a stack of loose crayons—and when that chore is complete, give him another task. As Explorers transition out of this stage, they become ready for more individual responsibility, but the primary responsibilities we have toward Explorers is to draw boundaries and guide and redirect their energy.

OPEN SPACE

As we've mentioned, Explorers are active and aggressive, which can be the cause of many behavioral issues with boys at this stage of development. As adult caretakers, we can head off a lot of potential problems (or broken lamps) by providing Explorers with plenty of open space. All boys, especially Explorers, need identified stations within the house and yard where it's safe to run, hit, kick, throw, spit, fart, dig, and jump. Boys need room to run and be wild. Explorers tend to get in the most trouble when they are in a confined space for an extended period of time. Preschool educators consistently say that rainy days are the kiss of death. They understand well the oil-and-water relationship of confined space and young boys.

My (David's) friend Micah is the mother of five. The first four are boys, and her youngest is a girl. Early in the game, Micah realized that in order to maintain her sanity, she needed a strategy for channeling the intensity, aggression, and activity involved in having that much testosterone under one roof. She implemented what she called "race time." Race time took place whenever the need arose—rain or shine, warm or freezing, day or night. She marched her little fellas out the front door to the steps, lined them up, and raised a flag. Then this little pack of boys would start running laps around the house, and Micah would count every time they crossed the sidewalk. When she wanted to mix things up, she placed obstacles on the sides of the house or in back. She could also require them to run backwards every other lap. The boys loved it—and Micah did too.

CONSISTENCY

Explorers are internally unstructured and inconsistent. Most Explorers have an attention span of only eight to fifteen minutes.

Explorers need a great deal of consistency from their parents. They thrive on structure and consistency. Preschool educators understand this, which is why they have children at this stage follow the exact same ritual every day. Music happens at the same time; recess is at the same time; stations are visited at the same time. They even visit the bathroom and wash their hands at the same time every day. This kind of consistency brings order and peace to the internal world of an Explorer.

Another way to be consistent with a boy in this bracket is to appeal to all of his senses. When you address him, make tactile contact (touch his back, shoulder, or the top of his head) while you issue the verbal command (and say his name with the instructions). Also, make visual contact by looking him in the eye as you speak. For example, "John [touch his shoulder], please go to the kitchen and put this in the garbage." You may be surprised how much more information sticks with an Explorer when you keep your requests short and make tactile and visual contact with him.

UNDERSTANDING

Last year, just after New Year's, I (Stephen) held a family meeting with my wife and our older two children to discuss some family changes for the upcoming year. We met during naptime for my twin two-year-old sons and talked about a variety of things, ranging from finances to ministry outreach, that affected our family. During the meeting, it became increasingly more difficult for Elijah (who was four at the time) to maintain focus, so I allowed him to walk around the room at different points and then report back when the conversation more directly involved him.

An Explorer needs for his adult caretakers to understand that his wiring differs from that of his female counterparts. Therefore, our expectations should be different. We've already mentioned how the female brain secretes more serotonin, making it easier for young girls to sit still and be less impulsive in their decision making. In chapter 6, we will discuss in greater depth the differences between male and female brain chemistry. But for now, suffice to say that boys need for us to understand the uniqueness of their wiring and to respond to them accordingly. For example, with an Explorer, we must be more concrete and directive in our communication. Boys get lost in a lot of verbiage. We've found that Explorers do better when we make our requests very specific, instead of using a lot of words and asking a lot of questions.

Likewise, Explorers are more responsive when we give them a command rather than ask a question. Instead of saying, "Now, where should the dirty clothes go once you take them off? Do they go on the floor or in the dirty-clothes basket?" we should simply say, "Put your dirty clothes in the basket." This approach sounds somewhat disarming, but it's actually quite useful. Training a young boy is not much different from training a dog.

Putting the Principles into Practice

Explorers need choices and responsibility, boundaries, and lots of opportunities to succeed. The following are some suggestions for how to put these principles into practice with an Explorer:

TIP 1: **Don't confuse him.** Explorers can't process abstract ideas, so be specific and set clear, realistic boundaries: "You can play on the computer for twenty minutes. I will set the timer on the oven. When it goes off, you have five minutes to finish what you're doing and turn off the computer."

TIP 2: **Limit his choices.** Explorers need a limited selection of things to do that will help them burn energy and give them a sense of success: "We are going to clean for fifteen minutes. Do you want to dust the furniture, sweep the floor, or pick up toys?"

When my (Stephen's) boys were this age, they loved to clean doorknobs. My wife would give them a disinfectant cloth, and away they would go—happy little guys. With Explorers, the point is not that they have to do a good job with the task at hand (they probably won't), but that you are setting the foundation of what you will expect at later stages.

TIP 3: Anticipate changes, and announce transitions in the daily routine.

"Today will be a little different. We are going to _____ today."

"You have five more minutes to play; then we are going to read a book and you are going to take a nap."

TIP 4: Set a few straightforward rules that everyone can consistently follow.

"We are kind. We don't hurt people or things."

"We always tell the truth. We do not lie."

"We are helpful and obedient. We are not disruptive or disobedient."

Have your boy define what being "helpful" and "obedient" means to him. Ask him to give you one example for each, to make sure he has a clear, age-appropriate understanding of the terms.

TIP 5: Demonstrate how you would like him to behave.

"Watch how carefully I turn the pages of the book."

"Let's see how gently we can love on baby brother."

TIP 6: Have your discipline make sense. It's important to use logical consequences that boys can connect to their actions: "Remember, I asked you not to throw balls in the living room. You can throw balls only in the playroom or outside. Because you threw the ball in the living room, I'm going to put it up in the closet for the rest of the day."

TIP 7: Give him space to roam. Turn him outside every day, regardless of the weather or temperature, and take him to a park or indoor playground at least once a week.

TIP 8: Model self-control and self-regulation in your words

and actions when you are frustrated or angry as a parent, teacher, or caregiver. An emotionally charged adult only provides more fuel to an already emotionally charged child. Instead of raising your voice to get an Explorer's attention, use a quiet, controlled, confident tone, and make eye-to-eye contact that communicates authority. This will convey that you mean business.

TIP 9: **Keep it short and simple.** Avoid lengthy instructions, and get to the point with as few simple words as possible: "It is time to put your trucks away, please."

One big mistake that parents make with Explorers is giving instruction in the form of a question. Don't say, "Do you want to eat lunch?" Say, "It's time to go eat lunch." And avoid ending your sentences with the phrase "Okay?"

TIP 10: **Praise him like crazy when he does something you like.** When you see your Explorer being successful, pour on the positive affirmation. Experiencing success and affirmation is one of the best motivators of future behavior for an Explorer. Select activities that can be successfully completed, and affirm everything positive.

"I saw how hard you were working. I really like that you are a hard worker."

"You were so kind to your baby sister when you gave her the bear."

CHAPTER 2

The Lover

(ages 5–8)

When my (Stephen's) son Elijah was five, we noticed a real shift in his personality. He went from being a wild and rambunctious toddler to being a wild and rambunctious preschooler—but he also began to exhibit a much more tender side.

His older sister had recently gotten a new toy called a Webkinz. If you aren't familiar with Webkinz, think of them as the Pet Rock for the Internet generation. Webkinz are little stuffed animals that come with a "secret code" that allows kids to access an online world in which they can care for their virtual pets, decorate their pets' living areas, and play various games and activities related to the world of Webkinz. Kids can also earn points (called Kinz-Cash) that allow them to "buy" stuff (pretend stuff, not real stuff) at the W Shop or Curio Shop. Whoever thought of this was an absolute genius.

When Emma Claire first got her Webkinz, Elijah showed little interest, except to throw the stuffed animal around like a ball. But as he got closer to turning five, he became more and more interested in his sister's pet. Eventually, in order to keep peace in the house, we got Eli his own Webkinz pet.

He proceeded to sleep with Spotty Dog, carried him to the grocery store, toted him to church, brought him to the dinner table, and took him along to the bathroom. Elijah also made sure that Spotty Dog was healthy (via Webkinz World's Dr. Quack) and regularly fed him his vegetables. It was pretty amazing, because I could barely get him to feed the real dog in the back-yard. But let that Webkinz dog get hungry, and we never heard the end of it.

The Lay of the Land

For boys leaving the Explorer stage, this sudden attention to detail and engagement with the personal side of his surrounding world is very typical behavior. Though boys still exhibit many Explorer characteristics (such as curiosity, activity, aggressiveness, and self-determination), something different begins to emerge around age five and continues to develop and expand for the next several years. Though boys still tend to play shooting games and remain very active, in this next stage of development they become more tender, more relationally driven, and more artfully expressive. For these reasons, we refer to boys in this stage as Lovers.

Who He Is: The Lover

Lovers are more sensitive to the feelings and needs of others around them. They tend to be cheerful, full of life, and enthusiastic. They are much more chatty than they were in the Explorer stage and enjoy having conversations with other children and adults. Lovers enjoy painting, drawing (instead of just coloring), and reading (instead of just being read to), along with other forms of self-expression, such as dramatic play and pretending with other children.

It's during this part of the journey that boys begin to experience their first spiritual awakening, which includes a growing awareness and curiosity about God. One day when my (Stephen's) family were riding in the car, Emma Claire started talking about heaven and how people refer to it as "up." Elijah (who was almost five at the time) chimed in and said, "That's better than it being down." My wife and I laughed because we thought it was some sort of reference to hell, but then Elijah added, "Cause China is down. Heaven is up." Then there was the time after church one Sunday when Elijah said to Heather, "Sin . . . is that the good guy or the bad guy?"

A Lover sees God in very matter-of-fact terms—mostly because his thinking is very concrete during this season of his development. He won't start thinking more abstractly until later in the game. At the Lover stage, a boy will ask questions like Where does God live? What does God look like? and Can I e-mail God? Similarly, concepts such as *death*, *heaven*, and *hell* are understood in practical ways. Lovers only loosely understand the finality of death, but they grasp that it's different from being alive (i.e., a dead person can't breathe, can't move, or can't watch TV). They understand that dead people are in heaven, and they think of heaven in very concrete terms, such as being "up in the sky" or "in outer space." Mostly they think of death as having to do with old age.[1]

Lovers are more articulate than Explorers with their feelings and often express them physically (especially anger, disappointment, and jealousy). With their growing verbal skills, Lovers learn to appreciate the power of "bad" words, and they especially like talking about and making noises that have to do with bodily functions, whether it's belching, farting, pooping, or peeing. Other characteristics that define Lovers are *tenderness, obedience, attachment to Dad*, and *competitiveness.*

TENDERNESS

My (David's) sons attended their first wedding when they were five years old. One of their favorite babysitters got married and invited all three Thomas kids to her wedding. The boys particularly enjoyed the reception (also known as "the part when you don't have to sit still and be quiet" or "the part when you get to run, dance, and eat cake"). Baker loved the idea of throwing rice at people, and Witt was entranced by a cake big enough to feed hundreds of people. On the drive home, we somehow ended up in a conversation about how most brides choose to change their last name, and my daughter started saying things like, "So my name would be Lily _____," and she filled in the blank with various class members' names, trying to make sense of the concept. Baker let her finish her thought and then said, "I want to marry Mommy anyway, and since we have the same last name, she won't have to change her name again."

I looked over at my wife, and she was feasting on his words—the tenderness of what he had spoken and the innocence in which it was delivered. My wife taught middle school students for six years, so she is well aware that when Baker turns thirteen, she will be the last woman on earth he would ever consider marrying. But, for now, she is enjoying being highly adored by her boys.

Some psychologists and educators call the first half of the Lover stage "the kinder years."[2] Great kindheartedness can emerge with boys in these years, especially when their basic needs are met and they are treated well. This explains why it's common to meet a kindergarten or first-grade teacher who has been teaching for twenty-plus years. That isn't to say that five- and six-year-old boys are always kind, because they certainly aren't; but they have the ability to be extremely kind, and they have a tenderness about them that the world may one day rob from them.

With their heightened emotional sensitivity, Lovers have an increased fear of the dark, loud noises, animals (such as strange dogs), and new or different people. Many parents have commented that their six- or seven-year-old son has all of a sudden become afraid of monsters in the closet, dark rooms, and thunderstorms.

As the Lover soon learns, being tender has its drawbacks— relationships can really hurt. And as the Lover becomes more grounded in this stage, he begins to express defensiveness to the outside world by being obnoxious, critical, and rude. Typically, a Lover has a lot to learn about the size of his britches. He can show impatience (especially toward younger siblings), and he can come off as a smarty-pants. He argues and talks back, and he tends to lose it with his parents (especially with Mom).

OBEDIENCE

A significant difference between Explorers and Lovers is that Lovers understand when they are right and when they are wrong.

(Early Explorers sometimes don't have a clue.) Often boys will continue to struggle with managing their impulsiveness during this stage, but there is no doubt that they know right from wrong. Numerous studies have shown that the more secure a boy feels with his parents, the more sense he has of right and wrong.[3]

I (Stephen) remember one of my sons asking, "Why are we taking food into the movie theater in Mom's purse when the sign on the door says, 'No Outside Food or Drink'?" As I stammered, trying to make up a reasonable excuse, he added, "Aren't we lying?" That was the last time we bought our Raisinets at Walgreens before a movie. As my son showed me that day, Lovers are very moral, with a clear and heightened sense of justice. They have a strong sense of right and wrong.

Psychologist Jean Piaget, who is famous for his work with children, concluded that youngsters determine bad behavior based on the amount of harm or damage caused. In his research, Piaget told children a story about a boy who accidentally broke fifteen glasses and a boy who broke one glass while trying to reach the cookie jar when his mother wasn't looking. He then asked the kids which one was "naughtier." Younger children judged the boy who broke the most cups as "naughty," because there was more damage done.[4]

This is a stage of following the rules. Generally, a Lover wants to be a "good boy" and wants to please his parents and teachers. Much of his self-respect derives from his parents' and teachers' opinions of him. During this stage of development, you may notice that boys are extra sensitive to having done wrong. Guilt and shame are hard feelings for a Lover to bear, and at times it almost breaks his heart.

A Lover measures his behavior, and the behavior of others, and judges it on the basis of those he looks up to in his life. For instance, if his parents don't smoke, he's likely to see smoking as bad. If they do, you may find him emulating his parents with play cigarettes. For Lovers, the posted speed limit is *the* speed limit, and they know it's wrong to speed. Many parents have experienced being chided by a child in the backseat, "You're speeding. You need to slow down, or you're gonna get a ticket."

This is why Lovers often struggle with things being unfair. It's common to hear them play the fairness card with comments such as, "She got a cookie. Why can't I?" But often, especially in the first half of this stage, Lovers will miss the point about what is fair and what isn't. "I want to go outside. It's not fair that it's raining."

Caregivers of boys at this stage must make the transition from giving specific, black-and-white instructions (which works well with Explorers) to helping Lovers see what it looks like to make healthy and useful choices. Instead of simply telling your boy not to eat cookies (as you did when he was younger), you should explain to him why eating cookies is unhealthy. Then you need to affirm that eating healthy foods is good. (This is especially difficult for dads like us, who believe healthy foods are indeed better to eat, but who don't necessarily follow our own advice on what to eat.)

ATTACHMENT TO DAD

When a boy hits the Lover stage, his attention begins to turn away from Mom, and he becomes more attached to Dad. Dad's now the man of the hour, and boys put a lot of effort into being just like Daddy. When my sons moved into the Lover stage, I (David) recall them hovering beside me for long periods of time, watching me shave or tie a tie. They wanted to sit with me and watch me assemble something or replace the locks on the front door.

Michael Gurian refers to this connection to Dad as "a

foreshadowing to a gender identity surge" to come.[5] It is crucial at this stage for fathers to spend time with their sons, and a father's investment in his son at the Lover stage will pay big dividends down the road. Because a Lover naturally craves a relationship with his father, this is a great opportunity for fathers and sons to build pathways for connecting with each other. It doesn't have to be extravagant. In fact, some of the best ways for fathers and sons to connect are by doing ordinary things together—running errands, working in the yard, going to a movie, doing the grocery shopping.

For single moms, the Lover stage is an important time to facilitate your son's relationship with his father (if Dad is in the picture) or with another significant male, such as a grandfather, uncle, or family friend.

Many dads choose to participate with their sons at this stage by coaching their teams. This is certainly a great way to connect with boys, but it's far from the only way. Spending a morning building with Legos or a Sunday afternoon hiking in the woods are also great ways for fathers and sons to spend time together.

COMPETITIVENESS

One striking difference between boys and girls is their competitiveness. Boys are far more competitive (some studies suggest as much as twenty times more), and this shows itself at a much earlier age.[6] For boys, it's during the Lover stage. Even though tenderness and relationship are hallmarks of this season in a boy's life, he still manages to be competitive. Go figure. Given the opportunity, boys will race to finish dinner first, brush their teeth first, and get in the car first. And once they're in the car, they'll compete to get the best seat.

I (Stephen) coached David's sons and my eldest son on the same soccer team—the Black Ninjas. The first season we were together, the boys were four and five years old. Despite it being a developmental league that year, with no official scores kept, the boys always knew at the end of a game which team had won, who had scored and who hadn't, and who had gotten to take the most throw-ins.

Parents, teachers, and coaches can use this competitiveness to their advantage at times. For example, you can turn a routine task (such as cleaning the boy's room) into a timed event, and he can try to beat last night's record.

It's worth noting that even though boys at this age are competitive, their competition is not aggressive. It's been shown that among groups of first- through third-grade boys, the boys will work to discourage individual physical aggression when they are engaged in a competitive game. Competition and cooperation are not mutually exclusive among boys at the Lover stage. Instead, as Eleanor Maccoby puts it, competition and cooperation are "woven into the same web of social relationships."[7]

What He Needs: Compassion and Restraint

The Lover's tender, relational heart, paired with his active competitive drive, can make him seem rather quirky at times. Because Lovers have such a strong mix of such disparate characteristics, they require a present and steady hand from the authority figures in their lives—and they really appreciate it too. If discipline, structure, and patience were established in the Explorer stage and consistently enforced throughout the Lover stage, by this time most of what a Lover needs from the adults in his life is mercy. If Explorers need mostly boundaries and reinforcement, what Lovers need is compassion and control. For Lovers to thrive, they need *reprieve, relationship, routine,* and *regulation.*

REPRIEVE

Like Explorers, Lovers need room to be boys. The challenge is that the Lover stage typically corresponds with the age when most boys start school. Unfortunately, most early childhood educational environments are not designed to help boys succeed. Think of the typical elementary school setting. Boys quickly learn that they will be required to sit still for long periods of time. Further, they will be required to self-regulate and self-initiate. They also discover that school draws heavily on written and oral expression (two areas in which girls tend to be stronger than boys at this age).

Often some of the most gifted boys have the most trouble in formal educational settings. History is full of famous examples, such as Albert Einstein, who struggled with his schoolwork.[8] Thomas Edison had a hard time concentrating during school and was eventually homeschooled by his mother.[9] Mohandas Gandhi was "often boisterous" and described school as "the most miserable years of his life."[10]

Much of the current research on boys and school recommends that boys wait to start first grade until they are six and a half. There's a real maturity lag in young boys in the Lover stage, compared to girls, and this is an obstacle to boys having a successful school experience in the early elementary years.[11] "Rather than start children too early and have them fail," writes Louise Bates Ames, former associate director of the Gesell Institute of Human Development, "we suggest giving those that need it an extra year before kindergarten or before first grade. The goal should be to ensure that at each stage they receive an education that is developmentally appropriate, rather than being pushed along on a rigid schedule."[12]

In the early years of school, boys need the reprieve of home that allows them to be who they are. They need a chance to come home, get a snack, and play outside before they can engage in homework or chores.

You will often find that boys in this stage will choose to go to their rooms for alone time. You may also notice that they have shorter fuses when it comes to siblings crossing into their personal space and belongings.

I (David) counseled a gregarious, creative eight-year-old boy who told me that he put a Keep Out sign on his door. "But," he said, "it didn't work. My four-year-old sister can't read, so I don't know what I was thinking. But she got it when I tied a string to my door that was hooked to a little can on top of my door that I filled with water. She opened that thing up like she always does, and I soaked her. It was perfect, except the can hit her on the head, too, and she went crying to my mom, of course. Now I have to leave the door wide open, and I'm back to square one."

We've noted the tendency of boys at this stage to be aggressive and wild. Let's add a caveat here: Some boys don't ever enjoy roughhousing. And most boys go through a season as Lovers where they think that other boys are too rough. Some boys go through a time of preferring dolls to weapons. These boys are not abnormal. In the prepubescent years, it is often damaging and shameful to force a boy into masculine stereotypes. More often than not, as he matures in the journey of boyhood, his internal development and the influence of culture will move him toward masculinity. (Having said that, it's important to pay attention to your boy's progress. If you notice that he's having problems with developing and maintaining same-sex peer relationships as he nears the end of the Lover stage, it's appropriate, and often necessary, to consult with a pediatrician or a trained therapist for adolescents.)

RELATIONSHIP

Boys need adult attention. Between the ages of five and eight, a window of development opens up in which boys begin needing and craving more one-on-one time with their parents. As we've mentioned, there is an intense search for male attention in this stage. It's a vital time for a boy to experience his father's presence—and especially his father's tenderness—both physically and emotionally.

Boys at this age really enjoy dinner as a family—not so much for the food, but for the fellowship. In fact, they'd rather be talking than eating their mac 'n' cheese. Mealtime is a chance for Lovers to hear stories and tell stories of their own. My (Stephen's) wife and I found that dinner is a great time to share stories of our lives. We tell our kids stories about when they were younger. We tell them stories about ourselves as children. We talk about what it was like before they came into our family. We also give them the opportunity to tell stories of their own lives—which they love.

Some friends of mine (David's) gave my wife and me a jar filled with colorful slips of paper as a Christmas present. It's one of the best gifts we've ever received. It's called the "Thomas Jar," and each colored slip contains a different question. The questions range from, What is your favorite book and why? to If you had a million dollars given to you, how would you spend it? We take turns drawing from the jar as a family. Sometimes we simply answer the question we've drawn, and sometimes we get to pick someone else at the table to answer the question we've drawn. My kids love the Thomas Jar, and it has become a rich, relational experience that is a part of our dinnertime routine.

ROUTINE

Speaking of routine, Lovers need a lot of it. In fact, they thrive on it. Don't believe us? Try substitute teaching in a K–4 classroom for a day and change the daily routine. We can't emphasize enough how important routine is for boys at this stage of their development. Lovers behave and learn best by repetition and consistency. Developing a regular routine for them is crucial for their happiness and well-being. For example, a Lover needs a predictable routine for getting ready for bed at night. Taking a bath or shower. Putting on his pajamas. Brushing his teeth. Going to the bathroom. Reading a book with Mom and/or Dad. Saying his prayers.

My (Stephen's) wife adopted an effective idea called the "Routine Chart," which she got from the book *Positive Discipline for Preschoolers*.[13] She asked our kids to tell her all the tasks involved in their daily routine (such as getting out the door for school in the morning and getting ready for bed at night). Once they had everything in the right order, they made pictures of each step in the routine and hung the chart where each kid could see it. When our kids got distracted from something they were supposed to be doing, all Heather had to do was ask, "What's next on your chart?"

The sense of accomplishment, independence, and self-satisfaction a boy experiences by progressing though his rituals serves to fuel his confidence and self-esteem in other areas of his life. Having a routine also gives a boy direction for his energy and trains him to think ahead of the immediate moment. Some areas of daily life where you may want to develop rituals and routines include mornings, after school, dinner, and bedtime.

REGULATION

As with Explorers, redirecting a Lover's energy and intensity toward something useful can be a very helpful technique. Along with continued redirection, boys in the Lover stage need a great deal of regulation. Though Lovers need affirmation and attention, they also need to have their unwanted behavior named and reprimanded. "Jimmy, you threw a rock at the car. That is destructive." Naming unwanted behavior helps a boy learn to control his impulsiveness. "Tanner, you took a cookie when I told you not to. That is deceitful." Notice how this feedback is straightforward, accurate, and specific. It's not belittling or personally attacking: "I can't believe you. You're so selfish." It's not expansive: "How many times do I have to tell you?" "You never listen when I talk to you." "I can't believe you did that." It's not nagging: "Oh, come on. Please . . ." Instead, effective feedback is short, firm, and measured.[14]

Frequently, after this kind of interaction, a boy will begin to cry or be sad and need a hug or other affection. If there is any sign of authentic remorse, most often no further discipline is needed, and it's time to immediately redirect his energy to a positive way of doing penance. "Tanner, come into the kitchen with me, and we'll make some more cookies together and give them to your grandfather. He will like that." He's been named, and he's been redirected. Job done.

If a boy doesn't show signs of remorse, it is imperative that you follow through with a natural consequence. "Tanner, when we have cookies for dessert tonight, you won't be able to have one."

You will save yourself many headaches down the road if you master what Michael Gurian calls the "Two-Times Rule." By this age, it is appropriate to expect a boy to follow through with an instruction by the second command.[15]

"Please go upstairs and pick up your toy cars before bed." A few minutes pass. "I've asked you to pick up your cars. I will not ask you again."

If these two times don't work, the boy's behavior needs to be regulated through a natural consequence—such as losing his cars for the next day, or sitting in a time-out, or losing his bedtime story privilege for a night. Some delay in response time is normal. After all, what boy at this stage is not going to get distracted? But a boy needs to learn to regulate his impulsiveness if he is going to successfully continue on his journey through boyhood.

Competition is one big area in which boys struggle with regulating their impulsiveness. They need help understanding that all of life is not about winning and losing. (If you've ever watched the coaches and parents at a Little League game, you know that a lot of grown men have the same problem.) Be prepared to redirect and regulate much of their behavior. Instruct them about the proper place for competition—in sports and games and belching contests, for example—and when it's not appropriate, which includes many aspects of life. Without this training, boys may establish relational patterns rooted in competition, which will end up sabotaging them in the long run. For an example of what this looks like in adult males, think about a man who has difficulty receiving input or accountability from other men because he is accustomed to always positioning himself on top of the pecking order. Or think about a woman you know who has said about the man in her life, "It's as if he 'won me over' and then wasn't interested in me anymore." Both are examples of what "life as a competition" looks like in adult males.

Putting the Principles into Practice

Lovers find themselves at a complex spot on their journey to manhood. Though they still exhibit many of the traits of Explorers (such as curiosity, activity, aggressiveness, and self-determination), these are balanced by more tender and relational characteristics. Our job as parents and caregivers is to nurture and help Lovers find the balance they need during this season. Here are some tips to help you nurture your boy during this stage.

TIP 1: **Give him lots of love and affection.** Boys at this stage desire and respond well to positive, healthy touch from trusted adults. Let him sit in your lap while you read to him, rub his back during nighttime prayers, or hold hands while on a walk.

TIP 2: **Reward good behavior.** Boys in the Lover stage are motivated by rewards (this is also true for dogs and adult males). Provide a lot of natural rewards when he does right. For example, if he takes his dinner plate to the sink on his own one night without being prodded, give him a high five and a hug. "Way to go buddy! You cleaned your place without having to be reminded."

TIP 3: **Get him involved.** Instead of trying to stuff your boy with rules and principles, find ways to involve him in the decision-making process. Be curious with him by asking engaging questions that rope him into the agenda at hand. "What do we need to do to get lunch ready?" Getting him involved will support the Lover's emerging sense of responsibility and personal power, while at the same time keep him moving in the direction you want him to go.

TIP 4: **Focus him outward.** The Lover stage is the time to introduce community service/outreach/volunteering into a boy's life. Show him that generosity and service are a vital part of what you want to be about as a family. When he reaches adolescence, he will desperately need opportunities to get outside of himself; so, by teaching him to regularly serve others during this stage, you will have laid a foundation for this type of experience, and it will be familiar to him later.

TIP 5: **Help him with hygiene.** Lovers often have problems with personal cleanliness. They may resist taking a bath, dislike getting their hair washed, and may not clean themselves well after going to the bathroom. As far as bathing goes, you don't have to require a daily bath. Most cultures don't bathe nearly as often as we do in the United States. You can decide how many times a week your boy should bathe, and then let him choose the days and times. You may also choose to let him decide between taking a bath or a shower. Regarding good bathroom habits, we're stumped. You may just have to tolerate some "skid marks." But somewhere around the time he starts middle school, he will become so self-absorbed with personal hygiene that it will make you sick.

TIP 6: **Take him to the movies.** This is a time to introduce your boy to some good movies. Don't turn the DVD player into a babysitter, but this is a great opportunity to watch some movies with your son and talk to him about the themes he is encountering. Ask questions like, What did you think when _____? or How did it make you feel when _____? He may not answer very thoroughly or articulately, but you are laying the groundwork for dialogue with him. You are also helping him take the beginning steps of connecting his inside world with the outside world. Ty Burr wrote a parents' guide for watching movies with your kids, called *The Best Old Movies for Families*; and Michael Gurian wrote an excellent book called *What Stories Does My Son Need?* Here are ten great movies for boys this age:

1. *The Adventures of Robin Hood* (1938)
2. *Stagecoach* (1939)
3. *The Wizard of Oz* (1939)
4. *Old Yeller* (1957)
5. *Miracle on 34th Street* (1947)
6. *The Ten Commandments* (1956)
7. *Where the Red Fern Grows* (1974)
8. *The Lion King* (1994)
9. *Babe* (1995)
10. *The Iron Giant* (1999)

For older boys in this stage (say, ages seven or eight), we suggest the following classics:

1. *It's a Wonderful Life* (1946)
2. *E.T.* (1982)
3. *The Princess Bride* (1987)

TIP 7: Encourage his imagination. Boys in this stage of development tend to love superheroes and are fascinated by the concept of superpowers. Much of their imaginative play will revolve around these two ideas. Be willing to put on a cape and let your son give you a superhero name, identify your powers, and direct the play. Don't be afraid to get ridiculous with this one. You were a kid once too. Remember?

TIP 8: Take him camping. This is a great time in your son's life to start camping if you haven't already. Camping is a fantastic family activity—it's all about relationship. If the outdoors is not your thing, plan a family campout in your playroom or den. Move the furniture back and pitch a tent. Roast marshmallows in the fireplace or over the grill. Sleep in sleeping bags and use flashlights after lights out.

TIP 9: Plan family game nights. Boys at this stage love games (and they need practice with winning and losing). Game nights encourage relationship and are an inexpensive way to spend time together as a family. Be sure to throw in some games that help boys develop emotionally and socially as well, such as the Ungame, Cranium, or charades.

TIP 10: Read *Parenting with Love and Logic*. This excellent book by Foster Cline and Jim Fay is one that every parent or educator should read by this time in their boy's development. It's an excellent resource for raising kids who are confident, self-motivated, and ready for the real world.

CHAPTER 3

The Individual

(ages 9–12)

The movie *A Christmas Story* is the tale of Ralphie Parker, a
nine-year-old boy growing up in the 1940s with Christmas
dreams of "an official Red Ryder carbine-action 200-shot Range
Model air rifle BB gun with a compass in the stock and a thing
which tells time." Ralphie plots various ways to obtain his prize,
but every grown-up he encounters tells him, "You'll shoot your
eye out!" In the course of the movie, Ralphie learns a lot about life
and growing up on the cold streets of northern Indiana.

In one scene, Ralphie and a pack of boys are on the school playground during recess. It's just before Christmas, and it's cold and
snowing. One of Ralphie's friends, Schwartz, is bragging about

how his dad said if you stick your tongue to a cold flagpole, it will stick. Another friend, Flick, doesn't believe it and challenges Schwartz, "You're full of beans, and so's your old man!"

In classic boy style, the conversation becomes increasingly competitive and begins to escalate in intensity:

Schwartz: Oh yeah?

Flick: Yeah!

Schwartz: Says who?

Flick: Says me!

Schwartz: Oh yeah?

Flick: Yeah!

The boys jab back and forth with challenges and retorts while Ralphie and the rest of the boys look on. Schwartz delivers double dares, double-dog dares, and eventually, in "a slight breach of etiquette," he goes right for the throat by issuing "the sinister triple-dog dare."

Not to be shown up, Flick takes the challenge and sticks his tongue to the flagpole, quipping, "This is nothin'."

And then, as Flick realizes that his tongue *is* stuck to the pole, he begins bawling and panicking. The crowd of boys stare in shock and in stunned speechlessness—afraid of not knowing what this means or what to do. In amazement, all Schwartz can manage is a baffled, "Jeez! It really works. Look at him. I can't believe that." Just then, the bell rings, and the boys obediently bolt for the classroom.

Flick cries to his friend, "Ralphie! Come back! Come back! Don't leave me! Come back!"

Ralphie, terrified in his own right, stops and looks back at Flick and says, "But the bell rang!"

Schwartz, in a moment of clarity, asks, "Well, what are we going to do?"

Ralphie responds, "I don't know. The bell rang."

The Lay of the Land

A Christmas Story provides a clear view into the life of a boy as he moves from the Lover stage further into the heart of boyhood. The movie captures well the heart of a boy at this stage: the mischief, the competition, the camaraderie, the prepubescent displays of machismo. Sometime between the ages of nine and eleven (remember, these are approximate ages), boys begin the transition from boyhood into adolescence. As they pass from childhood into preadolescence, they will experience a great deal of confusion— which is why they need a great deal of support and instruction from the adults in their lives.

This is an age of transformation. It's important enough in a boy's overall development that many developmental theorists refer to it as the second set of formative years. During this time, boys will begin experiencing significant shifts in their physical and emotional development that need to be met with information and support.

Bobby was in the sixth grade when he got called to the principal's office for the first time. For reasons that were never entirely clear, Bobby and his friends came up with the idea of greasing all the doorknobs in the school with Vaseline. The date was set, and the boys all came to school with jars of petroleum jelly in their backpacks. The plan was to pull the prank right after lunch, when they had an extra fifteen minutes before classes resumed. Each boy would slime as many doorknobs as he could.

It didn't take more than five minutes for Bobby to get caught. And it took even less time for him to give up the names of his coconspirators. By the time his parents made it to school, Bobby had figured out that he had really blown it and was in for some big trouble. He was so glad to see his mom and dad enter the school office, and it wasn't until then that he started weeping.

Like Bobby, boys begin to understand that they're not kids anymore around the time of fifth or sixth grade. Some of the energy and aggressiveness of the Explorer years has subsided, and the power and autonomy they began to embrace as Lovers is fully showing itself. Now they start to buck the system more and more.

Though boys at this stage are beginning to feel that boundaries and regulations are confining, they still need (and want) to maintain dependence on their caregivers for limits and a sense of purpose. They still need (and want) physical affection such as hugs, kisses, back rubs, cuddling, verbal praise, attention, and family time. They also need intentional emotional and spiritual guidance.

For those who care for boys, this can be a season of grieving as we watch the last remaining evidence of their childhood begin to pass away. At this stage, boys begin the transition into adolescence that will usher them into manhood. As this stage progresses, we'll see fewer glimpses of the little boys we knew and loved, and we'll get a taste of the young men they are becoming. This is why we call boys Individuals during this part of their journey through boyhood.

Who He Is: The Individual

By the time a boy is nine or ten years old, he is developing a stronger sense of self, and his search for masculinity has intensified.

He is starting to consider what it means to be a man. As the Individual passes from childhood into adolescence, the journey is about to get really rocky and more challenging. Emotionally, he is a wreck. Feelings like sadness, hurt, fear, and loneliness are all expressed as anger. Individuals cry a lot less and spend a lot more time alone in their rooms. Boys who were constantly underfoot only a few years ago are now hard to find at times.

With all these changes, the Individual's relationship with his parents often becomes strained. He begins to withdraw from his mother more and more (as well as from Dad), and for many moms, this separation can be difficult. He starts to have greater conflict with his male friends. He is, at times, afraid of girls, and at other moments profoundly curious about them.

In short, he is coming of age, and he is much more aware of the outside world and his own reaction to it. The Individual is trying to figure out how to fit in, and he has a new and clearer appreciation for the social pecking order and the chain of command as he comes to understand his place in the world. Some characteristics that describe the Individual are *searching, evolving, experimenting,* and *criticizing.*

SEARCHING

By the time a boy reaches nine or ten years of age, he is beginning to look deeply into what it means to be a man. His brain and body are beginning to experience significant shifts, and the search for masculinity has begun in earnest.

How this all plays out will look different from boy to boy. Some may want more responsibility, more privacy, or more time with their friends. Some boys at this stage are still engaged in what we would define as boy play (Legos, action figures, hide-and-seek), while others are becoming more curious about the opposite sex.

Don't be concerned if your boy seems stuck in boy play while his peers are chasing girls. (Actually, you can celebrate.)

Christopher is a fifth grader. He loves football, baseball, and swimming. When he's home alone, he still loves to build with Legos, and he likes to read. At the neighborhood pool during the summer, one of his buddies announced that he was working on "getting a six-pack" by August (referring to his abdominal muscles). One of the other boys looked at Christopher in his bathing suit and told him there was no chance he'd ever have a six-pack "with that much flab hanging around your trunks." Later that day, at home, Christopher asked his mom if she thought he looked fat. She looked at his little frame with shock and said, "Why would you even ask that question?" Later that night, she found him in his room, on the floor, doing one hundred sit-ups.

With Individuals, it's normal for there to be a lot of closed doors, increasingly longer showers, and the choosing of friends over family. The Individual is becoming more private about his body, more determined in his opinions, and highly concerned with his ranking in the family and among friends.

Equally so, as the Individual develops a stronger sense of himself, he becomes keenly aware of the possibility of being humiliated, and he grows increasingly emotionally isolated. It is during this stage that boys often decide "they'd rather hide out than take any more hits."[1] Emotional isolation becomes commonplace for Individuals. Throughout their middle school years, boys get better and better at disguising their feelings and denying their emotional and spiritual sensitivity.

EVOLVING

Some years ago, I (David) had been counseling a twelve-year-old boy for a while when I started noticing some signs of distress and depression. I explored my observations with Eric and finally got him to admit that he had something he hadn't told anyone in the world that was making him feel really sad and scared. I asked him if he felt he could tell me. He finally buried his head in his hands and said, "I need your help. I need you to help me tell my parents that I'm dying."

"Tell me what you mean by that," I said.

"My body has been leaking spinal fluid for almost three weeks now. I wake up every few nights, and there is this wet, sticky substance on my sheets and all over my pajamas. I finally figured out what it must be, and I don't know how to tell them."

I began asking him questions. "So, it's only at night when this happens?"

"Yes."

"And is it slightly colored, like milky colored?"

He sat up in distress and said, "Yes, yes it is."

"But there's no hole at the base of your back where it's coming out, is there?"

He looked confused and said, "No, and I can't figure out how it's traveling out of my spine."

I looked at him with compassion and said, "Eric, you're not dying. You're not leaking spinal fluid. You're having wet dreams."

He looked at me with confusion and relief.[2]

At this stage, the Individual's emotions will be changing more than his body. Most boys will experience a growth surge around thirteen or fourteen years of age, though there is no need to be concerned if the change seems slow and gradual. Even if on the outside he still seems boyish, it's important to be aware that on the inside (hormonally, emotionally, psychologically) he's experiencing "the Invasion of the Body Snatchers." For example, depending on when his adolescence begins, a boy's body will secrete between five and seven surges of testosterone each day. With these fluctuations in hormones, preadolescent and adolescent boys experience emotional shifts along the lines of volcanic eruptions. Ruled by testosterone, boys often feel driven to seek independence sooner than girls. Compared to their female peers, pubescent boys experience testosterone levels that are ten to twenty times greater.[3]

It's important for parents to stay ahead of the curve here. Adolescence can begin at nine, with some reports as early as seven or eight. Though Eric's experience at age twelve is typical, a boy can have his first nocturnal emission as early as nine or ten.

EXPERIMENTING

The Individual wants to make his mark on the world and to discover who he is as a man. In order to do this, he needs to find ways to stand out from his peers and separate from his parents. One way that he can begin this process is through experimentation. He may experiment in a variety of ways, such as with smoking, alcohol, drugs, deception, and sexuality (primarily masturbation and pornography, but also with gender identity). Two other common "tests" are using profanity and breaking the rules away from home.

Experimentation with profanity is primarily a means of gaining power. It feels powerful to use dangerous and taboo words. It also feels powerful to break the rules. We've heard parents report everything from stealing electronics to painting graffiti to destroying property. This type of experimentation needs to be met with strong consequences that communicate a very clear message: "This behavior will never work for you; it will only bring consequences that you don't want (such as grounding, suspension, juvenile detention, or mandatory community service)."

Boys are more at risk than girls when it comes to experimentation—especially with regard to alcohol and drugs. Boys are three times more likely than girls to use alcohol before the age of twelve. Almost 20 percent of twenty-one-year-old males report that they first experimented with alcohol before the age of fifteen. And what is eye-opening to many of the families we work with is that white children are the highest risk group.[4] (There goes the myth that the suburbs will save your kids.)

CRITICIZING

In his journey of separating out from family and friends and finding his place in the world, the Individual can become highly critical. It's not uncommon for the Individual to be critical of himself, his parents, his siblings, his peers, and other adults in authority. Boys can develop a belief that adults are against them and never for them. It's not uncommon for a boy to say, "My teacher hates me," or "My coach is committed to seeing me sit on the bench." Boys at this stage are also very hard on themselves. A mother told me (David) recently that when she picked her son up from track practice, he would regularly say, "Did you see Jim running at the end? Don't you think he runs like a girl?" This particular mom was attuned to the "criticizing" phenomenon, and she eventually responded by saying, "I notice you talk a lot about how Jim runs. It makes me wonder if you are a little concerned about the way you look when you run. Has anyone said anything to you about it?" The young man didn't answer; he stared straight ahead and his eyes filled with tears.

What He Needs: Limits and Opportunities

You may be familiar with the Greek myth of Icarus. Icarus was the son of Daedalus, who was a prisoner in King Minos's labyrinth. In an effort to escape the prison, Daedalus fashioned a pair of wings made of wax and feathers for himself and Icarus. Before they took off from the prison, Daedalus warned his son not to fly too close to the sun (because the wax would melt) nor too close to the sea (because the wax would dampen). But Icarus, overcome by the magnificent feeling of flying free, soared through the sky higher and higher, so close to the sun that the wings melted and he fell into the sea to his death.

As an Individual begins to show autonomy, confidence, and maturity, it's easy to assume he's ready to be independent. Well, the truth is, he's not. There's a big difference between *individuality* and *independence*. Much of a boy's pull away from authority is more of a test to see whether those with power over him can handle and corral his strength and presence. If an Individual knows the rules and lives within a culture of healthy boundaries and wise limits, he will feel safe and be compelled to remain good.

Individuals are much like Icarus. They need chances to stretch their wings and test their capabilities, but they also lack the wisdom and experience not to fly too close to the peril of the sun or the ocean. A boy's parents and other caregivers need to help him strike more of a balance between limits and opportunities. To love an Individual well, we must provide *supervision, information, involvement,* and *outlets.*

SUPERVISION

The Individual stage is a time when many boys begin to wander off the beaten path and venture into the darker corners of the landscape. Because of a boy's tendency to experiment at this stage, it's also a time when his caregivers must increase their level of observation.

Parents often ask us when they should worry—which red flags to watch for in order to minimize the chances that their son will get lost in the wilderness. We recommend that parents keep an eye on several observable and measurable indicators: *grades, hobbies, friends,* and *moods.* These outward expressions are often indicators of internal realities. A decline in a boy's grades (either precipitous or gradual) could be one sign that something is amiss emotionally or spiritually. Likewise, a declining interest in hobbies, sports, or talents that he previously showed promise or interest in may signal that something is wrong. A loss of friends, or a significant change in the type of friends he has, may also be a sign that a boy is being lured off the trail. Another thing to monitor is his mood, as compared to that of his peers. Is he more sullen, surly, or sulky?

Because the warning signs are not always obvious, even with boys who are severely struggling psychologically, parents, teachers, coaches, and youth workers must keep a watchful eye so they can detect the signs of impending trouble.

When parents notice changes, they should interpret them as warning signs, and they shouldn't hesitate to offer their son help or to seek help from others. The problem is that boys at this age often can't articulate what's wrong—and even if they can, they may be unwilling or afraid to trust others. Parents need to ask themselves the question, How would the CIA keep tabs on my son if they wanted to?

Though we're taking a stab at some lighthearted humor here, thinking in terms of espionage is not a bad idea. Here are some practical suggestions:

- When he is out of the house, periodically browse through his room and backpack.

- Monitor his e-mail, text messages, and MySpace and Facebook accounts.
- Keep tabs on the Web sites he visits.
- Compare notes with his friends' parents.
- *Always* talk with the other parents to confirm plans and adequate supervision when he is spending time at someone else's house.
- After you drop him off at the mall or a movie, it's okay to circle back around from time to time to make sure he's heading in the direction he told you he'd be heading.

If right about now you're thinking, *My son would go through the roof if I invaded his privacy like that,* give us a minute here to explain ourselves. Although we recommend that parents read their kids' e-mail, Facebook, MySpace, IMs, and the like, we also strongly urge you to talk to your son before you do this. You can say something like this: "Son, as you get older, there will be more opportunities for you to get harmed in ways that can really hurt you. Because we love you, and to help you stay safe, we will from time to time be checking up on you. . . ." Talking to your son up front will let him know that you care, and it may cause him to think twice before he makes a bonehead decision. When he knows in advance that his media usage, friendships, and personal space can be inspected at any time for any reason, he has less cause to accuse you of "invading his privacy" when it happens. We do, however, strongly recommend against reading his journal, if he has one. It's important that he have a safe place to explore and process his internal world.

If you still feel reluctant to monitor your son in the ways we've suggested, we ask you to consider the alternatives and count the costs. Boys at this stage need limits and accountability from their parents and other caregivers to help them stay on the right track.

It won't always be that way, of course, but at the Individual stage of a boy's development, it's vitally important. It's far less complicated to be involved with a boy at this stage than it is when he is a teen. If you get involved when he is young, it is much, much easier to stay involved as he gets older.

INFORMATION

Boys like it when we shoot straight with them. And they like accurate information. I (David) had a young man named Brent tell me years ago, "I hate it when my mom tells me how great I am at basketball all the time. She thinks she's being encouraging, but it just comes off as fake. The truth is, I'm a decent basketball player, but I'm not that great compared to the other guys on my team. Now, baseball is my sport. When she tells me I'm good at that, I tend to believe her more."

Like so many boys his age, Brent could see straight through his mother's attempt at encouraging him. It didn't feel believable, because she said the same things about all his abilities. He could clearly tell for himself where his strengths lay and where they didn't. Boys at the Individual stage like accurate information.

This same rule applies to information about the changes that will occur to them, both emotionally and physically. Parents need to name for their sons all that is going on and all that is to come. Boys need education regarding the physical and emotional changes that will take place throughout their development.

Toss aside the idea of a "birds and bees talk." This conversation should be an ongoing dialogue throughout all stages of a boy's development. If this idea feels foreign to you (as it does for most adults) because your own parents never talked to you about anything when you were growing up, and thus you have no idea what these conversations are supposed to be like, spend some time preparing before you talk with your son. Meet with a pastor, friend, or therapist to talk it through. Take advantage of some of the excellent books and videos that provide examples, outlines, and questions to ask.[5] The more comfortable you are with the material, the more comfortable your son will be with having these kinds of conversations. For example, your son needs to know what a nocturnal emission (wet dream) is. He needs for you to dialogue openly with him about erections, masturbation (more on that in the next chapter), and pornography.

Even if there are no physical changes taking place yet with your son, begin a dialogue with him. You want to stay ahead of the changes that are coming. He needs for puberty to be put in a physical and spiritual context. He needs more than a single talk—or even several—about the birds and the bees. He needs for you to keep the lines of communication open throughout the biggest time of change that will take place in his life.

INVOLVEMENT

There are two primary influences in a boy's life—*parents* and *peers*. At this stage of a boy's development, parents are still the primary authority. The power of peers will increase later. Your son may appear not to need you as he moves through the Individual stage, but it's an act. This is a period in his life where he still needs strong parental involvement and supervision.

Jeff is an incredible dad. He purchased NFL tickets for himself and his nine-year-old son to attend together. Every other game, Jeff lets his son decide whether or not they will wear body paint. He understands the importance of time with his son, the magic of attending games together, and the sense of wild adventure his son gets from wearing body paint and screaming like a crazy man. (We suspect that doing this isn't much of a sacrifice for Jeff, either.)

This is a great time to make family time very intriguing. It doesn't have to be expensive or extravagant; you just want to turn up the volume a notch. For example, if you've had a tradition on Friday nights of ordering pizza and watching a movie, you may want to add in a night of playing Xbox, PS3, or Wii games that the whole family can join in.

This is also an important time in your son's life when you'll want to make certain you have close contact and relationship with his friends' parents. Dialogue with them about their rules for watching movies and television. Ask questions about Internet access and exposure to social networking. The majority of boys I (David) work with had their first exposure to pornography in this stage of their development, and it happened at a friend's house.

Because their physiology is going haywire during this stage, Individuals need a lot of love and attention. "The way we interact with [a boy]," says clinical psychologist William Pollack in his book *Real Boys*, "and the connections we make with [him], can have a permanent effect," not only on his emotional and spiritual development, but also on his "biology, his brain, and his social behavior. Scientists have found that early emotional interaction can actually alter a boy's brain-based biological processes."[6]

Pollack calls this phenomenon "the potency of connection." He adds, "The level of testosterone in any boy—and the way that testosterone affects him—has less impact on his behavior than how the boy is loved, nurtured, and shaped by his parents and by the context of the society in which he lives. . . . The people in a boy's life—moms and dads, teachers and siblings, coaches and ministers, day-care providers and doctors—may have an effect equal to that of testosterone in shaping a young boy, not only by influencing his formative experience but by affecting his brain structures and neurotransmitters."[7]

OUTLETS

Mark and his family have traveled together to a family camp since he was seven. He's thirteen now and confessed to me (David) that "I act like I'm not that into it anymore, but it's actually a lot of fun. We go white-water rafting as a family. My mom always screams like she's on Space Mountain or something. My dad and I always go to the firing range together, and it's cool. They even have a talent show, and we come up with something crazy to do." Mark will likely never let on to his folks that he has these positive memories from their time together or that he enjoys going on these vacations, but the family times are meeting a significant need for him.

The Individual needs strong outlets for testing his identity. These include athletic and extracurricular opportunities through which he can develop his sense of self and be led by responsible adults, teachers, and coaches who are committed to the development of his character first and his abilities second. He needs the outlet of time spent at friends' homes where he is exposed to strong families with house rules that are similar to yours.

Just as he did when he was an Explorer and a Lover, a boy at the Individual stage still needs plenty of opportunities to be outside. Many Individuals love activities that involve wide-open spaces and groups or teams. They also enjoy engaging in family activities (even if they won't admit it). Here are some suggestions that boys are almost sure to enjoy:

flashlight tag
paintball
flag football
night golf
Ultimate Frisbee
Wiffle ball
White-water rafting
high-ropes challenge courses
rappelling or rock climbing
horseback riding

As the Individual gains a better grasp on his individualism and his *place* in the world, he needs to be exposed to his *position* in the world. For the Individual, the outdoors has an important spiritual quality. God instructs us through the natural world—and he humbles us too. "There is a humility and a seasoned wisdom to be learned *in* the natural world," writes John Eldredge.

> Turn a canoe sideways and it will tip. Approach an elk upwind and it will spook. Run your hand along the grain of wood and you'll get a splinter. *There is a way things work.* Oh, what a crucial lesson this is for a man. In the realm of nature, you can't just order room service, or change the channel, or write a new program to solve your problems. You can't ignore the way things work. You must be taught by it. Humility and wisdom come to a man when he learns those ways, and learns to live his life accordingly.[8]

Nature commands our respect. It's mysterious and wild (much like God). Learning to live in accord with nature is vital to a boy's survival, maturity, and happiness. This doesn't mean he has to take weeklong hikes on the Appalachian Trail (though it could). There are so many adventures to be had: sailing, hunting, fishing, mountain biking, canoeing, walking down a country lane, or stargazing with binoculars or a telescope, to name just a few. What's important for Individuals is that they spend time engaging with and contemplating the bigness and awe-inspiring power of creation.

Another important outlet involves outreach or service. A boy at this stage needs opportunities to develop a sense of self and to be affirmed for giving of himself. He will enjoy new responsibilities, such as tutoring a younger student in a favorite subject, helping out with a team of younger players in a favorite sport, or giving music lessons on an instrument he plays.

This is also a good time to increase his chores and responsibilities at home. Tell him that the greater responsibility comes from greater trust and will be met with greater reward (more freedom, increased allowance, etc.).

Putting the Principles into Practice

Individuals find themselves on the fault line of childhood and adolescence. As caregivers, we need to expect some earthquakes. We need to prepare for them. We need to know what to do when they hit. And we need to prepare our boys for handling them as well.

Individuals are at the beginning of some very bumpy years. Our job as parents and caregivers is to equip ourselves and equip them for the rough ride and the aftershocks that follow. Here's a list of some things you can do when the tremors strike:

TIP 1: Be intentional with summers. A number of great
    camps across the country are doing excellent work with

boys. Camps provide a rich opportunity for boys to experience appropriate risk—physically, emotionally, and relationally—in a completely different way than they can on their home turf. The Individual stage is a valuable season to incorporate camping as a part of your boy's experience.

TIP 2: Keep the dialogue going. This is the time when you need to specifically address some important issues head-on. Your son needs to hear your views on sex, drugs, alcohol, and suicide, and he needs to be taught how to handle these issues.

TIP 3: Engage with him. Dads, consider taking your son on an experiential day or weekend to initiate a dialogue about the changes we've discussed. Make it a memorable time in which you intersperse conversation with doing something fun and meaningful. Moms, to maintain connection with your son during this season when he starts the journey of separation, you'll want to figure out a ritual that is specific to the two of you. Consider stopping for donuts on the way to school (or on the way home; there's never a bad time for donuts), or take him to a batting cage once a month and then buy him a milkshake afterward.

TIP 4: Enlist his doctor's help. Prompt your son's pediatrician to begin talking with him more openly about the upcoming changes with his body and emotions. A boy can't hear about this from too many sources.

TIP 5: Get ready for a steak dinner. A good friend of ours started a rich tradition with his sons. When they reached a specific age, somewhere between eight and ten, he told them all about wet dreams. He also told them to come and get him out of bed the first time they awoke to a wet dream (no matter what time it was), so they could celebrate. The next day, they would go out for a steak dinner to celebrate that the boy was becoming a man.

TIP 6: Make him read the book before you let him see the movie. Yes, even *The Lord of the Rings.*

TIP 7: Don't follow the crowd. Just because "everybody else's parents" let their sons have a cell phone or be on MySpace or Facebook doesn't mean you have to.

TIP 8: Keep him active. This is the time in a boy's life when he can become obsessively absorbed with media. A good rule of thumb is that he should never spend more time watching sports than actually playing them. He should never spend more time talking to friends on the phone, or via text, e-mail, or MySpace/Facebook than actually being with his friends. He should never spend more time playing video games than playing outdoors—or playing indoors with something that doesn't require batteries or need to be plugged in.

TIP 9: Watch and discuss *A Christmas Story* together.

TIP 10: Fasten your seat belt. The changes that are coming in your boy's life (which we'll discuss in the next chapter) are gonna knock the wind out of you.

CHAPTER 4

𝕿𝖍𝖊 𝖂𝖆𝖓𝖉𝖊𝖗𝖊𝖗

(ages 13–17)

The Body is a coming-of-age tale by Stephen King that was originally published as part of a collection called *Different Seasons*. You may be familiar with the story, because it was adapted into the 1986 film *Stand by Me*, starring River Phoenix and Wil Wheaton.

The story takes place in the fictional town of Castle Rock, Maine, during the summer of 1960. A boy named Ray Brower has gone missing. When Gordie (the narrator of the story) and his three friends—Chris, Teddy, and Vern—find out that Ray has been hit by a train and killed, they set out to find his body near the tracks. Along the way, the boys encounter numerous adventures:

they're chased by a junkyard dog, and Gordie and Vern are almost run over by a train themselves while crossing a bridge.

The boys eventually make it to the spot where the corpse is, but soon after they arrive, a gang of older teenagers shows up. The older boys confront Gordie and his friends, and during the ensuing argument, Chris pulls out a gun (which he had taken from his father's dresser) and fires a shot. Ace Merrill, the leader of the older gang, realizes that Chris means business, and after promising to get the boys later, he and the rest of the thugs leave.

After the boys arrive home, Ace and a friend make good on their threat. They break Gordie's nose and fingers and kick him in the groin. Chris is also beaten, left with a broken arm and a face "looking like a Canadian sunrise." Teddy and Vern get off with less severe beatings. When the four boys refuse to identify their assailants to the authorities, they gain the respect of their peers.

The Lay of the Land

The next stage of boyhood parallels the themes found in Stephen King's story: deep friendships, adventure, being lost, danger, significant loss. If your boy is at this stage of life, there are three foundational things you'll need to best care for him:

1. Prayer
2. Chocolate
3. The ability to laugh

You will need to pray often—for wisdom, mercy, and forgiveness—because you will likely say and do a lot of things you will later regret. You'll also want to pray for your boy's safety, because he will likely do a lot of things that *he* will later regret.

You will need chocolate (or whatever bad-for-you food brings you comfort). You'll want to eat it alone and sometimes in the company of friends.

You'll need friends to laugh with when your son is at his absolute worst (a place he'll visit often at this point in his life). You'll need to laugh about him (but not at him). You'll need to laugh silently to yourself when he comes out with lines like these:

"You're ruining my life."

"You are the worst mother I have ever known or seen. God messed up big time when he let you be a parent."

"You get a kick out of trying to control me, don't you?"

"When you get old, I'm putting you in a nursing home. A lousy one. And I'll never visit you, except to make sure they are neglecting you."

"I'm counting down the days until I turn eighteen. I used to count the years, and now I'm counting down the days."

"The only time I don't hate you is when you're asleep."

"You will regret this [whatever indignity you're visiting upon him] for the rest of your life. I will make sure of that."

"Some people get embarrassed by their parents; I live in a state of humiliation."

Tragically, these are all things we have actually heard adolescent boys say to their parents, or had parents report that their sons said to them. Somewhere in this stage of development, your son will become the worst version of himself. This is the "Invasion of the Body Snatchers" stage—in which the tender, funny, resilient, happy-go-lucky little guy you once knew is stolen in the night and replaced with an angry, argumentative, sullen, contemptuous, grumpy clone.

At this point of their journey, boys are self-determined and craving independence more than ever. In so many ways, they've left the reservation, flown the coop, and gone AWOL. Because of their willful independence and self-centeredness, we refer to boys in this stage as Wanderers.

Who He Is: The Wanderer

When a boy enters the Wanderer stage, it sometimes seems as if he is bound and determined to make those who care for him miserable, to resist authority at all costs, to ignore every request, and to wander as far away as possible. Boys in this stage of development will careen back and forth between their desire for us to be involved with them and their need for us to leave them alone.

Dan Allender, author of *How Children Raise Parents*, says that kids ask two questions simultaneously throughout their adolescence:

- Am I loved?
- Can I get my own way?[1]

Allender discusses how an adolescent's responses and behaviors are always rooted in these two questions. The Wanderer will live with one hand held out in resistance that says, "Get away from me," while the other hand (hidden behind the hand of resistance) is motioning, "Come toward me." In so many ways, he has us held hostage. If we come toward him, we aren't respecting his privacy or "space." If we keep our distance, we "don't care." And if we do nothing, we are "idiots."

Like boys in the previous stages of development, The Wanderer has his own set of defining characteristics, which includes *physiological chaos, arrogance, individuation*, and *argumentativeness*— and did we mention arrogance and argumentativeness?

PHYSIOLOGICAL CHAOS

I (David) remember this stage well. When I was in late middle school, my acne was so bad that my family helped finance the local dermatologist's addition to his home. By the time I got to high school, we had put his kids through college. I made monthly visits to his office for a range of brutal treatments, such as one in which he tried to freeze the millions of red, lumpy, volcanic craters on my face by spraying them with liquid nitrogen. I'd go home with a flash-frozen, red face and multiple prescriptions for creams and solutions to lather on my zits morning and night—all with limited results.

When I had my senior picture taken at the end of my junior year of high school, they offered an "airbrushed option" for those adolescents who had "complexion issues." My senior picture is so airbrushed that I'm not quite sure it's still me. The chaos around my mouth, on my chin and neck, and across my forehead was an outward indicator of the turmoil that boiled in my internal world.

Such is the case for many boys. If you thought the changes you observed in your boy during the Individual stage were something, you ain't seen nothin' yet. Now that he's a Wanderer, his physiological world is pure bedlam. The chemical reactions in his body now are like a fireworks stand on fire: excessive surges of testosterone, serotonin spikes and dips, and other chemicals and hormones pouring through his body.

These chemical shifts cause everything from out-of-control acne to intense mood swings that mirror those of menopausal women. They cause hair to grow on his body, his voice to deepen, and his attitude to sour.

For the Wanderer (and his parents), this is a season marked by insecurity, uncertainty, confusion, and instability. In addition to triggering acne, hairy pits, voice changes, and mood swings, testosterone can also cause boys in this stage to seem fidgety and impulsive—reminiscent of a two- or three-year-old Explorer.

I (David) lead a weekly meeting with a group of boys in this age bracket. If I leave them alone for even two minutes, they're likely to break out into wrestling matches, pillow fights, or experimentation with something in my office. The reason is that boys often get a buildup of testosterone in the hypothalamus (the part of the brain that acts as a thermostat of sorts that controls body temperature, hunger, thirst, fatigue, anger, and sexual urges). When this buildup happens in a boy's brain, a kind of alarm will go off, indicating the need to cool down the system. This is why boys get fidgety and need some kind of quick tension release. (This is another stage in a boy's development when we do him a disservice by requiring him to sit still and stop fidgeting.)[2]

Speaking of quick release, this is a time in a boy's development when he begins to masturbate . . . a lot. Most adolescent boys will admit to masturbating anywhere from once a week to once a day. As parents, we need to create an open dialogue with our sons about this topic in a way that creates less shame. It is especially important for fathers to engage their sons in discussion on this topic.

There are usually three reasons why parents don't talk with their sons about sex: fear, laziness, and shame. Parents are often afraid to reveal to their sons how little they actually know about sex. Moreover, they may be too lazy to educate themselves and prepare appropriately for these significant conversations. And they often are too ashamed of their own sexual history and practices to talk with their boys without feeling like hypocrites. Our advice is simple:

1. Get some educational books and/or parenting videos. Educate yourself on what to say, when to say it, and how to say it.

2. Get some courage. It's hardly ever as bad as you expect. Think of all the shame and self-contempt you've experienced because your parents did a poor job of teaching you about sex.

3. Get some counseling. If you are one of the millions of American men or women who are sexually addicted or deal with other shameful sexual issues, the only real shame is in not getting the help you need. Go to a counselor. Visit a Sexaholics Anonymous meeting. Talk with your pastor.

And while we're on the subject, masturbation usually goes along with pornography. Get involved in your son's life. Educate yourself on the epidemic of pornography (and sexual abuse). Ask the tough questions. Talk with him about the dangers. We realize that talking about pornography is as difficult as talking about sex. But get out of your comfort zone. Your son is worth it.

"Often when a child gets into inappropriate material," one advocacy Web site says, "we dismiss it as 'kids being kids.' Well, parents should be parents. It is our responsibility to monitor and control the content that comes into our homes. We are called to protect our children to the best of our abilities. That beckons for us as parents to actively understand where our kids go and what they do online."[3] The reality is that Western culture offers the most sexual stimulation to youth with the least amount of teaching. That needs to change; but until it does, we need to guard our sons and instruct them well.

ARROGANCE

The other day, I (David) was catching a flight and found myself walking behind a Wanderer and his parents. He refused to walk beside them and instead stayed about four steps behind and to the side. They frequently asked him to pick up the pace, and he steadfastly refused to do so. Further, with his shambling gait, he was taking up more than half the walkway, completely oblivious to the people who were trying to get around him. His cap was cocked sideways, and his pants were sagging. (I think it's fascinating how these kids wear big, thick leather belts that still don't manage to hold their pants up above their boxers.) His mom periodically turned around to make sure he was still behind her, and he responded by holding both his arms out and grunting, as if to say, "What? I'm walking as fast as I can." On one occasion, the mom caught my eye, and her face seemed to say, "I can't seem to train this dog. I brought him home from the pound, and he won't do a thing I say." I looked at her with a knowing and compassionate look that said, "I know. I train the same kind of dogs, and they make me want to lock them in a crate (for days on end)."

I enjoy watching Wanderers when I'm in public places, such as a mall or an airport, because when I'm not charged with influencing them, I can simply observe. You can just smell the attitude on them, a mixture of arrogance, bravado, and cluelessness. The way they carry themselves—the saunter that seems to say, "Whatever." The way they greet you (or don't) by slightly nodding upward without saying anything at all. The way they often refuse to make eye contact, in a way that smacks of insecurity but has a hint of "I'm above you" about it.

No one loves a Wanderer more than the Wanderer himself. At this stage, boys border on narcissism. They appear confident, cocky, and full of themselves, but deep down they are often confused, fearful, and insecure. Even though they feel afraid of the changes taking place in their bodies, their emotions, and their relationships, Wanderers will most often act as if they've got the world by the tail. They want the adults in their lives to be completely interested in them, and yet they act put out when they're asked questions—which smack to them of invading their privacy. Wanderers are walking contradictions.

Navigating your boy's bravado and digging down to his insecurity will require a good bit of decoding and reading between the lines. (In chapter 10, we offer some ideas for how to look and listen for what's not being said.)

INDIVIDUATION

To complete the process of individuation (that is, forming his own distinct sense of self, apart from his parents), a boy needs growing autonomy, increased responsibility, and manageable opportunities to figure out who he is. He wants to be himself—even though he has little idea who he is. The hardest emotional, psychological, and spiritual work a boy will do is in becoming his *own man*. During this time of transition, he will beg, borrow, and steal elements from his family, friends, church, culture, and strangers as he tries to piece together his own construct of masculinity.

I (Stephen) once met with a man who confessed that as a teenager he had "tried on" two dozen different identities in an effort to find one that felt like a fit. He had been a "Goth," a "player," a "jock," a "prep," a "druggie," a "Christian," and the list went on and on. He said, "I never liked smoking the three weeks I did it, but it was part of the package so I kept it up until I decided to try being a prep for a while."

After a season of conforming to his peers, it's normal for a Wanderer to desire a more individual expression of who he is. One dilemma that comes with this shift is a phenomenon that developmental theorists call "the imaginary audience." It's an adolescent style of relating in which he acts at all times as if there is an audience present that is observing and critiquing his every move and response. This irrational belief is extremely real to the adolescent and can complicate the individuation process and peer relationships. By this point in the game, peers have become the primary influence in a boy's life, while his parents begin to take more of a secondary, supporting role. Relationships with his friends become his top priority.

I (David) saw an extreme example of playing to the imaginary audience in a young man I counseled years ago. One day, he marched into my office and announced that he wanted the day's session to be with his mother. He had evidently announced it to her in the car, saying, "When we get to David's office, we're meeting together so he can back me up on how you're humiliating me." This was a family I had worked with for a couple of years, and the mom had fantastic instincts. She had taken my Nurturing Boys class and had a sense of the imaginary audience phenomenon. I pulled her into the session, and here's how it played out:

Son: Mom, do you have any idea how embarrassing it is when you pull into the pickup line at school wearing your workout clothes?

Mom (dressed in modest exercise shorts, a T-shirt, and a zip-up jacket): No, I didn't.

Son: See how clueless you are? Everyone notices but you.

Mom: Who is "everyone"?

Son (exasperated and motioning with his hands): Everyone in the universe. And you look ridiculous.

David (glancing at the mom with a knowing look and addressing the son): What I'm hearing is that you've got concerns about your mom picking you up from school in her workout clothes. And you're uncertain how that's reflecting on you.

Son: Not just on me, but on her. I'd be embarrassed for myself dressed like that.

Mom: What do you think is a compromise for the both of us? I want to be sensitive to this being an issue for you.

Son: The compromise is that you work out in the morning and take a shower before you pick me up.

David: Actually a compromise is when two people meet each other halfway and you both give up something. I'm not sure you're giving up anything in this.

Son: I've had to give up respect. That's what I've been giving up.

David (fighting back laughter): Well, your mom is entitled to exercise whenever she wants. And you are entitled to everything you're feeling about this, whether she gets it or not. I'm thinking a decent compromise would be that on the days your mom picks you up straight from exercising, she parks about a quarter mile down the road, so no one sees, and you walk to her.

Mom: Oh, I'm great with that idea.

Son: Well, that's a long way to have to walk.

David: Sure, but I'm afraid any closer and you run the same risk. Why don't you just try it, and we can reevaluate.

The next time they came in, the mom reported that her son had walked to the car one time and then miraculously didn't have an issue with her exercise clothes anymore.

The Wanderer's separation from his parents is inevitable, and the parents' response is crucial. During this time of intense individuation, their son is at risk. For years, he has leaned on his parents and other authority figures for guidance and discipline. Now he is increasingly without that support. If he has not had consistent discipline before entering this stage, it's really difficult for his parents to enforce that structure now.[4] During a boy's Wanderer years, some basic rules need to be in place and consistently and lovingly enforced. These include, but are not limited to, the following examples:

- Significant responsibilities and chores around the house (washing the family cars, mowing the grass, washing clothes, etc.)
- The expectation that he will call home to tell his parents where he is and where he is going
- The requirement that he speak respectfully to his parents and other authority figures. This includes no name-calling and respecting his parents' wishes on what kind of language is used in their presence.
- A set curfew that is enforced

ARGUMENTATIVENESS

The Wanderer will often use words like *always* and *never* in responding to his parents.

"You *always* point out things I do wrong."

"You *never* extend my curfew on the weekends."

"I'm *always* the *only* one who has to call home and report in."

"You *never* listen to a word I'm saying."

He will verbally push up against authority—and what's surprising is that this jousting has a purpose. Arguing is one means of his separating out from his parents. Having different ideas and opinions identifies him as distinct from the adults who care for him. In those moments when you feel as if he's arguing just for the sake of arguing, he probably is, and that's why.

We've had plenty of boys confess to us that they didn't even like certain films or music, but they acted as if they did for the purpose of getting a rise out of their parents or choosing something they knew their parents would oppose. Arguing almost always feels harsh and oftentimes disrespectful, but it can be experienced differently if we arm ourselves with the knowledge that it's actually a part of a boy's developmental agenda.

When your son is argumentative and extreme, it's important that you coach him in the art of negotiation and delivery. I (David) will often say to adolescent boys, "I hear exactly what you're saying, and I think your delivery is off, causing people to miss the importance of your message." I will also often role-play conversations with Wanderer boys and their parents, and sometimes I end up saying, "Try it again," four or five times before the boys nail the delivery without the attitude.

What He Needs: Inputs and Outlets

Toward the end of his sophomore year in high school, Anthony got his driver's license, and his parents gave him a used pickup truck. Soon after his birthday, however, Anthony showed some real changes in his behavior and attitude. He started talking back to his mom and dad more often. He even got to the point of shouting and cursing at his mother. And after a call from the school, his parents found out that he had skipped a couple of days of English. Anthony had taken the plunge headfirst into being a Wanderer.

Anne Lamott writes, "Living with a teenager can feel like living with an ex, or with a drug addict who has three days clean and sober."[5] Amen, sister! This stage of development can put a real strain on the relationship between a boy and his caregivers. Because this is such a critical time in his journey toward manhood, his needs are especially intense. To love him well, we must provide some basic support through other voices, outlets, understanding, and boundaries.

OTHER VOICES

During this stage of development, it is crucial that a Wanderer have adults who care deeply about him (other than his parents or primary caregivers) speak into his life. As the voices of his peers get louder and louder, the voices of his parents are dampened. He still needs adult input, yet he is more resistant to receiving it from his parents than ever before. We need to make sure that his path crosses with those of respected adults who really understand and relate well to teens, and let them have a voice in his life, people such as youth leaders, coaches, scoutmasters, teachers, pastors, counselors, and other mentors.

Here's Anne Lamott's perspective on her own teenage son:

> I make Sam go [to church] because the youth-group leaders know things that I don't. They know what

teenagers are looking for, and need—they need
adults who have stayed alive and vital, adults they
wouldn't mind growing up to be. And they need
total acceptance of who they are, from adults they
trust, and to be welcomed in whatever condition life
has left them—needy, walled off. They want guides,
adults who know how to act like adults but with a
kid's heart. They want people who will sit with them
and talk about the big questions, even if they don't
have the answers; adults who won't correct their feelings or pretend not to be afraid. They are looking for
adventure, experience, pilgrimages, and thrills. And
then they want a home they can return to, where
things are stable and welcoming.[6]

Mentors serve as intermediary or transitional parents as a boy
moves closer to manhood. This is also a great time for boys to
connect with their grandfathers or uncles, if possible, or even
older siblings, depending on the age difference.

Mentors are also imperative in the development of male
friendships. These men serve as gatekeepers and architects for
the context in which boys create friendships. As boys get more
engaged in social activities, it is often these mentors who create
opportunities for relationship and community. For example, the
guy who volunteers at the neighborhood skate park three days a
week sets the tone and provides the opportunity for boys to be
together. Likewise with the man who serves as a scoutmaster in
his community. He facilitates when, where, how, and how often
boys will be together. Boys gather to do a task (such as practicing golf, going camping, racing motor bikes, making a short film,
etc.), and through the process of completing the task, they bond
with each other and develop strong friendships that often last into

adulthood. It is often up to mentors to create the environment for all of this interaction.

OUTLETS

As he did when he was in the Individual stage, the Wanderer needs outlets—places where he can release the intense energy that comes with the physiological chaos going on inside of him. Physical activity is an imperative for the Wanderer, but not necessarily competitive activities. Organized sports can be an excellent outlet for boys who need release when testosterone is building in their systems, but the competitive nature of sports can actually make things worse, because testosterone levels are elevated during intense competition. If competitive sports are a boy's only outlet for the release of pent-up energy, he's actually just pouring gasoline on the fire. Competition creates a cyclical effect on testosterone levels that looks something like this: release/surge/ release/surge/release/surge. The Wanderer needs to have other physical outlets that don't involve intense competition, activities such as woodworking, playing in a rock band, participating in debate club, sailing, kayaking, lifting weights, rock climbing, cycling, learning martial arts, or doing construction.

UNDERSTANDING

Wanderers need for their caregivers to understand that this part of the journey toward manhood is painful, scary, and disorienting. Wanderers are emotionally, spiritually, and psychologically lost in a cloud of ambivalence. They simultaneously want to wander away and come home. Their physiology is in turmoil, and it changes several times in the course of a day.

Even when a Wanderer is most abrasive and self-determined, he needs for the adults in his life to act like adults; to not take things personally; to be able to laugh—not *at* him, but to be able to laugh off some of his intensity. He needs love. He needs mercy. He needs kindness and forgiveness. He needs to be shown compassion. He needs for his parents and others to provide moments, events, and situations that ease his distress and pain. Moments that he does not deserve.

One father told us of the time he drove to the site of his son's second car accident (in one year) to find his son on the side of the road, his face buried in his hands, and wet, sloppy tears pouring down his face. The son knew he had screwed up, and he was swimming in the shame of having botched up twice in succession. The father realized that his son didn't need to hear a lecture; he needed mercy and understanding.

It can be hard to love someone as "unlovable" as a teenager. We're not talking about some ooey-gooey feeling. The kind of love a boy at this stage needs is purposeful, willful, and desirous. It's the kind of love that compels us to pray for our children. It calls us to remember the times when they were enjoyable, and to hold that in our hearts. It calls us to prepare and plan ways to delight in our boys. It moves us toward them in curiosity about what they are like with interest in who they are becoming.

And when those times come when we can't seem to laugh or love, or we completely blow it in relating to our boys (which will most definitely happen at least two dozen times during their adolescence), they need us to ask for forgiveness. And they need us to go *first* in asking for forgiveness, even when they should be the ones to go first. They need for us to be the grown-ups (because we are).

Wanderers need for us to understand how confusing and complicated a time it is for them, and not to throw stories at them about how hard it was for us when we were their age. Times have changed, and being an adolescent in the twenty-first century is a lot more complicated than it was when the current generation of parents was growing up. Technology alone makes it a whole new world. Don't pretend to know all the challenges your son faces on a daily basis. Yes, it's an extremely valuable time to share stories with him. Stories are actually one of the most beneficial ways to teach and dialogue with your son—but not at the expense of coming across like you really don't understand his reality, what it's like to live inside his skin.

Wanderers need for us to respect them; to respect who they are becoming and what it takes to get there. They need for us to respect that they will make mistakes and be able to learn from those mistakes. They need for us to acknowledge that adolescence involves trial and error.

One of the ways you can show your son you respect him is by engaging in his world. Be interested in the things he loves (even though he will act put out by that at times). Respect what interests him (unless it's pornography or something equally harmful), even if it makes absolutely no sense to you at all. For example, boys at this stage like really stupid movies. One way to show your teenage boy understanding is by learning to appreciate movies by Adam Sandler or Will Ferrell.

We demonstrate understanding and respect for Wanderers when we validate their opinions (even those we disagree with) and acknowledge what's happening that feels like a big deal to them. We also respect them when we empower them to come up with their own solutions rather than always giving them advice. Show your Wanderer that you believe he's capable of working his way out of tough situations.

BOUNDARIES

At this stage of their development, boys crave structure and despise it, all at the same time. This can be maddening for the adults in their lives. But regardless of how much a boy acts as if he doesn't need limitations, and no matter how many times he mutters some version of "leave me alone," he needs boundaries. Underneath the rebellion, resistance, and bravado, he feels safest when there are firm boundaries in place.

I (David) counseled a young man whose family had bought a new house. The market in Nashville had slowed down significantly, and they were having trouble selling their old house, but they decided to go ahead and move and do some work on their old house in hopes of increasing its value and appeal. They left a handful of items in the garage at the old house and some other things in the house for a possible garage sale at some point. Periodically, they sent their sixteen-year-old son back over to the house to pick up some of the items left behind.

One Saturday morning, the mom went over to the old house to check on the work that had been done during the previous week. When she opened the door, she discovered that her son had lied about his plans the previous night. Scattered throughout the house she found pizza boxes, beer bottles, and six teenagers sleeping on the floor. It seems her son had invited his friends over to the old house for a party on Friday night, and some of the kids had slept over with the promise that they'd be out first thing in the morning.

Five of the six teenagers—including the party's host—had told their parents they were spending the night at another friend's house, and these parents didn't have an established boundary of confirming such plans with the friend's parents. The sixth boy said, "You can call my mom if you want to. She won't care where I spent the night. I didn't bother calling her last night because she doesn't know where I am half the time anyway." The mother who owned the house, in retelling the story to me, said, "David, the greatest tragedy to me wasn't in hearing this kid say that his mom didn't know where he was; it was the sadness in his eyes that no adult in his life cared enough to require him to report in."

In Margaret Wise Brown's classic children's book *The Runaway Bunny*, a mother bunny is confronted by her son, who announces he is leaving home. Over the course of the book, he tries everything he can think of to get away—from climbing a mountain to joining the circus to hiding in a trout stream. But to every threat, the mother bunny responds with the same consistent message: "If you run away, I will run after you."

The little bunny keeps trying to outsmart his mother, and she keeps responding with the same boundary: "If you do that, then I'll do this." Finally, the little bunny gives up and says, "I might as well stay at home and be your little bunny." Though it's a book for much younger children, *The Runaway Bunny* paints a beautiful picture of the steady, consistent, *nonemotional* response that adolescent boys need from their parents and other caregivers. At no point in the story does the mother bunny start screaming, "You stupid rabbit, get a clue! You keep pushing me like this and I'll nail your cotton tail to the floor," although it might have crossed her mind at some point during the game. Instead, she kept restating the boundary every time he pushed. He acted like he hated the boundary (and her) and had every intention of turning up the volume on her, but she calmly kept drawing the same line in the sand.

Putting the Principles into Practice

Wanderers need other voices, outlets, understanding, and boundaries. Here are some ideas for how to help your boy navigate this complicated season of his life.

TIP 1: Call your parents and apologize. If your parents are still living, call them and apologize for everything you said between the ages of fourteen and seventeen. Thank them for loving you during a very unlovable time in your life.

TIP 2: Enter his world. As much as your boy will allow, involve yourself in his outlets. If he loves basketball, stand at the goal and pass the ball back to him every time he shoots. If he loves football, throw him some passes. Use it as an opportunity to talk with him. Boys are more apt to talk when they don't feel cornered, and they talk well when they are in motion. But don't cling, nag, or pester him for affection or attention if he clearly wants to let go. With Wanderers, you have to get good at picking your times to connect emotionally and physically—and then be ready to pounce like an alley cat.

TIP 3: Commiserate with him. Demonstrate that you understand the mess he's in. It's helpful for a Wanderer when the adults in his life show that they know how difficult and painful adolescence can be. With compassion and understanding, show him that you haven't forgotten your own journey through the teenage years.

TIP 4: Don't panic. If he starts to resist spiritually, give him some room. As part of the individuation process, many boys start to question what they believe at this stage. Sometimes, after years of believing in God, they will announce that they're not quite sure anymore. Struggling in this way can actually be a means of deepening their faith and figuring out what they really believe in.

TIP 5: Partner with another family. If you have some friends who have boys that your son enjoys, sign up together to work on a Habitat for Humanity house, or go on a spring break missions trip together. Boys are much less apt to resist this kind of opportunity when they have friends who are participating as well. Also, spend some time with parents of boys who are between the ages of eighteen and twenty-two (the next stage your boy will enter). Have them tell you stories about how normal and enjoyable their sons are, so you have something to look forward to.

TIP 6: Affirm your son as much as you can. Look for (and create) opportunities to tell him you love and respect him. It's important during this stage to emphasize specific things you respect about him.

TIP 7: Feed him. There's great truth to the saying that the way to a man's heart is through his stomach. Food is one of the best ways to engage with an adolescent boy (or a grown man, for that matter). Take your boy out to his favorite burger joint, or his restaurant of choice, with no agenda but just to hang out with him.

TIP 8: Make him get a job. If he hasn't already started working, he needs to now. Many of the lessons he needs to learn to get him ready for the next stage of development he can learn at an after-school job, working on the weekends, or getting a summer job.

TIP 9: Make regular dates with him. During this time in your boy's life, it's particularly important for you to play with him. Whether it's going to a hockey game, out for a hamburger together, or to the new Adam Sandler movie, make it a priority to spend regular recreational time with your son. Tell him you heard that *Zoolander* and *Napoleon Dynamite* were great films, and you're sorry you missed them when they hit the theaters. Ask if he'll watch them again with you.

**TIP 10: Talk with him about dating and romantic relation-
ships.** At this stage of his development, your son is
entering a minefield of fresh challenges. Having already
grown up in a highly sexualized culture, constantly
bombarded with provocative images, he now must
contend with massive amounts of testosterone coursing
through his system, girls who are physically maturing
and catching his eye as never before, and peer pressure
to step up and "prove" his masculinity. In short, he's a
walking time bomb. Regardless of what you have done
thus far as a parent, now is the time for increased diligence and wisdom in your relationship with your son.
Almost half of all boys will lose their virginity by the
time they're eighteen.[7] If they are going to be responsible
and avoid the many pitfalls along the way, they need as
much help as we parents and caregivers can give them
at this stage. This includes teaching them about birth
control and your views on sex and dating. This is not a
season for the faint of heart. But with care and compassion, it is possible to help your son successfully navigate
these treacherous waters.

CHAPTER 5

The Warrior

(ages 18–22)

I (David) remember leaving home at the crack of dawn on a chilly Saturday morning back in the 1980s, my parents' car packed to the brim with clothes, towels, posters, a microwave oven, a new comforter, some cleaning supplies, extra toilet paper, and all the other odds and ends a kid needed to go to college. We caravanned there with two other friends from high school and their parents.

I had absolutely no clue what I was getting myself into. All I knew was that I was headed to one of the largest universities in the Southeast, known for good times and SEC football. (No wonder my parents were freaked out about my choice of college.) The school had twenty-five thousand students, which equaled the population of my hometown, Shelbyville, Tennessee. And there was more alcohol on fraternity row than one could purchase at every liquor store in Shelbyville as well. It was all so new, so big, and so frightening to a small-town boy from rural middle Tennessee.

I can remember helping my dad assemble the loft bed, while my mom organized the cleaning supplies. And I remember the noise up and down the dorm floor and how I had never seen so many beautiful girls in one place in all my life. I remember finishing the room and my parents taking me out for dinner. My strongest memory, however, is standing in the parking lot and saying good-bye.

My mom was starting to cry and looking away, and then my dad embraced me, and he just kept holding on to me. He was weeping and saying, "I'm so proud of you, David." He just kept saying it over and over and over, and he held me the entire time he spoke. I remember being overwhelmed. I was overwhelmed by his words, by his tears, and by everything stirring inside of me. I remember having some sense of "this must be a really big deal for my mom—and even my dad—to be in such a state at the idea of leaving me here."

As it turned out, my parents had no idea what I would put them through over the course of my undergraduate experience. At summer orientation, the advisors had asked each of us to declare a major. I recall choosing accounting, because (at the time) I thought it was a stable career and would make me good money. "Besides," I told my roommate, "what woman wouldn't want to marry, settle down, and have a family with a good CPA?" Excellent logic. I held true to my choice of majors for some time, despite earning a D in Introduction to Accounting and failing Statistics—twice!

When I finally admitted that accounting wasn't my strong suit, I changed my major to English. When that also didn't quite pan out, I moved on to advertising, and then marketing, took a brief look at hotel and restaurant management, and finally landed in the study of psychology my junior year. By this time, my mother's only request was that I would "just pick one and graduate. We don't care what, just pick one." I'm certain my parents were thrilled to learn I would finish with a B.A. in psychology. Without graduate school, I would be well suited to manage any Ponderosa Steakhouse or be a night manager at Kinko's.

The Lay of the Land

I'm a parent myself now and just the *idea* of sending my kids away to college nearly undoes me. I now understand what my parents went through. The idea of spending eighteen years pouring into someone, sacrificing on their behalf, lying awake worrying and wondering about them, investing all of who you are, and then being required to send them out into the world is just so backwards. Yet it's exactly what every parent is called to do in this season of a boy's life. If we've done our job, he's ready to be sent out. He's been preparing for this moment for years and years, and we can only hope that we've prepared him well enough for it.

For most guys, this stage in their development is a time of launching out into a dangerous world. They will now go into battle in the world of independence. As parents and caregivers, we can't go to battle for them (though many of us will try). It's time for them to fight on their own. That's why we call boys in this stage of development Warriors. The word *warrior* is defined as "a soldier, a fighting man, someone engaged in or experienced in warfare." In sending our boys out into the battleground of the adult world, it's important that we understand what they will face there.

Not all boys are ready for the Warrior stage when they arrive there. Some seem closer to still wanting to be tucked in at night than they are to having the world by the tail. Some boys are just downright lazy and seem more like warts than Warriors. They aren't reflective, and they don't search for what's next. Instead, they sit around the house, mooch off their parents, and become experts at PS3. For the most part, they are still immature.

What may inhibit a boy from stepping into being a Warrior are things such as birth order, temperament, transitions or traumas, developmental lags, and a parent's response to the launching out.

If a boy got stuck or short-circuited somewhere along the way, we will see strong evidence at this point in the game. He will have great difficulty stepping into life on his own. He won't have a sense of who he is. He won't know how to be his own man. He won't know how to exercise his strength or demonstrate his tenderness.

Who He Is: The Warrior

Rocket Boys is Homer Hickam's award-winning memoir of growing up in the depressed coal mining town of Coalwood, West Virginia, and his struggle to find his way out.[1] For most boys, the only way out of Coalwood was by getting a football scholarship. Fourteen-year-old Homer, however, was miserable at sports and feared that he would be destined to work the coal mines after high school. After watching Sputnik streak across the night sky in October 1957, Homer became inspired to build a rocket and someday join the Army Ballistic Missile Agency.

His dreams inspired other Coalwood boys to join his cause, and the group dubbed themselves "The Rocket Boys." Against Homer's father's wishes, and in the face of the town's derision, the boys struggled with their dream. Yet, with the help of their teacher, Miss Riley, the boys overcame various obstacles and set-backs and successfully launched a rocket. Before it was all said and done, the boys would launch thirty-four rockets, achieving a maximum altitude of more than six miles.

Homer's book, which later became the basis for the movie *October Sky*, gives us an excellent illustration of the evolution from Wanderer to Warrior in a boy's life. The opening paragraph of *Rocket Boys* says it well:

> Until I began to build and launch rockets, I didn't know my hometown was at war over its children and that my parents were locked in a kind of bloodless combat over how my brother and I would live our lives. I didn't know that if a girl broke your heart, another girl, virtuous at least in spirit, could mend it on the same night. And I didn't know that the enthalpy decrease in a converging passage could be transformed into jet kinetic energy if a divergent passage was added. Other boys discovered their own truths when we built our rockets, but those were mine.[2]

When a boy reaches the Warrior stage, he is full of promise, pur-pose, innocence, and insight. He is in the home stretch of a long journey. Warriors are *finishing, reflective, searching, romantic*, and *ambivalent*.

FINISHING

Though Warriors are prepared for the fight, they are largely untested in battle. Every time I (David) teach the Nurturing Boys class, I ask the adults present to identify the age at which adolescence ends for males. I have yet to teach the class without at least one woman in the room yelling out something like "forty-five." The room erupts into laughter, because every woman present has at one time or another encountered an adult male who acts more like a fifteen-year-old boy. Many people are surprised to learn that adolescence for males ends around twenty-three or twenty-four (which is much later than for their female counterparts).

This stage in male development is a time of launching out. The Warrior is peaking in his physical development and has come to grips with the changes in his body. The biological tsunami that began when he was an Individual and continued when he was a Wanderer is dissipating. He is cognitively becoming more reasonable and analytical, and he is generally more focused on his goals.

A Warrior still may be experiencing a good deal of confusion, but it's a different agenda at this point. His focus has shifted from boyhood to manhood. He wants to become a man. He is learning how to manage himself and cope with his inner world and the world around him. Though his physical development is mostly complete, there is still room for growth in terms of his emotional, spiritual, and psychological maturity.

By the end of this stage, a Warrior will have become more of a peer to his parents. He will complete his education, find his own place to live, get a job, and begin paying most, if not all, of his own bills.

REFLECTIVE

In the classic teen movie *Say Anything*, Diane Court, the class valedictorian, gives a speech at her high school graduation ceremony. Though the character is a girl, she sums up the way of the Warrior:

Well, it's almost over. We've gone to school together
for three years, and we've been through a lot. But with
that training out of high school gone, what's going
to happen to us? We all know what the answers are.
We want to be happy, go to college, own a car, maybe
raise a family. But what if that doesn't happen? I have
... I have to be honest, though. I have all the hope
and ambition in the world. But when I think about
the future, the truth is, I am really ... scared.

Where once he thought the world was black-and-white, the Warrior now sees that certain things are gray. He no longer considers
things in such concrete ways, and he has developed the ability to
think abstractly. He is reflecting on things such as family, politics,
culture, faith, and romance, but the thing he is thinking about the
most is himself.

The Warrior wants to become a man, but he knows he's not
fully there yet. He still has questions—deep questions—about his
identity, his core values, his calling, and his relationships. Masculinity is hard for him to articulate, but it's something he craves
and considers often. He thinks about his place, how he fits in, or
his ranking in the pecking order. He often reflects on his purpose
and his past. He is asking questions like, What does it mean for
me to be a man? What do I want to do with my life? and What is
life all about? Even if you never hear him talk about it, he is thinking and feeling about issues of masculinity, and he is asking more
than ever, *Do I have what it takes?*

SEARCHING

The Warrior is searching for many things. In addition to wondering about his purpose and identity, he is searching for the

next steps to take and how best to take them. He feels a sense of urgency about becoming a man, and he is ambitious. The Warrior is searching for a context in which to express his passion and pursue his interests, and he has many options—college, military service, trade school, missionary work, starting a business, and public service, just to name a few.

He is also searching for a mentor, leader, or guide other than his parents (specifically, other than his father). This can be a professor, coach, campus minister, employer, or other older adult male friend. The Warrior is searching for the voice of other adult men that he respects who will speak into his life.

There's a lot on the line if a boy can't find his place as a Warrior. The consequences are painful and long-term. If a boy stumbles at the Warrior stage, he will struggle with it for years, and it will frustrate his growth as a man. Many of the thirtysomethings I (Stephen) see in my counseling practice talk about being "lost" or "unfulfilled" or "bored." These guys wrestle with feelings of incompetence and looking for connection. As we talk, it becomes apparent that they never got the key "questions of the soul" answered as Warriors. Often, to avoid the pain of this predicament, they quit searching.

ROMANTIC

The Warrior is also searching for a mate. Many guys at this stage of their development will become involved in a significant romantic relationship (sometimes even to the point of being preoccupied with it). As a Warrior's peer group and parents diminish in importance, romantic relationships often become center stage. He begins to practice and explore how things like love, self-sacrifice, and mutuality work in the adult world.[3] Some Warriors become sexually active. Some fall in love. Some do both. Some get married. Some even have kids.

As a college freshman, Jared met a girl at orientation and had an epiphany. These are his exact words: "She walked into my orientation group, and I couldn't breathe right for the first ten minutes. I remember the orientation leaders talking about how normal it was to feel lost and misplaced in the first month on campus and to question your decision about college. I don't remember anything else they said after that. I couldn't stop staring at her, couldn't stop thinking about how in the world to ask her out on a date, couldn't stop thinking about how not to come across like an infatuated idiot, but I was."

Though a Warrior may have dated in high school, he now begins to see how difficult love is and how rewarding it can be. He starts to learn about how the themes of commitment, love, and sex weave in and through each other. It's as a Warrior that a man ultimately decides whether women are to be loved or consumed.[4] He also begins to see that nothing is more gloriously disruptive to a man than a woman. Regardless of how brave he is as a Warrior, he is nothing if he doesn't learn the importance of compassion, beauty, and softness that a woman can bring into his life.

AMBIVALENT

Warriors are frequently perplexed as they begin to experience contrary simultaneous emotions: joy and sadness, fear and excitement, humility and hubris, uncertainty and confidence.

This can be a time of grieving, transition, and loss for a Warrior—a period of fear that involves such questions as, Will I make something of myself? or Do I have a future ahead of me? There's usually some grieving about leaving home; yet, at the same

STEPHEN JAMES | DAVID THOMAS

time, there's a great deal of excitement, as well. The Warrior stage is typically also a period of hope, ambition, and passion, in which he often declares to himself, "I can't wait to get started!" or "Nothing will stop me!"

A Warrior may struggle with grieving his current relationships (girlfriend, family, and friends) if he is leaving them to go away, even if it's not far from home. At the same time, he may be excited about the adventure of making new friends and building new relationships.

I'm fascinated by back-to-back pages in Maurice Sendak's *Where the Wild Things Are*. On the first page, Max is fully engaged in "the wild rumpus," riding high on the back of one of the wild things. With scepter in hand, and his eyes closed in confidence, he is leading the event. But turn the page and there sits Max with a look of fear and hesitation on his face. It seems that despite all the fun and adventure, "he was lonely and wanted to be where someone loved him most of all." It's a great picture of the ambivalence a boy experiences in the Warrior stage—full of strength and bravado at one moment; lonely and longing the next.

What He Needs: Guidance and Support

The movie *Ferris Bueller's Day Off* depicts a day in the life of high school senior Ferris Bueller, who takes a day off from school to go to downtown Chicago with his girlfriend, Sloane, and best friend, Cameron. It's hilarious. If you haven't seen it in a while and you have a boy in the Warrior stage, make a point of watching the movie together. Apart from the teenage antics, such as borrowing a meticulously restored 1961 Ferrari 250 GT California, faking reservations so they can dine in a five-star restaurant, and singing and marshaling a German cultural parade, much of the humor in the movie comes from Bueller's frequent, pretentious philosophical comments made directly to the audience. In one such soliloquy, Bueller remarks, "Life moves pretty fast. If you don't stop and look around once in a while, you could miss it." In another, he muses, "A person should not believe in an *ism*, he should believe in himself. I quote John Lennon, 'I don't believe in Beatles, I just believe in me.'" And Ferris's friend, Cameron, declares, "I am not going to sit [around] as the events that affect me unfold to determine the course of my life. I'm going to take a stand. I'm going to defend it. Right or wrong, I'm going to defend it."

Ferris Bueller and Cameron are Warriors fighting to declare their independence. And like most Warriors, they know a lot, but a lot less than they think they know.

Even though they are legally adults by this point, Warriors still need guidance, nurturing, and support. Though their journey through boyhood to the country of men is coming to an end, there are still some very important things they need: *a training ground, freedom, blessing, patience,* and *transitional parents.*

A TRAINING GROUND

Before he is launched into the fray of manhood, a Warrior needs to live life within the context of a training ground. He needs to be in an environment where he can begin experiencing what it looks like to carry his own weight. He needs a context in which life's logical consequences can play out, but in relative safety. He needs to be challenged with weighty responsibilities. Training grounds include such places as college, art school, or trade school; spiritual communities, such as L'Abri[5]; personal development experiences, such as Outward Bound[6]; or service organizations, such as the military, AmeriCorps[7], or the Peace Corps.[8] All these organizations provide a context for the Warrior to test and train himself.

I (David) remember the first time (because there were several before I really got the point) I walked out behind my dorm to take my car to work, only to find it missing. When I had pulled in a little before midnight the night before, I had somehow missed the small wooden sign tucked behind the bushes that read, "No parking. Tow away zone." I remember freaking out and calling my dad, who remained surprisingly calm and coached me through calling the number on the sign and lining up a buddy to drive me to the tow yard (not to mention figuring out how to get my hands on an extra seventy-five bucks). The next time it happened (yes, it happened twice more before it really registered with me, because sometimes adolescent boys are slow learners), I navigated the waters on my own. My dad didn't rush in with money to cover my mistake or offer to help line up transportation to get to my vehicle. He understood the error as part of my training and hoped it would serve as some sort of wake-up call for me to pay attention.

FREEDOM

A Warrior needs the freedom to leave (even if we don't want him to). He needs to experience our believing that he is ready (even if we have some reservations). And he needs for us to celebrate his leaving (even if we are grieving). He needs the freedom to go away and make mistakes, and to be welcomed home the way the Prodigal Son was welcomed home in the Bible.[9]

A young man in this stage of his development should experience reduced physical, emotional, and financial support if we are to prepare him well for adulthood. It's important to keep the larger objective in focus as we make decisions for boys in this stage.

Many parents we have worked with begin to panic during this stage, making mental lists of all the things they have failed to teach their sons. They then set out on a full-court press to make sure their son gets what he needs. Unfortunately, for most boys, if they don't have it by now, it's too late for their parents to give it to them. These boys will have to get it someplace else—usually in the school of hard knocks.

One mother I (Stephen) was working with was torn up that her son was not prepared for the academic responsibilities of college life. "All during middle school and high school, I studied with him. I checked over his homework. I quizzed him before his tests. We talked about the papers he was writing." She was now in tears. "He and I joked about how I was like his own private tutor. Now I realize that maybe I hurt him more than I helped him. Please tell me what I can do to get him ready for college by teaching him how to study well."

Dane Anthony, a friend of ours, served as associate dean of students at Belmont University in Nashville, Tennessee. Among other things, he was responsible for the orientation process for new students and their parents. After working with college students for almost twenty years, Dane says, "Over the years, college students have become increasingly less independent. When I started working in higher ed, they were expected to meet with their advisor, register for their classes, pay their bills, navigate financial aid, take care of settling in the dorms, and figure out their meal plans. Orientation was about building relationships. Now we have to spend all this time and energy teaching them things they knew how to do on their own a few years ago. It's weird. . . . On a whole, freshmen are more sophisticated than ever, but they are also less responsible."

When asked why he thought that was, Dane said, "Parents," without hesitation. "They are so afraid to see their kids fail, that

STEPHEN JAMES | DAVID THOMAS

they have hovered over the kids their entire lives. You've heard the phrase 'helicopter parents,' right? Well they are really becoming more like 'Apache attack helicopter parents.'"

If parents haven't let their son fail by the time he's a Warrior, they're going to have to let him fail now. Though the pain will be worse because the consequences are bigger, it is better for a boy to learn these lessons now, before he enters manhood. On a practical level, he should be washing his own clothes, cooking for himself, attending to things such as auto maintenance, routine medical appointments (physical exams and going to the dentist), grocery shopping, and managing his own finances. (Even if his parents are paying his tuition and college expenses, he should manage those expenses and a regular budget.)

BLESSING

There's a powerful scene in *There Will Be Blood*, the Oscar-nominated film starring Daniel Day-Lewis as an oilman in the early 1900s. Lewis's character, Daniel Plainview, is consumed with finding oil, drilling for oil, and the wealth he has accumulated from the industry. In a pivotal scene within the story, Plainview's son sits before him as a young man, newly married, wanting to inform his father that he is launching out, moving to a new state with his young bride to develop his own oil business with all he has learned from watching and working alongside his father. The father is unable to move past his own greed and anger to bless his son in this new venture. He merely sees it as competition. As he begins attacking and shaming his son, we watch the boy's spirit break in the presence of the man from whom he so desperately longs to receive a blessing.

A Warrior needs to experience our blessing and celebration of his becoming a man. He needs to hear our approval and that our good wishes and prayers are for him. We need to communicate to him that we are glad about who he is becoming and excited to see him take the last steps of boyhood.

Much of our role as parents to a Warrior lies in recognizing our power to bless him with our affirmation, recognition, and vision. Our affirmation and love reassure him that we are in his corner. Our recognition draws attention to his impact in the world. And our vision of who he is and where he is going gives him wind in his sails and a compass bearing to follow as he ventures out into manhood.

One way in which we can recognize and affirm our Warrior sons and help them complete the transition from boyhood to manhood is through rites-of-passage experiences and rituals. We believe these celebrations are so important that we've devoted an entire chapter to them later in the book.

PATIENCE

A Warrior needs to experience his parents and other caregivers being patient with his growing up. We know he is almost finished, and he knows he is almost finished, but we don't need to rush the process. Some boys are slow to move forward and reluctant to transition into the next academic and life phases. Boys at this stage need our understanding in terms of the grieving, transition, and loss that go along with leaving behind their boyhood. They need for us to acknowledge that this season can be plagued with uncertainty and change.

It's not uncommon for a boy who was fiercely independent in high school to struggle with the transition into college. He may go from being a no-show around the house as a high school senior to showing up at home every weekend (with his laundry) as a college freshman. Some boys at this stage make big plans for trips and adventures that never seem to take place.

Warriors need for us to give them room to ask questions of themselves. They need our help in identifying the parts of themselves that are still trying to settle in. However, if we want them to hear us, we must help them more through listening than through sharing. As parents and mentors, we must keep the lines of communication open with our boys so that they have a place to bat around ideas. But even though we should welcome them to call for advice, and they should know that we will hear them and support them at all times, there should be less advice and more empowerment taking place in this stage. When we do respond, our feedback should involve more than empty praise and "you'll do fine." We need to respond honestly, even if it's painful to say and hear.

It's important to note that being patient with a Warrior in transition doesn't mean there aren't some boundaries and parameters around his season of launching out. If a Warrior is living at home and not pursuing academic or vocational goals, he needs to do two things: pay rent and work full-time. Some birds need a bit of nudging out of the nest, which means making the nest more uncomfortable than it was when he was in high school.

TRANSITIONAL PARENTS

When twenty-year-old Glen comes home from college, he can't stop talking about Gary, his campus minister. Gary is a man in his late thirties, with two young children. Gary hangs out on campus, meeting students for coffee or meals, playing intramurals, and attending football games. He has a keen interest in Glen and his suitemates. They are studying texts from early theologians and thrive on having long, heady conversations. When Glen comes home for breaks, he talks endlessly about his emerging ideas on faith, politics, war, and the environment. His parents refer to the content as "the Gospel according to Gary."

In the Warrior stage, a boy still needs mentors, but they now serve a slightly different role than they did when he was in the Wanderer stage. Instead of reinforcing what was being taught at home, these significant adults in the Warrior's life serve as transitional parents (or what some call third parents).[10]

Oftentimes it can be painfully hard as parents to hear a son confidently quote what his philosophy professor says about the presidential candidates. Or what suggestions his pastor gave him for his prayer life. Or what his coach thinks he needs to do about his job offer. Or what his girlfriend's parents suggested he might do this summer.

Parents need to remember that these mentors and advisors are important figures in their son's life. They are helping him make the final steps into manhood. Without transitional parents, a boy can become trapped in adolescence. He will come much closer to being a man before he gets married if he has transitional adults in his life. So many of the men we see in our counseling practices are still, in effect, emotional adolescents. They often come to talk about their midlife crises, but what they end up learning through therapy is how to be a real man.

Putting the Principles into Practice

At the Warrior stage, your boy is poised at the cusp of manhood. Here are some suggestions for helping him take the next step.

TIP 1: **Don't squash his dreams—even if they seem impractical to you.** Warriors are great at dreaming big and
casting visions for themselves. At this stage, your boy
has more ambition than experience, but it's more helpful for you to blow wind into his sails than to clip his
wings. Would you rather he remember your encouraging his dreams, or your not believing in him?

TIP 2: **Let him overload.** At some point as a Warrior, your boy
will take on much more responsibility than he should.
Don't rescue him. He needs to learn to recover from his
own bad choices. (However, if you see him taking on
too much responsibility, keep an eye on him in case he
becomes excessively anxious or worried or has a panic
attack. If this happens, you need to intervene and help
him get the appropriate help through a physician or
counselor.)

TIP 3: **Recover the basics.** As your boy enters this stage, it
is important to review the family rules with him and
invite his feedback. He may have good reasons why
your expectations of him need to change, and he will
probably be able to offer you some sensible ways of
loosening his boundaries. Negotiating through this process with him will affirm his voice and show him you
value his ideas in the decision-making process regarding his life and affairs.

TIP 4: **Welcome his girlfriend(s) with open arms.** At some
point in this stage, the Warrior will return from battle
with a damsel he has rescued. Don't freak out. Don't
judge her. Remember, it is likely that this is the most
important person in his life. Your acceptance of her is
also acceptance of him. Likewise, don't be overly enthusiastic. You don't want to start making wedding plans

and decorating the grandbaby's nursery; you'll just look like a fruitcake.

TIP 5: Do your homework. Ask your son what books or movies are important to him. Read the books and see the movies and ask him to tell you what he appreciates about them.

TIP 6: Initiate him. Send him on a trip by himself, and orchestrate a season of rites-of-passage activities (see chapter 13).

TIP 7: Get him off the sofa. If your son is lazy, remember that's not unusual at this stage. With that said, he still needs to be active, even if he's hard to motivate. By this stage in the game, he should be motivating himself and not waiting for you to nag him. Ideally, there will be enough external motivators (such as needing to make money to pay for gas or to take his girlfriend on a date) that you won't have to do much of anything. If not, you may need to evaluate whether you've made life too convenient for him. Expect him to want downtime when he's on a break from school, but if you notice him quitting activities that he once loved, sleeping more (or not sleeping), or gaining or losing weight, he may need some professional help, because these are all signs of clinical depression.

TIP 8: Remember, he's not twelve anymore. If he comes home (either by flunking out or of his own accord), consider drafting a contract with expectations around his living at home as a young adult (paying rent, doing laundry, assisting with home management, etc.).

TIP 9: Keep the door open. Make certain that you are a safe person for him to talk with about the use of drugs or other risky behavior. Make certain that you communicate with him that you believe in his ability to regulate his own behavior. If you don't trust him in this area, state your expectations clearly and then remember that you cannot police this area of his life. Your attempts to do so will likely only keep him from wanting to come home or dialogue with you about it. If you have concerns regarding experimentation moving into addiction with drugs, or with other risky behavior, consult with a therapist about options for intervention.

TIP 10: Remember who is king of the castle. It's okay to have some expectations of your son when he comes home on break. As much as he should have ownership of his own schedule and disciplines (or lack thereof), once he comes back under your roof, he has to be respectful of those still living there. For example, I (David) once worked with a young man who kept ridiculous hours (like most college students) when on campus. When home for Christmas break, he would stay up watching TV until 2 a.m. and then take a shower in the bathroom next to his parents' room. His mom woke up the second time it happened to remind him that he was welcome to shower while at home, but his parents, unlike his suitemates, liked to sleep at 2 a.m. rather than hear the water running and doors slamming. So, welcome him home, but make sure he remembers whose house it is. It's never a good idea for a boy to be king of the castle.

Part 2

The Mind of a Boy

And the walls became the world around.

MAURICE SENDAK, *Where the Wild Things Are*

Some friends of ours, Ted and Ann, have three kids, two of whom are boys. A job transfer recently moved them just outside of Houston. The family has been settling into a new community, a new church, a new home, new schools for the kids, a new job for Ted, and a new life for all five of them.

Early in the transition, they met a family in the church who had a son the same age as their second son, Wilson. This discovery had all the makings of an emerging friendship. They invited the family for a Saturday evening dinner and hoped to connect as couples and nurture a friendship for their son.

Ann is a spectacular cook—not just a good cook, but a meal-that-changes-your-life kind of cook. She prepared a stunning dinner, the couples shared great conversation for hours, and the kids were seemingly content playing upstairs. As they concluded what appeared to have been a nearly perfect evening and got the kids down to bed, Ted and Ann reflected on how grateful they were to be laying down roots in Texas.

The following morning, Ann was making her way down the hall in the educational building of the church when she was stopped by the wife of the couple they'd had over the night before. Ann reached out to hug the other woman, assuming she was approaching to say what a great evening it had been or to comment on the dessert. They had no sooner pulled back from their brief embrace when the mom spoke up to say, "I need to tell you something, because you seem like the kind of mother who would want to know." (Now those are honestly some of the worst words we can hear as a parent. You know what's coming next is gonna be bad.) "Last night, just before bed, our son mentioned to us that Wilson had locked him in a closet and told him he'd have to 'kiss my butt' before he'd let him out."

The mother went on, "I didn't quite know how to respond, but I thought you would certainly want to know." Ann also wasn't quite sure how to respond in her state of humiliation and shame. When our buddy Ted retold the story to me (David)—and once I stopped howling—I immediately asked, "What the heck was he thinking?"

If you've had much contact with boys, you've probably asked yourself the same question a time or two: "What was he thinking?" Well, odds are, it's not the same thing a girl would have been thinking in the same situation. In many, many ways, the mind of a boy is different from the mind of a girl (and thus the Venus and Mars thing with men and women). These structural differences affect everything in the life of a boy—from how he thinks, to how he relates to others, to what he watches on TV, to how he needs to study, to how he takes discipline, to how he thinks about God. On the whole, boys tend to be

- spatial instead of relational (they understand the lay of the land instead of how things are interconnected)
- aware of objects instead of faces (they're more attracted to balls than they are to people)
- action oriented, as opposed to process oriented (they're oriented toward movement instead of toward emotions)

Gaining an appreciation for the mind of a boy is fundamental if we are to nurture him well. (And it may even give us the perspective we need to answer the question, What was he thinking?)

The development of the male brain from birth through boyhood to manhood is quite different from the same process in girls. It's not uncommon to find a three-year-old boy fascinated with balls while a girl the same age is transfixed on dolls; or adolescent boys zoning out in front of the TV while teenage girls are chatting it up on the phone. It's important for us as parents, educators, and caregivers to understand these distinctions in gender terms, because often what's needed for boys is different from what the girls need.

Parents, teachers, and other leaders often expect boys to do things that go against their wiring—for example, requiring boys to sit still for long periods in the classroom when everything about them craves space and movement. Many of the challenges that boys face in our culture, at home, and at school—things like aggression, competition, sexuality, depression, and ADHD—are intensified by how we expect boys to behave. Certainly, we can't adequately address these issues without a thorough understanding of how a boy's brain develops.

In the next four chapters we will look at some important categories that we must understand if we hope to nurture our boys with dignity, respect, love, and confidence.

- A Boy's Brain (chapter 6)
- Different Learning Styles (chapter 7)
- "Sit Still! Pay Attention!" (chapter 8)
- Deficits and Disappointments (chapter 9)

In these chapters, we will address many of the issues we frequently encounter as we work with boys and their families, mentors, and teachers. Though not every boy will struggle with all the same issues, the concerns are common enough that we want to provide you with a framework for understanding them. We've tried to explain things in a way that brings clarity, as well as offer you some specific tools for engaging, equipping, and encouraging your boy along his journey.

CHAPTER 6

A Boy's Brain

How does one kid end up with green testicles, another suffer a broken arm, and a third wind up lost in a field more than five miles from his house in the hours right after dawn? Easy—they're all boys.

Six-year-old Mark was visiting his friend Luke's house. Boys being boys, it wasn't too long before they found Luke's big sister's stash of green nail polish. Both boys loved to play superheroes, and it made sense to them that this fingernail polish was perfect for turning themselves into the Incredible Hulk. Luke convinced Mark he could become the Hulk only if he painted himself green—which Mark proceeded to do, right down to the green weenie. Later, as Mark's mother wiped off his genitals with fingernail polish remover, she asked, "What in the world were you thinking?"

When Derek was eight, he was sitting on the edge of a tree fort about twelve-feet high and accidentally pushed off his friend Gavin by slapping his back and saying, "What would happen if you got knocked off?" Gavin broke his arm. En route to the emergency room, Derek's mom said to Derek, "What was going through your head?"

Jeff and his dad got into a serious fight one evening over curfew. That night, after his parents had gone to bed, Jeff packed some clothes in a duffel bag and set his alarm clock for 5 a.m. When he got up, he took forty dollars and his mom's credit card out of her purse in the kitchen and then slipped out of the house on foot. When Jeff's dad came to wake him up at 6:30, he found an empty bed. After searching the house and calling Jeff's cell phone, he contacted the police. An hour later, the police found Jeff, about five and a half miles from the house, walking through a field on his way downtown to the bus station. As he was placing Jeff in the back of the patrol car, the officer asked, "Where were you thinking about going?" Jeff replied, "I don't know, I was gonna figure that out when I got to the bus station."

The common denominator in each of these stories is the question, What were you thinking? If there's a boy in your life, you'll ask that question at least a dozen times (a day). Often you'll wonder if he was even thinking at all.

The Not-So-Good News

Extensive research in the area of cognitive development has enhanced our understanding of the brain's function. This research has also furthered our understanding of the differences between male and female brains. Recognizing these differences can shape our responses as parents, educators, coaches, mentors, and other adults entrusted with the responsibility of caring for boys. The differences between male and female brains explain a number of the fascinating (and sometimes maddening) distinctions that we see between the two sexes. Let's do some of the arithmetic.

MORE ACTIVITY + LESS IMPULSE CONTROL + TESTOSTERONE = BOYS

We've already discussed how the female brain secretes more serotonin, which is directly related to impulse control. In addition to this, a girl's frontal lobes grow at earlier stages and are generally more active. For this reason, girls tend to make fewer impulsive executive decisions compared to boys. The male brain has more spinal fluid in the brain stem, which makes boys more physical than girls. Add to that the high level of testosterone in a boy's brain, and it's easy to see that he is programmed to be more aggressive than a girl and more of a risk taker.

LESS SENSORY DETAIL + LESS MEMORY ABILITY = BOYS

The occipital lobe of a little girl's brain develops more rapidly than a boy's, which means girls can take in more sensory data. This explains why women can multitask more effectively than men. Boys tend to (and need to) focus primarily on one thing. Also, the hippocampus, which is in charge of memory (both capacity and function) is much larger in girls than in boys. This explains why girls can recall every specific detail of their day.

MORE FREQUENT REST STATES +
LONGER REST STATES = BOYS

A boy's body may be more active, but that doesn't hold true for his brain. Estrogen provides a biochemical base for increased brain activity, and a female brain has up to 15 percent more blood flow at any given moment than a male brain. Furthermore, even when the female brain goes into a state of rest, it does not shut down the way the male brain does. (Think of a computer going to "sleep.") Thus, even when a female student is bored by a lesson, her brain is more actively able and willing to keep her eyes open, continue taking notes, and process the information. On the other hand, if you've ever asked a boy (or a man) what he's thinking about and he said, "Nothing," odds are he was telling the truth.

LIGHTS + SOUNDS + MOVING IMAGES =
ZOMBIE BOYS

By the time boys and girls are in third or fourth grade, media influences become stronger and more enticing. But boys can become obsessively absorbed with media (television, video games, or movies) at even younger ages. Fast-moving images, blaring sounds, intense special effects, and colorful characters enter his mind more quickly and intensely than other less-stimulating educational and life experiences.

FEWER FEELINGS +
LESS VERBAL EXPRESSION = BOYS

Structurally, the male brain is very different from its female counterpart. Though boys have bigger brains than girls, on average, some studies indicate that they may have a smaller corpus callosum (the part of the brain that connects the hemispheres and lets the different halves of the brain "talk" to each other). A bigger brain also means less white matter, which is the jelly that surrounds the brain and helps the different parts of the brain connect efficiently. Compared to girls, boys have less gray matter (the brain cells that perform thinking), slower blood flow in their brains, and slower electrical activity (which means girls are able to change focus more quickly than boys and explains why a boy who is playing Wii can "ignore" or "not hear" his mother, even when she stands directly over him and calls his name).[1] These distinctions, among other structural differences in a boy's brain, mean that he can't process emotional content as well as a girl can. Research has shown that, during the emotional process, there is not as much activity in a boy's brain, which translates to less emotional recognition and reduced verbal expression.

LARGER PREOPTIC AREA + ROUNDER SUPRACHIASMATIC NUCLEUS = BOYS

Another difference between the brains of boys and girls is in the hypothalamus, the part of the brain that controls sexuality and circadian rhythms. The hypothalamus is made up of two different parts: the preoptic area and the suprachiasmatic nucleus (SCN).

One difference, which shows up around the age of four, is that a boy's preoptic area (the part of the brain that controls sexual behavior) is more than twice as large in volume and has twice as many cells as the same structure in a girl.[2] The preoptic area is also responsible for maintenance of body temperature, and it receives nervous stimulation from thermoreceptors in the skin, mucous membranes, and hypothalamus itself. The SCN

STEPHEN JAMES | DAVID THOMAS

is involved with circadian rhythms and reproduction cycles. It orchestrates biological rhythms, such as the rhythms of hormones, body temperature, sleep, and mood. The differences in the hypothalamus (combined with the influence of our hyper-sexualized culture) begin to explain why boys are often more sexual than girls.

Now for Some Good News

Fear not. The news isn't all bad. Having a male brain brings with it some extraordinary gifts. The more scientists study the human brain, the more they are seeing that boys tend to have some innate cognitive abilities. As parents, teachers, and mentors, we can use our knowledge of this "hardwiring" to help boys be more of who they are made to be.

A BOY'S BRAIN IS IMAGINATIVE.

One day I (Stephen) went into one of my sons' rooms, where he was playing, to find twine running from one end of the room to the other. From ceiling to floor and window to door, he had wads of string. "What happened here, buddy?" I asked.

"Spiderman tried to catch the bad guy," he said, without pause or recognition of the amazing mess he had created. When I asked him to explain further, he told me that "the bookshelves are sky-scrapers, the bed is a neighborhood, the rug is a pit of acid, and the closet is a black hole."

Amazed, all I could say was, "Oh."

Imaginative play in the life of a boy is a natural and healthy thing. Imagination is a significant component of a child's emotional, psychological, and spiritual development. Imaginative play is not simply a time when a boy amuses himself. Imagination leads to other forms of learning and moral development. Boys, even teenagers, live in their imaginations. From role-playing to daydreaming, boys depend heavily on their imaginations to process and resolve inner conflict. In *Where the Wild Things Are*, Max's room becomes a forest that "grew and grew and grew until his ceiling hung with vines and the walls became the world all around and an ocean tumbled." Max used his imagination to come to grips with his poor behavior and his mother's discipline.

A BOY'S BRAIN IS SPATIAL.

The male brain is also hardwired to be strong at spatial relationships. Boys have an extraordinary ability to navigate building and design projects. Alongside being spatially strong, they are typically more skilled than girls in hand-eye coordination. A boy's ability to handle a ball and move it through space is oftentimes extraordinary. His ability to form Legos into a helicopter is wonderful. One reason that boys excel at video games is their ability to handle the complex process of interpreting the relationship of three-dimensional concepts from two-dimensional screens. This same ability explains why boys are typically better at tasks that require the ability to mentally rotate images, such as in interpreting graphs, reading maps, making architectural drawings, and reading X-rays.

Researchers at the University of Chicago demonstrated that boys have an advantage over girls in their understanding of spatial relationships as early as age four and a half (much earlier than once thought). Spatial skills are important to everyday living, as well as for performing well in school and on the job.[3]

The findings that sex differences in spatial learning develop so early is important, because it disproves earlier theories that these differences were brought on by biological factors (such as hormonal changes) or environmental differences (such as boys playing sports).

A BOY'S BRAIN IS SOLUTIONS FOCUSED.

In his book *The Essential Difference*, Simon Baron-Cohen explains his theory that the female brain is predominantly hardwired for empathy (the ability to identify and respond to another person's emotions) and the male brain for systematizing (the drive to explore and analyze systems).[4] This phenomenon would explain why boys tend to be weaker emotionally and relationally than girls. The female brain houses more oxytocin, a chemical that drives a caretaking response in girls and women. It's why we see little girls rocking and comforting baby dolls while their male counterparts are more inclined to slam a doll into the wall or pin it to the floor.

Boys Are Different. So What?

When we understand the essential differences in how boys and girls are hardwired, it helps us appreciate, rather than condemn, the behavior we observe. Though environmental influences (primarily family and culture), life experiences, socialization, and inherited genetic personality traits directly influence who a boy is, we cannot overlook his essential nature. And we can't nurture out the nature (nor would we want to). Instead of fighting against boys and their basic character, we must learn to work with how they were created and redirect them toward a noble vision of masculinity. Boys are largely created to be who they are—boys. As parents, teachers, and leaders, our best choice in guiding and shaping our boys is to understand how they are uniquely designed and why. When we don't intentionally channel and guide our boys' aggression, independence, tension, ambition, assertiveness, and competitiveness, we do them a great disservice. When we try to override a boy's basic wiring, the results can be disastrous (confusion, shame, self-doubt, aggression, and passivity, to name just a few).

Helping boys grow and mature into men means providing an environment that acknowledges and supports them in their maleness, not one that demands they be different. Understanding how their bodies are made to work is a form of loving them well. We will address some of these issues more specifically in the next few chapters, but in order to lay some groundwork for understanding, here are some common mistakes many caregivers make with boys: confining them, verbally or emotionally flooding them, sparring with them, rescuing them, squelching them, shaming them, guilt-tripping them, and sabotaging them.

MISTAKE #1: CONFINEMENT

It was 4:30 p.m., and ever since Andy had gotten home from school, he had been bouncing off the ceiling. Like any eleven-year-old, he left a trail of debris wherever he went. When he scratched the wall with his shoe and broke a lamp, his mom had had enough. "Go to your room right now!" she demanded.

What Andy needed at that point was not more restriction, but more direction; not more confinement, but more opportunity. Don't get us wrong, timeouts can work wonders, but so can inviting a boy to work alongside you, or putting him to work on a project or a chore. Often, parents send a boy to his room when he causes trouble. But this is like caging a tiger. What a rambunctious boy needs to correct his behavior is space, not confinement. He needs to have his energy redirected and channeled into something helpful and productive.

MISTAKE #2: VERBAL OR EMOTIONAL FLOODING

Harry's teacher, Ms. Pullman, pulled Harry out of class for teasing another boy. Once in the hall, she launched into an impassioned lecture about how the other boy must have felt, how disappointed she was in Harry, what his parents would think, how he would feel if he were the one being teased, and so on. Two minutes into the lecture, she began sounding like Charlie Brown's teacher: "Waa waa waa waa." Information was circling the hall, but nine-year-old Harry couldn't absorb it.

Because boys cannot process words and emotions as quickly or accurately as girls, Ms. Pullman was just blowing hot air. Instead of flooding Harry with words and feelings, what Ms. Pullman could have done was take any one of her emotionally centered questions and ask Harry to bring back an essay the next day with an answer to it.

MISTAKE #3: SPARRING

Twelve-year-old Jonah's dad had been waiting for him in the car for fifteen minutes to take him to lacrosse practice. When Jonah finally wandered out to the driveway, his dad was fuming. "Son, what took you so long? If you want to be on time, you need to get your bag ready the night before. Do you know how late we are? Did you hear me?"

Because boys already have a high level of aggression and assertiveness, one surefire way to turn a conversation into a war is to spar with them. Many boys will naturally escalate a confrontation. They don't know when or how to back down. When challenged, a boy's adrenaline starts pumping and his testosterone levels start building. If you want to lead him well, it is rarely good to set him up to go toe-to-toe with you. If you do that, you will have to win by exerting your power and dominating him. If he starts an argument with you, exerting your authority and power is one thing, but you can't ask him to respect you if you don't respect him. What Jonah's dad could have done was give a warning: "Next time you're late, we don't go." Or, if he had already given a warning, he could have given Jonah a five-minute grace period and then either parked the car back in the garage or left without him. Natural consequences are always better teachers than an argument.

MISTAKE #4: RESCUING

Carl, a high school sophomore, had known about an upcoming history exam for two weeks. His teacher had reminded the class every day to study and warned them that the test would be difficult. Carl spent the weekend at his dad's house, and they'd had a weekend-long *Star Wars* movie festival. On the way to school that Monday morning with his mom, Carl all of a sudden remembered the exam. He had honestly forgotten, and he knew he wasn't prepared. Now he was scared and almost in tears. Not wanting Carl to feel bad, his mom wrote a note to the teacher explaining that

Carl had "been away all weekend on a family trip" and needed to take the exam the next day.

Now, Carl's mom meant well. She loved her son and didn't want to see him hurt. But one of the biggest mistakes parents make is keeping their sons from experiencing natural consequences. Most often, the pain that boys experience for their own irresponsibility is far less severe than the consequences they will suffer as adults for being irresponsible.

MISTAKE #5: SQUELCHING

Ramsey had come up with a fabulous idea. He wanted to finger paint a picture for his preschool teacher. His mom was apprehensive, because she knew that there would be an enormous mess when it was all said and done. "Ramsey, we can't do that today," she said. "Can't you just color her a picture with crayons instead?"

Ramsey pleaded, "Please, Mom?"

"No, baby. It will be too messy and take too long."

Boys need to express themselves creatively—and, for many boys, the messier the better. Too often we squelch a boy's personality because it is too big, too loud, or too messy for our convenience. We're not saying that Ramsey should get everything he wants all the time, but we are saying that on those occasions when it is Mom's or Dad's own agenda that gets in the way, it's a good time to step aside and allow the child to express himself. Ramsey's mom could have thrown a tarp or an old shower curtain in the driveway, given Ramsey one of his dad's old T-shirts, and turned him loose. If it was too cold to go outside, she could have put him in the bathtub with some watercolors and let him paint there. Let your boy share his ideas and experiment as much as you can— even if it is impractical or messy.

MISTAKE #6: SHAMING

Jaquez had gotten in a fender bender on his way home from a date. When he got home, he was obviously nervous and guilty. He slunk into the living room, where his mom and dad were watching TV, and he told them what had happened to the car. His dad turned to him and blurted, "I knew it was a mistake to hand you those keys. Do you have any idea how much this is going to cost me in car insurance? You should have paid more attention to what you were doing."

Perhaps as cruel as some physical violence is the power of shame to corrupt a boy's heart. We cannot nurture a boy and shame him at the same time. Shame tells a boy that he is worthless or not good enough. It is humiliating for a boy to be attacked in this way. Coaches are infamous for this type of verbal abuse, but so are parents and teachers. Showering boys with contempt can have a long-term effect on them. Jaquez's dad may have been angry, disappointed, and worried, but it would have been far more helpful for him to engage with his son, instead of poisoning his heart with toxic shame. Instead of attacking his son's character, he should have been willing to hear his son's already guilty confession, show some concern, ask his son some questions about the event, and determine whether his son needed anything. Surely, Jaquez's dad had a right to share his disappointment, but never in a way that would make his son feel small or diminished—especially in the face of failure.

MISTAKE #7: GUILT-TRIPPING

Zane had been arrested for underage drinking at a frat party on his college campus. After being booked, he was allowed to call home to arrange his five-hundred-dollar bail. He got his mom and dad on the phone, and they double-teamed him with a guilt trip about how his father was going to have to work an extra shift to make up the difference. And how his mom was going to have to figure out how to wire money out of state. And questions like, "What will we tell your grandfather?"

Part of being a boy is making stupid and impulsive decisions and taking stupid risks. It's not terribly uncommon for boys to cross the line and get in over their heads. When they do get into trouble, they don't need a guilt trip. Guilt trips are just a passive-aggressive way of shaming someone. Zane's parents had a great opportunity to let the external authority (courts) discipline their child. Instead, they piled on. Guilt-tripping someone is always a form of manipulation, using shame-producing statements or actions in an effort to coerce someone into doing what you want, or making him feel worse about something he already feels bad about. Rubbing a boy's nose in shame is self-centered and demeaning. It is a codependent act that makes the child take responsibility for the parents' feelings.

MISTAKE #8: SABOTAGE

With one out in the top of the third inning, Ben's coach looked up to find eight-year-old Ben pasted to the center field fence, calling to a stray dog on the next field. "Ben, heads up! Pay attention!" the coach yelled. After the side was retired, the boys jogged into the dugout to take their at bat. But the coach stopped Ben at the edge of infield, bent down, and said, "If you can't pay attention out there, you'll have to sit on the bench." Ben was replaced in the lineup and watched the rest of the game from the dugout.

One way in which parents, teachers, and coaches do a disservice to boys is by setting them up to fail. Too often, boys have unreal expectations placed on them. We ask them to perform in ways they can't or that they're not ready for. Take the example above. We know two things for sure: eight-year-old boys can't pay attention, and baseball is a really slow game. Expecting a boy to maintain a laser-sharp focus all the time is unrealistic. We may want our boys to act like men and think like grown-ups, but they can't. Of course we need to discipline them for poor attitudes and for being disrespectful, and we must help them learn to be responsible, but we can't expect them to do what they're not capable of doing. As we've seen, there are biological factors that inhibit boys in the areas of focus and self-control. We must help them learn to control their impulses, but in age-appropriate ways. And we mustn't expect them to do things that are beyond their abilities.

Putting the Principles into Practice

As we said earlier, understanding a boy and how he is made is a sure way of loving him. Here are some tips for what you can do as a parent, coach, educator, or caregiver to nurture your boy's brain.

TIP 1: **Cut out the energy drinks.** We all know the benefits of a healthy diet. Along with your pediatrician's recommendations for eating, one sure way to help a boy's brain is to limit his caffeine intake. Caffeine crosses the blood/brain barrier very quickly, and its concentration in the brain is highly correlated to levels in the blood.[5] In other words, the more caffeine your boy takes in, the more ramped up his brain is. There's evidence that caffeine stimulates motor activity and that boys are particularly susceptible to this effect.[6] A boy's brain is already on the verge of igniting his body into activity—he doesn't need the help of caffeine. Be aware that caffeine is an additive in several popular soft drinks, not to mention all the so-called energy drinks.

TIP 2: Create ways for him to get exercise. Exercise is beneficial for boys not only physically, but also cognitively. Being active actually primes the brain for maximum functioning. In speaking with educators and coaching them on the rest-state phenomenon, we encourage taking frequent breaks and having boys stand, stretch, do jumping jacks or push-ups, and move about the classroom. This type of movement increases blood flow and stimulates the brain for increased functioning. At home, you can use this technique when your boy is stuck completing homework. Having him "sit still until you're finished" could actually be working against him. Have him do laps around the house, shoot hoops for fifteen minutes, or ride his bike around the block (and time him to make it competitive), and then come back and work ten more math problems. Repeat as needed.

TIP 3: Limit TV and video games. We know that boys want their MTV, PS3, Wii, and Xbox 360, but these kinds of media are bad news for their brains. There's clear evidence that the more visual media a boy takes in, the worse off his sleep, learning, and memory will be. The results of a study at the Sport University in Cologne, Germany, discovered that television and computer-game exposure (just one hour a day of gaming or two hours of television) affects a child's sleep and deteriorates his verbal cognitive performance. Both television watching and video-game playing affect children's sleep

negatively, but video games have an even more negative effect.[7] Visual stimulants, such as media watching,
inhibit development of the limbic system (the emotional center of the brain) and the neocortical (con-
scious thought and language center) areas of the brain.

TIP 4: **Make sure he gets enough sleep.** We've all heard Ben
Franklin's adage, "Early to bed and early to rise makes a
man healthy, wealthy, and wise." It has never been more
true than in our day and age. Researchers have found a
strong correlation between sleep-disordered breathing
(SDB)—snoring—and inattention and hyperactivity
among children. When doctors treated the sleep problems, they found that the inattention and hyperactivity
often improved.[8] Inattentive and hyperactive behavior
are highly prevalent among boys and are often associ-
ated with mental health issues such as ADHD.[9] But
unrecognized medical conditions are often the cause of
hyperactivity and inattentive behavior.[10]

TIP 5: **Teach him about his emotions.** Because of their brain
structure, boys have a greater difficulty in recognizing,
processing, and verbalizing emotional content. They
need our help. Boys who have a large vocabulary of "feeling words" are better at expressing their emotions using
language rather than behavioral outbursts. As caregivers,
we need engaging ways to teach boys a vocabulary for
emotions and to help them identify feelings within themselves and on the faces of others. We have to teach them
empathy. One way to do this with young children is to
open the door to feelings during story time. When reading to them, stop every so often and ask what a character
is feeling. Another powerful tool with boys is to role-play.
Switch roles with your boy and act out scenes with him.

With older boys, expose them to films and books that have strong emotional content (e.g., books such as *Where the Red Fern Grows* and *Bridge to Terabithia*, both of which have also been produced as movies, and movies such as *Remember the Titans* and *Radio*). Take your boy out for a snack and talk with him, not just about the plot and the moral of the story, but also about the emotional content of the characters.

TIP 6: **Read. Read. Read.** If your son isn't old enough to read for himself, read to him endlessly. We can't emphasize the importance of this enough. If he is old enough to read on his own, reward him strongly for completing books. (His school may already have an incentive-based program in place.) If he's struggling in this area, keep searching with him until he finds books or a series that pique his interest. If his school doesn't require summer reading, require him on your own and create strong incentives for completing a certain number of books.

TIP 7: **Give yourself a report card.** Grade yourself on each of the mistakes we mentioned above. Also, ask your spouse or a close friend to grade you, based on their observations. Focus on the areas where you scored lower, and create some strategies to avoid repeating those mistakes.

TIP 8: **Create opportunities at home that draw on his cognitive strengths.** Get your boy involved in projects that require spatial reasoning, games and activities that involve his vivid imagination, and tasks that utilize his ability to find a solution. Validate and affirm his strengths.

TIP 9: **Pick his brain.** Continue to gather information and insight about the functioning of the male brain. It's easy to respond to boys without considering the cerebral differences we've highlighted. Educating yourself about the unique characteristics of the male brain will help you understand and appreciate why your boy does or says some of the things he does.

TIP 10: Hide the green nail polish.

CHAPTER 7

Different Learning Styles

For my (David's) boys' fourth birthday, my wife asked her parents to give them gymnastics lessons at our local YMCA so they could climb, swing, jump, flip, twist, dive, leap, pounce, soar, and whatever else a four-year-old boy could dream to do in a giant room full of mats and bars. Into their fourth lesson, she called me to say, "Next week you have got to carve out some time to come see this, and bring a video camera." So, the following week I showed up with the camcorder to document the experience for the grandparents sponsoring the event and to add to our library of footage. I ended up with my own version of a documentary that I show from time to time in my Nurturing Boys class. It is a fascinating study in the differences between the genders.

The video begins with the well-intentioned instructors educating the coed class of ten in the morning's plan and leading them in some light stretches to prepare their bodies for the class. The boys in the class make it about ninety-two seconds into the instruction before the first one lies back, lifts his legs into the air, and stares at his feet. No joke. I clocked it. The guy next to him starts spinning on the mat in circles, and the guy next to him starts singing "The Star-Spangled Banner." My boys immediately become intrigued by the sideshow, and they quickly shift their focus to the trio of performers. The instructor, realizing that she's losing them, stands up and announces that it's time for stretches.

The boys proceed to stretch, but not the kind of stretches they're being instructed to do. Instead, it looks like a hybrid of martial arts, yoga, and Navy SEAL training.

At this point, I started chuckling, and the camera began bobbing up and down. My wife popped me on the arm to silence me.

The class was then split into two groups, and the instructors led them to different parts of the room, where they were to make their way through an obstacle course that had been set up before class. Each instructor demonstrated how to navigate the course, and then she lined the kids up to wait their turn. I kept the camera rolling through this portion of the class, and I've considered sending it in to *America's Funniest Home Videos*.

The girls are standing perfectly in a straight line, and the boys are scattered behind, between, and in front of them. As the first girl launches out, the boy at the back of the line edges out and makes his way to the bar designed for swinging. He pulls the bar out of the poles and begins swinging it like a lightsaber. The instructor has given her full attention to helping the first girl do a barrel roll down the mat, so the boy's mother jumps up from the sidelines and runs to take the pole from him. She scolds her little Obi-Wan Kenobi and places him back in line.

At this point, one of the other boys can no longer wait his turn. Jumping out of line (if he was ever really quite in it), he starts at the final obstacle and begins working his way forward. The instructor calls out to him to get back in line and wait his turn. He stops while she looks at him, but as soon as she turns her back, he continues his backward obstacle course. Obi-Wan starts doing some tai chi–type moves in line that end with a karate chop on the shoulder of the guy in front of him. That kid yells, jumps on Obi-Wan, and takes him down to the mat in a full-on World Wrestling Federation moment. Both their moms jump up and run to peel them off each another.

By now, on the other side of the room, two more boys are doing their own versions of the obstacle course. Instead of crawling over the moon-shaped mat, one boy tackles it, straddles it, and yells, "Ride on, Ranger." The boy is circling the room, in his own little world, and one of the girls—a classic firstborn, type A personality—is hollering, "He's not listening. He's running and not waiting his turn. Miss Jenny, he's running!"

By this point, I am hysterical, the camera is shaking, and I'm thinking that if I can't win a prize on *America's Funniest Home Videos* with this footage, it would at least make a good YouTube video.

"Boys, look with your eyes only, not your hands."

Early on, most boys are tactile and kinesthetic learners. The Explorer is a toucher and a feeler of things. He learns his letters best by tracing them rather than by memorizing them. Moreover, as we've discussed, he is designed to move. Many boys learn best when given the freedom to move about, rather than being confined to sit still and listen. This is one of the reasons that Montessori schools are such boy-friendly settings. Boys are allowed to touch and feel the manipulatives and to wander around the space, exploring at their own pace. Many preschool environments are set up similarly, allowing boys the freedom to move from center to center with limited "circle time" that would require them to sit still for extended periods.

Unfortunately, as boys transition from the Explorer stage to the Lover stage, the academic setting starts to look very different. Boys go from a school schedule that includes fewer and shorter days to five long days. They move from a fluid environment to a more ordered one. The classroom setting that once involved limited time sitting still and the freedom to move about and explore is replaced with one that requires sitting for longer periods with extended focus. Boys are given one or two opportunities a day to run without restriction or boundary and to exercise their gross motor strengths, and these times average twenty to thirty minutes total.

Whereas at one point we invited boys to touch and feel things as a means of learning, we are now saying more things like, "Stop touching!" and "Keep your hands to yourself." Boys are wildly familiar with phrases such as these:

"Sit still."

"Pay attention!"

"I need you to focus."

"Look at my eyes when I'm talking to you."

"Keep your feet on the floor."

"Look with your eyes only, not your hands."

"Stand still, please."

"Are you listening to my words?"

"This is not a time for playing."

Going through the Motions

As boys develop, they learn primarily in three ways: visually, spatially, and experientially. Schools, on the other hand, are mostly auditory, sedentary, and intellectual. This mode of learning is detrimental not only to boys, but to girls as well. A study from the American Academy of Pediatrics reports that "free and unstructured play" is "healthy and essential" for helping children reach chief "social, emotional, and cognitive developmental milestones, as well as helping them manage stress and become resilient."[1] The report cites changes in family structure, an increasingly competitive college admissions process, and federal education policies that have led to reduced recess and physical education in many schools. In settings like these, boys suffer the most. This loss of play and free time "in combination with a hurried lifestyle, can be a source of stress, anxiety, and may even contribute to depression for many children."[2] Boys who sit all day listening to lectures are being taught in an environment that is not conducive to their learning.

VISUAL LEARNING

Boys, in general, are wired to be visually stimulated. Sixty-seven percent of boys are visual learners, meaning they absorb information from illustrations, symbols, photos, icons, diagrams, graphs, and other visual models. Another way of saying this is that a boy's brain turns on when he *sees* words, whereas a girl's brain responds more readily to *hearing* words. This is important when it comes to teaching boys, because studies show that when children are deprived of vivid and regular sensory experiences, they develop brains that are 20 to 30 percent smaller than what is normal for their age, and they suffer parallel decreases in cognitive ability.[3]

Chance is a kindergartner with whom I've (David) been meeting for several months. His mom reported that he was pulling sticks (the classroom form of discipline) five out of five days.[4] She had met multiple times with his teacher, consulted with his pediatrician about the possibility of attention-related issues, and cried herself to sleep many nights before showing up in my office. I did some digging around with Chance over the course of several sessions, and he described getting bored and wanting to distract himself and other people. We did some testing and found out Chance is gifted. He's also an extremely active little guy. We talked a little about rest states and how his brain wants to go to sleep sometimes at school and stop listening, and how he understands a lot of what his teacher is saying when other kids don't and so he zones out. We came up with some strategies (such as having an object in his hand that he could manipulate) that he could use to occupy himself, without distracting others, and that would allow him to still pay attention. He's down to one pulled stick per week, and we both think we're making some headway.

As visual learners, boys benefit from seeing things play out in front of them. They benefit from charts, diagrams, overheads, and other visual stimulants in the classroom and at home. If instructions are simply spoken, there's always the chance they'll fly in one ear and out the other.

When working with an Explorer, we encourage his parents and teachers to draw diagrams that include pictures of his chores and responsibilities—such as a picture of a boy putting toys in a basket, a picture of a boy brushing his teeth, and a picture of a boy putting dirty clothes in a hamper.

With boys at the Lover stage and above, we suggest giving him an index card with a *short* checklist of responsibilities. (We emphasize the word *short*, because boys get lost and overwhelmed in too much verbiage.) He can place this list on the inside of his closet door, the inside of his school binder or locker, or on his bathroom mirror—wherever he'll see it often and be reminded. Consider duplicating and laminating several cards to place in multiple locations.

Visual learning strategies can be used with boys to help them grasp abstract ideas, show them how something works, and teach them new concepts. Because boys are naturally visual and spatial learners with limited language proficiency, visual learning is a powerful teaching tool.

That's why movies and art can be such useful tools for boys when it comes to their moral development. Films that introduce and reinforce the concepts of integrity, compassion, and empathy are an excellent way to engage a boy's attention. A great place to start is with the book *What Stories Does My Son Need?* by Michael Gurian. It's an annotated list of films and books recommended at different ages, and it includes questions about each film or book that you can use to initiate conversation with your boy.

Another helpful way to draw boys into learning visually is through art. Many classic paintings and sculptures have intense imagery that will stimulate a boy's brain and teach important concepts such as faith, history, culture, and emotions. A painting such as Emanuel Leutze's *George Washington Crossing the Delaware, 1851* is a great way to open a discussion about the Revolutionary War, tyranny, and nobility. *The Scream*, by Edvard Munch, is an emotional painting depicting an agonized figure against a blood red skyline—a great conversation starter to help boys talk about fear or anxiety. Michelangelo's *Pietà*, a sculpture portraying the body of Jesus on the lap of his mother, Mary, after the Crucifixion, is a way to initiate a conversation not only about faith, but also about suffering, parenthood, love, and sacrifice.

SPATIAL LEARNING

Boys are also spatial learners and succeed when working around a task. The male brain is hardwired to be better at spatial relationships. This explains why Explorers and Lovers thrive on building with Legos and Lincoln Logs and why boys in general can tend to succeed in math and science. These subjects involve a significant amount of problem solving, working with models, experimenting, charting out equations, etc. Anytime we can design academic learning as a spatially driven assignment, boys stand to benefit. A great example of this would be asking a boy to build a model or diorama and explain his work, rather than simply assigning a written report. We're not suggesting that boys shouldn't learn to write and develop their nonspatial skills, but much of the school setting is already designed around these disciplines, which favor the natural orientation of the female brain. We're simply suggesting that, for the sake of our boys, the scales need to be balanced with more opportunities for spatial (and visual) learning.

For boys to succeed, spatial thinking must be recognized as a fundamental part of K–12 education. Because many educators are women, they will have to pay special attention to building lesson plans around spatial learning and problem solving.[5]

Darren, a sixth grader, loves it when his class does math drills on the board. The teacher divides the class in half, and the two teams compete to see which one can work out the equations first. The teacher sits in the back of the room, announces the equations, and then clocks each player. Points are accumulated when a player comes up with a correct answer before the opposing team does. This strategy is extremely boy friendly because it appeals to their spatially oriented minds and their hunger for competition.

Teaching/parenting/coaching/mentoring a visual and spatial learner requires that we take into account that boys typically are weaker verbally than girls. One way to understand this is to think about how you might teach/parent/coach a deaf child. When you are talking, the spatial learner hears "Waa waa waa." Spatial learners need to *see* something in order for it to sink in. Boys often learn more holistically, and they struggle when asked to learn sequentially. That's why subjects such as reading, spelling, basic math, and handwriting are often problematic for boys. Here are some tips to help spatial-learning boys succeed in school and life.

1. Teachers and parents, when you give a boy a new concept, ask him to close his eyes and picture it in his mind's eye.

2. Teach a boy to close his eyes at each punctuation mark and picture what he just read.

3. When working with spelling words, ask him to picture words in his mind and make wild and crazy pictures out of the letters. Ask him to spell each spelling word backward by looking at the picture. If he can spell the word backward, he can spell it forward.

4. Help him to use his imagination to make a lesson or an assignment more interesting. Can he make a graph out of the information? Can he draw a picture of it? Is there a story to tell about it?

5. If he has trouble memorizing math facts (such as the times tables), ask him to try drawing a picture to represent the ones he finds most difficult.

6. For help in creating outlines for papers, suggest that he organize them visually. Developing a thought map, or drawing pictures and moving the icons around, makes it easier to organize the information. Also, check out the computer software Inspiration (or Kidspiration) to help him organize his ideas visually.[6]

EXPERIENTIAL LEARNING

Boys also learn by doing. They learn best when allowed to experience and practice a task, skill, or concept and then talk about what they learned. In this way, boys are experiential learners. They need to go through the motions for the experience to really lock in. For boys, most of life's lessons need to be experienced, not told. Aristotle said it this way, "The things we have to learn before we do them, we learn by doing them."

Experiential learning is "nature's way of learning." It is "education that occurs as a direct participation in the events of life."[7] It's learning that comes about through thinking about and reflecting on life's experiences. In experiential learning, emphasis is placed on the participant's individual encounter with the material.

This is a big deal with boys. Too often, we write off boys as stubborn or hardheaded, when perhaps the reason things don't stick for them is that they weren't allowed to experiment and they weren't asked to explain their experiences.

To help boys learn and grow, parents and other caregivers need to view their roles as that of experiential educators. An experiential educator's role is to arrange and facilitate a boy's interaction with material, circumstances, and events in hopes that it will lead to meaningful and long-lasting learning.

Think of a coach who is running a practice for a football team. Would we expect him to last long if he took his football team into the classroom every day and talked about how to play football? Absolutely not. A coach puts his players through repetitive drills that teach them, *through experience*, what they need to know. If you watch the practices of the most successful coaches, you will see them talking with players after plays and between drills, talking through different aspects of the activity; but when the activity starts, they shut up and stand back and let the practice itself do the teaching.

Can you see how different this is from a typical classroom? Most often, a teacher's role is seen as downloading information to students through oral instruction and assigning study exercises, which have as their main goal the transmission of knowledge. Think how boy friendly our classrooms would become if schools adopted more of an experiential-learning model.

What about parenting? Experiential learning can really change the way we parent boys. Instead of trying to tell our boys everything we want them to know, we can invest our parental energy in creating teachable moments that allow life's circumstances to do the teaching.

If real-life situations don't lend themselves to teaching certain concepts (or aren't appropriate for some reason), you can always role-play. For example, when my (David's) boys were Explorers, I introduced the concept of appropriate touch through role-playing. I set up a big play time with my boys, and we acted out different situations with adults who had permission to touch their bodies (such as Mom and Dad and the pediatrician) and adults who did not. I also used their favorite stuffed animals and our family dog to identify body parts that were private and not to be shown, shared, or touched by others. We used the stuffed animals to play out situations in which a child was touched inappropriately and went to a safe adult to tell what happened. These vignettes ended with the safe adults loving on the boys and praising them for telling the truth.

With very young boys, role-playing is a powerful tool for instructing and giving feedback (instead of giving verbal criticism or advice). In role playing, allow boys to play themselves, and then switch roles, letting them be the peer, parent, teacher, or other adult—the more dramatic or "in character," the better. Boys learn a range of concepts through this method.

With adolescents, experiential learning is a vital means of introducing concepts. For example, boys learn the value of money and possessions through work and labor. If you're trying to teach them about money, they need to work, earn, save, spend, and give long before they get their first job. If you're trying to teach them the concepts of poverty and privilege, boys need to see it with their own eyes. You can give them firsthand experience with cultural differences through opportunities such as missions trips and outreach projects.

When Carter was ten, rather than simply talk about homelessness, his parents took him to a local homeless shelter, a nonprofit organization that provided food and shelter for complete families. Carter and his family delivered a meal to help serve the families at the shelter, they volunteered to sleep overnight at the shelter together as a family, and they got sponsors for a hike that raised money to support the organization. How many times have you said, or heard another adult say, "There are starving children in Africa, and look at all the food on your plate that is going to waste." This approach only works to shame a boy; it does little to connect him to the pain of the hungry.

As parents and mentors of boys, we need to talk less and do more. We need to stop talking *at* our boys and start *exposing* them to moments and experiences right in our own cities that will impart the values we want them to have. After each experience, ask your boy questions about it, and encourage him to ask you questions about it. Remember, most boys aren't super verbal, and it can take some time for them to formulate their answers to the questions. Here are some suggestions for getting your boy involved in experiential learning:

- Sign up at a local soup kitchen to serve meals.
- Go on a missions trip to the inner city or another country.
- When a friend or extended family member is under the weather, ask your boy to make soup with you and take it to the person who is sick.
- Ask him to pick a charity for you as a family, or pick a group that he will work to raise money for.
- When he lies or steals for the first time (which he will), make him go through the motions of confessing, making things right, and restoring the relationship.
- To work on leadership, ask him to work with you in scripting a movie or play, or make up a game or activity to teach to the family, and then perform it or record it together.

There is an excellent picture of experiential learning in the movie *Radio*, the true story of a football coach and a mentally challenged young man (who goes by the nickname "Radio") who becomes a student at T. L. Hanna High School in Anderson, South Carolina, and transforms the small community. Radio has a passion for football and spends his afternoons wandering around the field, pushing a grocery cart and hoping a football will accidentally make its way across the gate.

In a powerful scene, Coach Harold Jones arrives at football practice to find that his players have tied up and gagged Radio in a storage shed and are throwing balls at the outside of the shed to torment him. Coach Jones exposes their strategy, releases Radio, and confronts the players with these words: *"Anybody got anything to say?"*

The boys stand in silence. He waits them out and then says, "Tell your folks practice is gonna run late tomorrow."

The following scene opens with the boys running around the field. They run for hours, to the point of exhaustion. It's a perfect picture of experiential learning and the concepts we've introduced.

First of all, Coach Jones understood that these young men needed to connect the dots with what they'd done, and that it wouldn't happen outside of their feeling the weight of the consequence. As he releases Radio and steps out to confront the players, there is evidence that he is full of anger. But he doesn't let his anger, or the players' apathy, dictate his response. He doesn't launch into a lecture on abuse or bullying. He doesn't even discipline them immediately (likely because he realized it would be from a place of anger and that the boys would feel the weight of his fury as opposed to the weight of their own choices). He simply speaks a few words, leaves, and then allows the experience to be the teacher.

Experiential instruction usually has three phases: *preparation*, *participation*, and *processing*. The two parts of the equation that parents need to pay attention to are preliminary prep and reflection time afterwards. The participation really takes care of itself. By setting up situations in which our boys can learn, grow, risk, succeed, or fail, we create opportunities for them to teach themselves important lessons about everything from math to morality. Boys learn best when life is their teacher.

Putting the Principles into Practice

By putting into practice some specific strategies that target a boy's unique learning style, we can set him up for success. Following are some ideas that can help you begin to think through and develop a tailored approach to learning for your boy.

TIP 1: **Less talk, more action.** For boys, this works for everything from baseball, to discipline, to algebra.

TIP 2: **Promote active, kinesthetic learning.** Because boys are tactile and kinesthetic learners, fill your home with Legos, Lincoln Logs, Magnetix, puzzles, marble runs, and other building tools when your boy is young. As he grows, find other age-appropriate toys, games, materials, and supplies to keep him actively involved in learning, experimenting, and creating. Make certain he has at least one room in the house with a significant amount of space and room to exercise and utilize his gross motor skills.

TIP 3: **Schedule his summers.** Once he hits stage three of his development (the Individual stage), put some parameters around his summer vacations. Boys aren't mature enough yet at this age to structure their time well. Your boy will likely want to spend a lot of time with video games and other media, but it's important to begin broadening his horizons. He's too young at age nine to get a job, but he can still make some money and learn

STEPHEN JAMES | DAVID THOMAS

the value of work doing odd jobs. It's also good to give him some parameters for how to break up his day. For example, he should spend x amount of time per day doing something physical outdoors; x amount of time reading; x amount of time contributing to the household, etc. He can choose the order in which he does those things, and he has some flexibility in what he chooses to do outdoors, what books he reads, etc., but he still has some general guidelines for ordering his time.

TIP 4: **Help him get experience.** A boy who is too young to get a job can spend some portion of his summer vacation volunteering as a means of occupying part of his time and tapping into experiential learning. It's called "working for free." A number of camps have counselor-in-training programs for late elementary- and middle-school-age boys. You can also volunteer as a family at many organizations.

TIP 5: **Plan family movie nights and take turns choosing the movie.** Spend fifteen minutes to half an hour talking about the film once it's over. Taking turns will give your boy a chance to sacrifice, and the dialogue will help him connect with the visual learning. For some help with choosing good, age-appropriate movies, see Michael Gurian's book *What Stories Does My Son Need?*

TIP 6: **Get him involved.** Have him pick an organization or cause that he is passionate about and ask him to commit to serving that organization for a year. He can do that by contributing financially, volunteering, attending educational or fund-raising events, and bringing about awareness for others.

TIP 7: **Use reminder cards.** Rather than nag him about specific tasks, try putting reminder cards or charts in different rooms of the house. You can simply prompt him to check the kitchen card or the bathroom card. You can choose to reward him for successful completion or dock him for not completing the list.

TIP 8: Allow him to experience natural consequences. And remember, you're not obligated to talk after an experiential consequence. Try letting the experience do the teaching without adding anything on to it.

TIP 9: Volunteer at his school. Make yourself available to create more visual aids, or for experiential-learning practices. Graciously let his teachers know that you are interested in helping to make the classroom more boy friendly. If his class in starting a new unit on Egypt, for example, ask if you can supply the boys with do-it-yourself pyramid kits.

TIP 10: Model service. Consider choosing an outreach opportunity as a family every other spring break, fall break, or summer trip. Let your boy see that you place that much value on service that you would use vacation time for that purpose.

CHAPTER 8

"Sit Still! Pay Attention!"

Not long ago, I (Stephen) got an emotional voice mail from my wife: "These boys! Call me! Seriously!"

She sounded fed up, so I took a deep breath and called her back. When she answered the phone, she was on her hands and knees in the bathroom adjacent to our sons' rooms.

"Guess what I am doing?" she asked. "I'm cleaning up the mess our boys made."

"Are you okay?" I asked. "What happened?"

She had heard a ruckus in the bathroom that, she soon discovered, included water, poop, urine, splashing, and laughing.

Exasperated, she had sent all the boys to their rooms while she cooled off.

"I walked into the bathroom to find our three sons laughing and splashing as the commode was overflowing."

It was hard for me not to chuckle.

"It's not funny," Heather said.

"Of course it's not." I tried to sound as sympathetic as possible.

When she interrogated the three boys, she learned that one of them had stuffed a towel into the john, for reasons known only to him. A short time later, our eldest son went *numero dos*. When Heather asked him if he had seen the towel, he said he had, but he'd plopped one anyway. Our third son, from what she surmised, apparently watched the entire thing and egged it all on.

It was the middle of January, and the cold and wet weather had confined the boys indoors for several days. This was the climax of a day of many incidents. One son had gone to the doctor for a nearly fractured toe. Another son had taken the sheets off the mattress and the mattress off the bed during his nap time. It was chaos all around—and sadly familiar. You see, this kind of stuff is pretty common in our house. When caged in, our three sons build up an energy that often leads to disruption and destruction. Remember the Tasmanian Devil from the old Looney Tunes cartoons? Times three.

Later that night, Heather and I were talking, and she said, "You've heard of a father and his children waking up one morning to find the wife and mother gone? . . . I get that." She wasn't talking about running off with another man. She was talking about running away from the chaos of three sons and the futility of trying to craft harmony out of their pandemonium.

This story is not only a great snapshot of some of the realities of living with boys, it also illustrates their need for movement and their propensity to be rambunctious and mischievous—especially if they are confined indoors or are asked to sit still for long periods of time. These needs and tendencies don't go away, and though by the time they are school age, most boys have learned to "sit still, and pay attention!" this isn't the best thing for them.

Requiring boys to sit still for extended periods of time is a disservice. In school, young boys are squirmy and restless. Older boys become rebellious and resistant. School requires something of them that is in opposition to their wiring, and it makes the academic setting a challenge for boys.

According to statistics, boys make up 73 percent of learning-disabled students in special education classes.[1] This is significant and more arbitrary than you might think. When learning-disabled students are identified via diagnostic criteria, there is no significant gender difference between boys and girls. But if learning disabilities were identified by teachers (either general ed or special ed), Dr. Nathlie A. Badian, a Harvard researcher, discovered, twice as many boys were identified, as compared to girls.[2]

The problem doesn't just lie in special education. Male high school seniors tend to have lower educational aspirations than their female peers, and they are less likely to enroll in college following graduation from high school.[3] "Thirty years ago, men represented 58 percent of the undergraduate student body. Now they're a minority of 44 percent. This widening achievement gap, says Margaret Spellings, U.S. Secretary of Education, 'has profound implications for the economy, society, families, and democracy.'"[4]

In elementary school, boys often fall behind girls in reading and writing. For instance, girls did better than boys at every grade level on the 2002 National Assessment of Educational Progress (NAEP) writing assessment. And boys often show signs of behavioral problems early in life. This poor academic achievement is related to higher rates of school dropouts and juvenile delinquency. "In 2004, 12 percent of males ages 16 to 24 were high school dropouts, compared with 9 percent of females. Although males comprise one-half of the population, they make up 57 percent of the dropouts in this age group."[5]

These statistics are only a handful of the alarming facts that speak to the state of boys in the academic setting. A longitudinal study done in Chicago beginning in the 1960s found that "almost fifty percent of males rated as moderately or severely underachieving in first grade reported a high level of depressed symptoms ten years later."[6]

Making the Grade

As we've already seen, most schools aren't set up to draw on a boy's strengths. In fact, the deck is stacked against him.

- Most academic settings rely heavily on written and verbal expression (and girls typically score higher in those two areas).
- The bell rings at different intervals, requiring the singularly focused male student to shift gears quickly, move to his locker (which is often an organizational nightmare), think about what items he needs to be prepared for his next class, and then shift his mind to a completely different subject.
- In class, he is required to sit still and focus for an extended period of time.
- At most, young boys get two recess periods a day (often only one). When they get older, they might have a P.E. class, but it may not be every day, and it may not come at

a time that allows them to burn off enough energy to sit still the rest of the day.

The model of education that has been in place for the past one hundred years or so is known as compulsory schooling. If you do some research into the history of education, you will find that the compulsory model was birthed out of the Industrial Revolution. The academic calendar and the very structure of school (length of day, amount of time spent in class, etc.) were designed as a means of fashioning great factory workers, not students. They weren't designed with the cognitive and emotional development of kids in mind. And they certainly weren't designed to correlate with the developing brains of boys. If they had been, physical education would happen four times a day, and boys would be at school only three to four days a week for four or five hours at a time. Boys would spend the other days engaged in apprenticeships or internships, learning and utilizing skills.

What's the Solution?

Clearly, if we want to do a better job of nurturing and educating boys, some changes are in order. But we don't have to scrap the current system altogether. There are several possible ways to create a workable scenario within the structure we already have. But in order for the system to work for our boys, parents and educators must collaborate.

One way for parents and teachers to work closely together is in understanding a boy's unique learning profile. It doesn't have to be an expensive process, such as formal testing with a learning expert (though you should absolutely do this if you have concerns regarding learning disabilities of any kind); it can be as simple and cost effective as asking good questions and taking good notes at every parent-teacher conference from preschool on. For starters, you can ask questions such as these:

- Does he have difficulty with focus or impulsivity that seems abnormal for a boy his age?
- What subjects does he seem most drawn to?
- In what areas do you see him excelling?
- Does he prefer to work with others, or on his own?
- Is he more engaged and apt to learn in the morning, or in the afternoon?
- Is he an external processor of information who likes to discuss solutions and ideas, or does he prefer to think things over before sharing them?

Every teacher, from preschool on, will have an educational checklist that basically determines if your son is meeting educational milestones and is tracking with other kids his age. Ask about this, and request candid feedback. Teachers aren't trained (or encouraged) to diagnose learning disabilities or developmental disorders; but they have vast experience in working with children and can give you insight into how your son learns best. If learning or behavioral concerns are identified, your son's teacher may recommend that you meet with an educational consultant or have psychological or educational testing done.

Another way to improve the current system is for parents, teachers, and academic institutions to find ways to support each other. For parents, this means not joining your son in his negative opinions about teachers, administrators, or policies. If you, as a parent, disagree with something taking place in the classroom, go talk to the teacher—and please go with a spirit of curiosity, not judgment. If you can't dialogue effectively with your son's teachers, involve the principal.

Recently, our local public school system adopted a policy of standard attire. Students in the county were instructed to wear khaki or navy pants or shorts with a belt (skirts or jumpers for the girls) and collared shirts (in certain prescribed colors) that had to be tucked in. As you can imagine, the decision was met with both support and resistance. The *Tennessean*, our local paper, ran an article the month before school began, citing opinions and responses of both students and parents.

One mother was quoted as saying that she was planning to let her child decide if he wanted to wear the school uniform or not, and she had no intention of letting the school punish her child if he chose not to wear it. Directly below her statement was a photograph of three middle-school boys standing on top of garbage bags. The photograph was next to an article about local agencies that were taking clothing donations to help public school families who couldn't afford to buy new clothes to meet the standard attire. The three boys photographed were volunteering with their families to sort clothes at one of the agencies to prepare for the demand they would likely encounter when they opened their doors for school purchases.

What a contrast. One mother decided to oppose the school's decision, while another group of families chose to create a teachable moment by taking their sons to serve those who couldn't afford the school's decision. My guess was that none of the boys in the photograph were jumping up and down when they heard they had to trade in their jeans and T-shirts for new khakis, tucked-in shirts (with collars), and belts. But who cares? That's the rule. Why stand in opposition when it's already been decided? How could that possibly stand to benefit your student?

It's also important for parents to remember that you may know your son best outside the classroom, but the teacher knows him best within the classroom. Children function differently under different authority and in different groups. I (David) can still remember the first time I went to a parent-teacher conference and my daughter's kindergarten teacher announced that my shy, timid little girl's favorite thing to do in the classroom was to sing with the karaoke machine. We may have no idea what our kids are capable of (good and bad) when under different authority.

For teachers and schools, it's essential to create parent-friendly, meaningful opportunities for parents to assist their sons. Things such as "family fun nights," art shows, plays or musicals, community events, and public meetings can help make schools a center of community activity. Schools need to bring in experts to speak to teachers and parents on male developmental and learning differences. Boys stand to benefit strongly from the direction many schools are moving in making it easy for parents to check grades online, communicating school events and activities readily to parents, and creating a forum for more open dialogue between educators and parents. A friend of mine (Stephen's), who is a sixth-grade language arts teacher, posts regular blogs about his classes for parents and students, with a special section for the students to chat with each other, as well as for the parents to interact with what is going on in the classroom.

Although research shows that boys (and girls) score higher in same-sex environments, these environments aren't the only places where boys can succeed.[7] Many coed environments are experimenting with having certain grades or certain subjects take place in same-sex classrooms.

Lastly, educators must expect healthy physicality and aggression among boys at times. To accommodate this, teachers can make their classroom environments boy friendly. Here are a few suggestions for how to do this:

- Teachers, make sure that you move around the classroom and are animated.
- Declutter. Too many diagrams, posters, objects, or fast-moving images can be distracting and overstimulating for boys. Good lighting is also important.
- Whenever possible, make learning into a game or competition.
- Choose boy-friendly books to read, and bring in male authors.
- Have boys write journal entries on a favorite scene from a movie they loved or a sporting event of their choice. Better yet, have them team up and act it out.
- Create opportunities for boys to get up and move around.
- Use physical activity and athletics not only to release all that pent-up male energy but also to prime their brains for learning.
- Allow boys to stand (when appropriate) or squeeze an object in their non-writing hands to jolt their brains out of regular rest states. (Silly Putty or stress balls work well for this.)
- Consider using single-gender strategies, such as splitting up boys and girls for certain assignments, projects, or even subjects.
- Make certain that much of the learning centers on life lessons and values. Use books on diversity, relationships, leadership, and service. Bring in books and other media (movie clips and TV clips) that teach compassion, empathy, and the concept of integrity.
- Get boys reading things like graphic novels and comics. Assign them technical and mechanical books and articles—such as those in car, aerospace, or skateboard magazines.

- Involve the school counselor or psychologist in curriculum development.
- Integrate the arts and athletics into learning whenever possible. Music can be a powerful tool to utilize with boys. Make your teaching experiential whenever possible, such as using the popular "egg drop" or "egg catapult" experiments to teach physics.[8]

Discipline and Direction

When boys misbehave, we strongly advocate physical consequences. By "physical," we don't mean spanking or paddling. We're talking about engaging them in a physical activity. Have them pull weeds, move firewood, clean out the garage, sweep the driveway, pick up sticks and debris, or do push-ups, sit-ups, and jumping jacks.

One mom keeps a reflective vest, a package of garbage bags, and a stack of *Real Simple* magazines in the trunk of her car at all times. When her son acts out, she takes him to some stretch of country road, and he picks up trash like a chain-gang prisoner. She parks the car on the side of the road and reads her *Real Simple* magazine while her boy does his community service. He's not allowed to get back in the car until he has filled a bag or two with trash. (Size and quantity of bags depend on the offense.) A dad we know has his sons run laps or do push-ups (like in the army) or sit-ups. Then the boy under discipline follows that by picking up a chore or responsibility from the person he harmed (by his words or actions). For example, if he harmed his younger brother with his words and it was his little brother's night to empty the dishwasher and set the table, the older boy takes over that responsibility for the night as a way of repairing the relationship.

If you're a single mom or a married mother whose husband isn't involved or invested in parenting, we recommend enlisting the help of a male family member (granddad or uncle), mentor, teacher, or coach to oversee certain parts of your boy's discipline. We've had parents report to us that coaches have said things to their sons like, "If you can't be a man off the field and respect your mom, then you won't be a man playing on this field. I'll get a report from your mom on a weekly basis. Your practice will either be practicing with the team or running laps around the field, depending on what she tells me. And you'll dress out for games, but you won't play (or start) until you work on this area of your life." For boys who care a lot about sports, having to run during practice and ride the bench during games can be an extremely powerful consequence.

(This suggestion comes with a caveat, however. It's usually a mistake to take away sports or physical activity from a boy as a form of discipline. We only rarely advocate this course of action, because boys so desperately need competition, camaraderie, and activity. When this is taken away, their behavior often gets worse, not better.)

For the same reasons that we recommend tailoring methods of discipline to conform with a boy's tendency to learn spatially and experientially, we also want to match his natural inclinations when we're imparting instruction or relaying information. In addition to what we've already said about making things visual, spatial, and experiential, we recommend taking advantage of a boy's natural desire for activity by using on-the-go instruction.

Once a boy grows out of the first two stages (Explorer and Lover), some of our best conversations with him will take place while in motion. Though younger boys (up to about age eight) can lose track of a conversation if we're moving, older boys thrive in active settings. Once they move into the Individual stage and beyond, boys can feel threatened by eye-to-eye contact and may actually prefer more shoulder-to-shoulder or activity-based conversations. Some of my (David's) most valuable conversations with boys in counseling happen outside the office (throwing a football or shooting hoops out behind my office) or on the floor of my office (playing checkers, Jenga, or Blockhead).

A good friend of ours decided that he would take his son away for the weekend when he talked with him about entering adolescence and the changes that would begin to occur in his body and emotions (birds and bees). They rented a cabin in the woods, and the two spent the weekend fishing, canoeing, hiking, and cooking together. Every time they engaged in an activity, they'd talk about another concept or two. They talked throughout the weekend without ever once having an awkward, eyeball-to-eyeball "talk." This dad understood that sitting across a table from his son and trying to have these kinds of conversations would not have worked for either one of them.

The more proactive we can be with our boys, the better off we'll be. And the more we can center their moral, emotional, intellectual, and spiritual development on activity, movement, and experience, the more receptive they will be. If we want to develop their character, encourage their moral development, instill a spiritual sensitivity, and tend to their intense physical needs, we need to plan ahead and construct environments of engagement, shepherding, and direction on their behalf. Too many parents, teachers, and coaches base their instruction on *reaction* rather than *planning*.

When boys act out or buck the system (which they will), that's not the time for teaching or the time for them to learn. Instead, it's time to corral them, redirect them, and contain them. Effective teaching and instruction for boys comes most often before (in the planning of) and after (in the processing of) experiential instructional moments.

Putting the Principles into Practice

As we've said repeatedly, boys in general need to learn and process information in different ways than girls. Here are some suggestions to get you thinking of ways to help your boy succeed.

TIP 1: **Get him on the chain gang.** Make a list of work options for your son for when you need to pull a consequence out of the hat. Keep a running list at all times.

TIP 2: **Be concise.** The more words a teacher or parent uses, the greater the odds that a boy will tune you out. Boys are better suited to symbols, pictures, and experiences. Try to keep your verbal instructions to no more than a minute. And be sure not to layer instructions one after another.

TIP 3: **Keep good notes.** Parents, make a list of things you've learned about your son as a student over the course of his academic journey. Document the feedback you have received from teachers over the years. Identify areas of strength as well as areas of deficit.

TIP 4: **Let him move.** Use physical teaching methods so your boy can work in a larger space. Boys need room to learn. Plan active moments that are centered on a topic you want him to learn. If most of your interactions are reactive, you need to rethink your approach and try to get ahead of the curve.

TIP 5: **Parent his brain.** "Our job as adults is to serve as external frontal lobes," says psychologist Barbara Green. "Teenagers are these emotionally pulsating creatures," so adults have to be ready to guide them by helping them think through situations. Bombard your teenager with hypothetical situations: "If you go to the mall to hang out, what will happen to your homework?"[9]

TIP 6: Join forces. Work in tandem with, not in opposition to, those who are educating your son. Ask his teacher to guide you in how you can do an even better job of supporting the investment he or she is making. Any teacher would welcome that question.

TIP 7: Pack the trunk. Get a reflective vest and put trash bags and magazines in the trunk of your car.

TIP 8: Get moving. Plan activities for conversations with your son that are better suited to have while in motion.

TIP 9: Take good notes. Every time you attend a parent-teacher conference, take good notes and look for emerging themes.

TIP 10: Listen, and run. If your son is under the age of six and you hear laughter coming from the bathroom . . . get in there!

CHAPTER 9

Deficits and Disappointments

J. D. Salinger's *The Catcher in the Rye* is the story of a boy, Holden
Caulfield, in the days immediately following his expulsion from
Pency, an elite East Coast boarding school. Told in the first person,
Catcher takes readers inside the mind of a boy—the profanity, the
sexuality, the angst, the confusion, the foolishness, the hunger to
be loved, and the disappointment that comes with it all. By seeing
the world from Holden's perspective, we get a better appreciation
of what it feels like for boys as they struggle toward manhood.

It would be somewhat of a stretch to say that Holden Caulfield
is a typical boy, but like many characters in literature, he is a great
archetype for understanding boys. A tall, skinny teenager full of

adolescent angst, Holden is simply trying to cope. After getting kicked out of school, Holden makes his way to New York City, where he makes plans, grows increasingly depressed, and tries to figure things out. As a way of coping with his disappointment, he is most often critical of others and tries to convince himself to be apathetic; but he is, at the same time, introspective, caring, and hopeful.

In a scene near the end of the book, Holden reconnects with his younger sister, Phoebe, who loves Holden very much. It's through his relationship with Phoebe that we get a deeper picture into the love and maturity of which Holden is capable. They walk to the park, and Holden buys his sister a ticket for the carousel. As he watches her ride the carousel, he is filled with regret, desire, and joy, and soon he is almost crying.

The mind of a boy is a complex and confusing place, and Holden gives us a clear example. At once intelligent and sensitive, he is also cynical and jaded. He finds the pretense, hypocrisy, and cruelty of the world around him almost unbearable—while at the same time he puts up a front that is quite unattractive.

As the novel comes alive, it's easy to see that Holden is projecting his own ambivalence and disenchantment onto the world around him. It's as if wherever he goes he finds a canvas on which to paint the disappointments of his boyhood. It's this disappointment and ambivalence about his life that make Holden a great picture of male adolescence.

In one of the more significant passages in the book, he mentions that he is being "psychoanalyzed" and finishes with the words, "Don't ever tell anybody anything. If you do, you start missing everybody."

With his future very much in question, Holden's hope is obvious, and yet his recognition that he needs other people, and needs to give to other people, is almost unbearable for him. He desperately wants to reach out, and yet he's tired of being disappointed by people and by life.

Disappointment is one of the primary struggles that many boys face as they move from childhood to adolescence and into their young adult years. Around the age of ten and onward, boys have difficulty handling failure—and they are more apt to stuff their disappointments than to name them and work their way through them. Boys talk less about what they are feeling and isolate themselves more than girls do. They go to their rooms and kick, brood, sulk, and hide in whatever emotion they are experiencing.

Unless we intervene with behavioral redirection, emotional coaching, and relational modeling, boys will carry these habits into their adult lives. It's one reason why boys disproportionately commit violence against society and themselves, and why men in general head the charts in terms of substance abuse, sexual addiction, rage, arrogance, adultery, and the use of pornography. Boys who never learn effective ways of dealing with their emotional lives grow into men with great struggles in terms of addiction of all kinds.

Boys who aren't taught how to deal with their disappointments will bury their heartaches, hide their weaknesses, and compensate for their incompetence. When they grow into men, they will be emotionally defensive, performance driven, or both. Boys who don't know how to handle disappointment will come to believe that their worth is based on what they achieve or what they have to offer. They're left to try to manufacture their own self-esteem and base their self-worth on performance or behavior. These are the guys who keep score.

Whether consciously or not, these boys, and the men they become, believe that their value is based on what others think about them, and they wear themselves out trying to seek approval or win affection. Too often, this exhausting quest to feel good about themselves creates a need or desire for some external substance or behavior to alleviate the pain of their unmanaged disappointments. Often, it turns to lust. Boys and men who can't handle their disappointments end up lusting for sex, money, power, fun, drugs, escape, TV, vacations, or whatever else they can find that works.

Military Parents

As these boys grow into men and have families of their own, we see them trying to compensate for their perceived shortcomings. Having never learned to cope with their own sense of disappointment in life, they feel ill-equipped to teach their children how to cope. So, instead, they try to cushion the blow for the next generation. We've seen parents go to great lengths to help their kids avoid experiencing pain or having to struggle. Parents generally do this in one of two ways: either by rescuing their children or by controlling them. Unfortunately, both methods teach kids to operate on the basis of fear and shame. Foster Cline and Jim Fay, authors of *Parenting with Love and Logic*, call these parents Helicopter parents and Drill Sergeant parents.

Helicopter parents "hover" over their children and rescue them from "the hostile world in which they live."[1] Some Helicopter parents take their vigilance one step further, crossing the line from excessive involvement to fraudulent behavior such as doing their kids' homework, writing their college admission essays, and calling professors and deans when they see grades they don't like. These overly aggressive and protective parents are called "Black Hawks," after the U.S. Army's military-attack helicopter. Another term for these parents is "tether parents," according to Patrick Heaton, director of the freshman orientation program at Florida State University. "It's like a leash. Students are afraid to make decisions about classes or anything without calling home."[2] The parents generally pay very close attention to their children and swoop down to stop any harm, heartache, or failure from happening.

Another way in which parents do a disservice to their children is by being *Drill Sergeants*. These parents command and direct their children's lives. They make lots of demands and have high expectations about responsibility. They dictate to their children how they should handle responsibility, how they should feel, what decisions to make, and when things should be completed. Drill Sergeants most often use emotional or physical pain, along with humiliation, to motivate their children's behavior and control their attitudes. They use verbal outbursts to intimidate, but they don't always see it that way. As one father said about his son, "I'm just trying to raise him like a man."

Though Helicopter parents and Drill Sergeant parents may go about parenting in different ways, they often produce the same kind of child. Neither approach—hovering or controlling—allows kids to learn from their failures. The Helicopter parents rescue their children before they can fail (or they shield them from the natural consequences), and Drill Sergeant parents simply don't tolerate failure. Thus, we now have an entire culture built around the avoidance of pain and disappointment. Unfortunately, our efforts to avoid pain and make life easier for our kids may very well backfire on us, because teaching our kids how to cope with pain and failure is an important part of preparing them well for life.

In our fast-food, instant-messaging society, we've eliminated waiting as much as possible, and we're working hard to eliminate pain and disappointment as well. Inventions ranging from cell phones with text messaging, to coffee shops, fast-food stops, and drugstores with drive-throughs, to epidurals in the delivery room are all designed to eliminate physical pain or the "pain" of waiting.

Despite our best efforts, however, we can't get around the fact that disappointment, pain, and struggle are all a part of life. When we don't allow the boys we love to suffer with the disappointments of life, we undermine their manhood by sending them messages that say, "You're weak. You can't handle life." Intentionally or not, by our words and our actions we communicate to our boys that they're not capable or responsible.

When we shield boys from life's natural consequences or demand perfection from them (which of course they can't achieve), we often have only one place left to turn as parents when our boys inevitably fall short of the mark—guilt and shame. Helicopter parents and Drill Sergeant parents often complain about their sons' mismanaged responsibilities. These parents are left to whine and nag (Helicopters), or demand and threaten (Drill Sergeants):

> "After all I've done for you, you go and _____."
> (Helicopter)
> "How many times do I have to tell you to _____?" (Drill Sergeant)
> "You never clean up after yourself when I ask." (Helicopter)
> "You clean up your room right now!" (Drill Sergeant)
> "Why do you make my life so hard?" (Helicopter)
> "If you don't bring your grades up, you won't leave this house for three months." (Drill Sergeant)

Do any of these phrases sound familiar? The styles are different, but the effect is the same. A boy's confidence is shattered; shame and guilt are induced; and the fear of a broken relationship is constantly present.

Parents as Guides, Mentors, and Models

Allowing boys to struggle is one of the greatest tasks and biggest challenges of parenting. It teaches them to grieve, to take responsibility, to overcome loss, and to develop confidence. Guiding boys through life's losses and difficulties helps prepare them for manhood—a manhood marked by both strength and tenderness. As parents, we must decide which is more important, material success or character. Too often, parents, educators, and coaches focus on behavior modification with boys and not enough on character development. Too often, parents manipulate or shut down their sons' emotions instead of drawing them out. Too often, parents see their sons' mistakes as failures instead of as opportunities for them to learn how to face the consequences of their choices and the futility of life. If we ourselves aren't comfortable with the pain of life, we will raise shortsighted and immature boys.

If, however, we focus on developing our sons' character, then the momentary setbacks of life become a fertile ground for teaching empathy, deepening sorrow, embedding hope, and developing strength. Admittedly, it's hard to watch our children suffer the pain of failure and disappointment. We love them, after all. But it seems that parents who don't let their kids struggle in life are more concerned about avoiding their own pain from watching their children suffer than they are concerned for the kids themselves. One of the most difficult—and yet beneficial—things we can do as parents is to sit with our boys while they are in pain and let their suffering soften our hearts as it softens theirs. We will address issues of the heart in more detail in the next section, but in the meantime, here are some categories to consider in understanding how suffering can help our boys grow into men of strength, responsibility, diligence, insight, and compassion.

BOYS DEVELOP STRENGTH THROUGH STRUGGLE.

For as long as I (David) have been teaching my Nurturing Boys class, I have invited some of the young men I've worked with in counseling to come to the final session and share bits and pieces of their stories and to be available to answer questions from the adults in attendance. Over the years, I've invited dozens of boys who have been willing to share their lives and illuminate the inner world of boys.

Struggle builds great resilience in boys. Every young man I've invited to speak to my class has tasted significant struggle—whether it's abandonment, separation and divorce, the loss of a parent to death, a struggle with drugs and alcohol or pornography, rejection by peers, or bullying. As they speak, these young men give testimony to the anguish of those life experiences and the resilience they gained as a result of living (at times) in agony. They are living examples of the painful beauty of refinement and redemption—the kind of redemption we all long for our children to know and believe but are afraid for them to experience.

BOYS LEARN RESPONSIBILITY THROUGH REGRET.

We cannot care more about a boy's academics than he does. I (David) have worked with valedictorians, National Merit Scholars, and countless other boys who have gone away to school on partial or full rides and managed to flunk themselves out in the first one or two semesters of college. These are young men with IQs in the superior range of intelligence—guys who had the cognitive ability to do just about anything they wanted, but who couldn't manage to stay off of academic probation. How do you explain that?

It began to make more sense to me years ago while counseling a nineteen-year-old National Merit Scholar who was on academic probation after his freshman year in college. His mother looked at me with tears in her eyes one day and said, "His accolades were always more mine than they ever were his. I hounded him academically for twelve years, straight to graduation day. By the time he reached college, I don't think he had any internal motivation or ability to self-initiate. When I wasn't around to stand over his shoulder and demand he work to his ability, he chose to play video games and watch mindless reality TV. I basically trained him to always need external motivation."

Despite her best intentions, she had trained her son to need her nagging, her organizational skills, and her regulations. He had absolutely no idea how to motivate himself outside of her presence.

Our guess is that most parents reading this are saying something along the lines of, "Not me. I would never allow myself to control that much of my son's academic life." Others are perhaps saying something like, "Well, if I don't care about my son's academics, no one in our household would care. He certainly isn't motivated on his own."

Regardless of your response, it's important to realize that your son must take ownership for himself. And it's not just about his academic performance—this is a life skill. Every boy needs to experience the satisfaction of working hard for something he cares about (or doesn't) and reaping the rewards of his hard work.

Every boy passes in and out of periods of his life when he feels unmotivated and disinterested. That's normal. Your role is simply to have expectations (based on his ability, not your dreams for him) and bring or allow consequences when he doesn't meet those expectations. Many schools now offer an online grading system that allows parents to log on and track their student's academic progress. We recommend that you set aside time once a week to take a look at this with your boy. Sit down together and have him walk you through the online report. With older boys, it's a good idea to do this on Thursday evenings and have his weekend plans directly correlated to what you find. He then gets a fresh start on Monday. Grounding a boy for an extended period of time for grades isn't always helpful, because some boys simply lose motivation and throw in the towel. We've had boys say things like, "My parents grounded me for six weeks because of my grades. Six weeks feels like six months. What's the use? By that point I won't remember anything I liked to do anyway."

Keep in mind that no college or university ever takes a look at your boy's elementary or middle school transcripts. These are useful times in his development to allow him to fail and learn how to motivate himself. See these years as a training ground, a time for him to practice taking ownership of his academic performance, and using natural consequences (not *Waa-waa-waa* lectures) as a means of instilling this core value.

BOYS LEARN DILIGENCE THROUGH DUTY.

Forcing a boy's involvement beyond his interest is a good thing to do. Yes, you read that right. Effective parenting means being disliked, or even despised, at times. We know they didn't tell you this when you brought your boy home from the hospital. But you simply can't wrap your mind around this concept when you first hold that tiny, beautiful, sleeping bundle. When he's a newborn, it's inconceivable that he could ever grow into a hairy, sullen, smelly, angry adolescent who will resist you over the most insignificant things.

Boys tend to be weaker than girls emotionally and relationally, so we fill their time with media and sports, and then we wonder why all they know how to do is either zone out or compete. We've each worked with young men who needed nothing more than to spend a month or two of their summers working or engaged in acts of service. We're talking labor and outreach. And it's not about whether they're happy doing it or not.

If you're having trouble getting your mind around this concept, read the book (or rent the movie) *The Ultimate Gift*. You'll get a great picture of what we're talking about. *The Ultimate Gift* is the story of Jason Stevens, a trust fund baby. When his wealthy grandfather dies, Jason anticipates a big inheritance. Instead, his grandfather has devised a crash course on life, with twelve tasks—or "gifts"—designed to challenge Jason in improbable ways, sending him on a journey of self-discovery and forcing him to determine what is most important in life: money or happiness.

How we accomplish this can differ from boy to boy. For example, when we see a boy who is struggling emotionally or relationally, we might recommend to his parents that they give him some time away from intense competitive sports and plug him in instead to activities that develop his emotional and relational muscles (while keeping his gross motor muscles well intact). Instead of a highly competitive environment, it might be helpful to look into activities such as camping, hiking, rock climbing, or cycling.

We've recommended that some parents send their boy on a wilderness experience for the summer, or a service project, to help him adjust his perspective or focus.

We've recommended sending some boys to visit their "country cousins," to work on a farm for spring break or a portion of their summer vacation.

With certain high-achieving boys, we've actually suggested to their parents that they pray for their sons to get cut from a sports team or fail a test, so that their first taste of failure doesn't come during their college years.

BOYS GAIN INSIGHT THROUGH INCOMPETENCE.

Help your boy identify and acknowledge his deficits. This may sound controversial or in conflict with everything you've heard about a child's self-esteem, but it's actually very much in line with it. Boys can gain wisdom and humility only through failure and ineptitude. Allowing a boy to practice his areas of weakness, rather than covering them up, is for his benefit.

A great picture of this can be seen in the movie *Remember the Titans*, the story of two Virginia high schools that are forced to integrate in the early 1970s. As part of this process, the white head coach of the T. C. Williams Titans is replaced by a black coach from North Carolina, and the impact of this decision reverberates throughout the community. Tensions rise when players of different races are forced to play together on the same football team. The team, like the greater community, is struggling to come together. At preseason training camp, the new head coach, Herman Boone (played by Denzel Washington), makes the players face their deficits and forces them to work within their weaknesses.

In one scene, Boone rises in the dining hall and calls out one of the players to educate the team on something he has learned about a teammate of a different race. A young man stands to report in. He then asks for a second volunteer, and no one is willing. He calls out the team's captains (one black and one white), and neither one is willing. Then he says, "Each one of you will spend time every day with a teammate of a different race. You will learn about him and his family, his likes, his dislikes. You will report back to me until you meet every one of your teammates. Until that time, we go to two-a-day practices. You continue to ignore each other, we'll go to three-a-day practices. Now, is there any part of this you don't understand?"[3]

A coach's mentality is to help his players focus on weak areas in order to build greater strength. It's a brilliant and intentional strategy. When a team shows up for a Monday practice following a Friday-night loss, they know that practice will likely center on the deficits from the game. They might watch film from the game or have some discussion about "what went wrong." The players then spend the remainder of the practice giving attention to those deficits on the field.

This is exactly what Herman Boone does with his team. He understands that until these athletes learn to come together on *and* off the field, the outcome will continue to look the same. Their differences would be reflected on the scoreboard.

This is also a great picture of what it looks like for a coach to be more concerned with the development of character in his players than their performance. We need more coaches who help boys win, but also teach them how to lose—coaches who care more about the development of character than winning the game.

BOYS DEVELOP COMPASSION THROUGH COMMUNITY.

Teach your boy empathy. Boys need help in broadening their emotional range. In *I Don't Want to Talk about It: Overcoming the Secret Legacy of Male Depression*, Terrence Real talks about the emotional deadening that boys experience while growing up. Boys come into life with a full range of emotions—lively and expressive—but over time, through a combination of socialization and biology, they begin to limit their experience and expression of feelings. Research shows that most men struggle with identifying and expressing their emotions accurately. (The clinical name for this is *alexithymia*.)[4]

Biologically, a boy's emotional palette is usually less colorful than a girl's. Differences in some of his brain structures and processes make emotions more difficult to distinguish. Socially, boys are discouraged from expressing their emotions. It's not nearly as acceptable for boys as it is for girls to express tender emotions such as sadness, hurt, loneliness, and fear. Unless we help our boys develop their full emotional range, they're likely to grow into men who are left with a dichromatic spectrum of emotions: anger and shame.

If we are to love and lead our boys well, we must be intentional in modeling and teaching them about such relational categories as sympathy, kindness, and concern. This will help them develop not only the necessary neuropathways in their brains, but also the emotional maturity they will need later in life to maintain healthy relationships as adults.

Boys need help in discriminating among their feelings. We can help by teaching them to develop a rich emotional vocabulary. Beginning when he is very young—but you can do this at any age—help your boy connect words to his feelings. You might say, "Your face looks hurt. Are you feeling disappointed?" Or, "You seem to be sad." Or, "I can understand why you might feel frustrated right now."

Boys are naturally good at being angry, but they need help identifying their other feelings. For instance, when your boy says he's angry, affirm him and confirm his feelings. Then help him identify other feelings that may be caught up with or covered over by his anger.

Son: "Mom, I'm ticked off at the coach for not letting me start the game. I barely played."

Mom: "I'll bet you're mad about that. That really stinks. If it were me, I would be really hurt, too. And probably embarrassed. Does it hurt, too?"

It can also be extremely helpful to talk with your boy about your own feelings (if you can do so without making him feel responsible for them). You can say, "I was afraid. What about you?" Or, "That movie really made me sad when the father died. How did you feel about that?" Sharing our emotions gives a boy permission to feel and express his own. Though we don't want to pelt him with questions or overload him with emotional freight, a simple exchange like this will begin to give him a vocabulary and a reference for other feelings he has.

It's also important to model curiosity and ask him to do the same. When he's telling you a story, listen well and ask him questions about his inner world. "What did that feel like?" "What were you thinking?" "What do you think the other person was feeling?" These types of questions teach boys to look inward and pay attention to themselves and others. You can also ask these same sorts of questions about characters in movies you watch with him. Listening well, and teaching your boy to do the same, is an important part of his emotional development.

Another way to build compassion into your boy is to model it when you are disciplining him. Maintain a courteous tone and focus on putting feelings into words and identifying natural consequences.

Son: "I hate this food, Mommy! Why did you make this?"

Dad: "I'm sad that you chose to speak disrespectfully to your mother. Now you won't get to eat dinner, and we won't get to watch the game together on TV, because you will be in your room."

Son: "No, Dad. That's not fair."

Dad: "I'm disappointed, too, buddy. I was really looking forward to hanging out with you tonight."

This technique accomplishes several things:

- It teaches a boy that feelings are a normal part of life.
- It allows the boy to have his own feelings rather than blaming them on the adult.

- It reinforces and maintains the authority of the adult-child relationship.
- It shows the dad as being kind and strong and not freaked out by his son's behavior.
- It demonstrates to the son that his parents care about him.
- It shows the son that his father isn't going to back down. The discipline is firm *and* loving.

The more we can let a boy struggle and learn how to struggle well, the better off he will be later in life. It is only through suffering that we grow spiritually and emotionally. Boys need far more help in developing their emotional skills than they do their motor skills. The more we focus on developing their character, the more they will become men of character. As parents and caregivers, we need to look deeply into our own lives to see where we tend to avoid pain, and we must learn to put words to our own emotions. If we don't, we will likely lead our sons from a place of guilt, shame, and fear, instead of love.

Putting the Principles into Practice

Helping boys to be more available to their emotions is an area where we really need to help boys develop and grow to their fullest potential. If we do this well, they will be well served throughout their lives. Here are a few suggestions:

TIP 1: Say "hello" to Rover. One way to teach a boy compassion is to get a dog (or other family pet) and give him much of the responsibility for taking care of it. For instance, make him responsible for feeding the dog, and let him know that he can't sit down to eat dinner until the dog has been fed. Inevitably, there will come a day when he is hungry and wants to eat without feeding the dog. Gently say something like, "I bet Sparky is hungry just like you are. I bet she also feels upset that she can't eat." Another way that pets can be used to teach empathy is by taking your son along to the vet appointments. Talk about how the dog is scared or nervous, and ask your boy to think of some ways that he can comfort the dog on the way to the vet, while at the vet, and on the way home.

TIP 2: **Don't wait for kindergarten.** Consider sending him to preschool as a three- or four-year-old. Most preschool programs cover foundational relationship structures such as sharing, awareness of other people's needs, taking turns, patience, personal space, etc., that are sometimes harder to teach at home.

TIP 3: **Allow him to suffer.** Don't shelter him from the greater sorrows of life. As we have mentioned, service opportunities are a great way to teach boys empathy. Working at a soup kitchen, sponsoring another boy through a relief agency, going on a missions trip, or doing a Scout service project are all great ways to teach compassion and concern for other people. When your boy sees firsthand the sorrow of life, and that he can have a positive impact, his heart will grow along with his self-image.

TIP 4: **Don't run his show.** Evaluate where you are overly invested in his academic performance, in ways that stand to hinder him rather than benefit him, and back off. If you have trouble identifying this in yourself, be courageous enough to get feedback from his classroom teacher, your spouse, or friends who have observed your involvement.

TIP 5: Help him evaluate. At different stages in your son's development, have him make a list of his strengths and weaknesses. Help him accurately identify these areas and watch for his inability to do this accurately. For example, if he can list ten things he does well and can't identify one area of weakness, his ego may be a bit inflated. The opposite scenario is equally troubling. If he can only list things he says he's not good at and can't manage to identify any of his strengths, this is a concern as well. Lastly, watch for accuracy in terms of his self-reporting. It's not uncommon for boys to believe themselves strong in areas of weakness and vice versa.

TIP 6: Show him his strengths. Be certain that both you and your son identify areas of emotional strength. Boys are likely to list only physical attributes, such as, "I'm good at basketball," and may need help identifying emotional and relational strengths. You can help him by reminding him of situations you have observed. For example, you might say, "You were compassionate to your sister when she found out she didn't get chosen for student council," or, "You were a good friend to Jacob when he didn't make the team."

TIP 7: Don't ignore deficits. Strategize with your son to address some of his deficits. For example, say, "I notice that you listed _____ as something you're not good at. What are your ideas for how to get better at that?" If he has trouble coming up with ideas, prime the pump by offering a few of your own ideas.

TIP 8: Be kind. It's important to recognize that the world will do its part in toughening up our boys. As caregivers, one significant role we play is in working to soften their hearts. Boys will inevitably be hit by life's disappointments and difficulties. When they experience life's pain, the best way we can help is by offering them compassion, support, and tenderness.

TIP 9: **Take a deep breath and count to ten.** Because boys are inclined toward anger, it's a smart move to remain calm and respectful when dealing with problems and providing discipline. Call a timeout if you need it, or wait a few moments (or hours) to think through your response. It's important to steer clear of yelling at or shaming a boy; this will only escalate the tension and incite his anger.

TIP 10: **Cut yourself some slack.** No parent, teacher, or coach is perfect. Mistakes will happen, and adults inevitably lose their temper, shame boys, or manipulate them with guilt. But what matters most is that responsible adults work to repair their relationships with boys when they break down. If they don't, a greater sense of disconnection between adult and child will occur. We must make this clear: When the relationship between an adult and a boy breaks down, it is always the adult's responsibility to repair it. If the grown-ups can't swallow their own pride and admit their mistakes, how can we expect our boys to do it?

Part 3

The Heart of a Boy

*And Max the king of all wild things was lonely and
wanted to be where someone loved him best of all.*

MAURICE SENDAK, *Where the Wild Things Are*

The Horse and His Boy, one of the books in C. S. Lewis's popular
Chronicles of Narnia series, recounts the mystical journey
of an escaped slave boy, Shasta; a talking stallion, Bree; and
their companions, Aravis and her horse Hwin, as they journey
toward Narnia—and freedom. In the book, Shasta and his friends
overcome trial after trial (including lions and a pursuing army) in
an effort to secure the freedom and dignity for which they were
made to live.

In many ways, the story of *The Horse and His Boy* mirrors the
emotional and spiritual journey that every boy takes as he moves
from childhood dependence and folly to masculine authority and

responsibility. Much of the narrative involves Shasta's shedding of his insecurity and foolishness and discovering his dignity and wisdom. Likewise, for our boys, the dangerous and beautiful journey they will take from childhood to manhood is much more than a series of physical and sociological changes. For every boy, this is a journey of the heart, a journey that will either confirm him as a man or leave him trapped as a boy in a man's body.

Shasta's expedition into the wilderness toward his freedom, like the typical passage our boys will take from boyhood to manhood, is a journey from innocence to wisdom, and from pride to humility.[1] And, like Shasta, our boys cannot find the way on their own. Though beautiful, the wilderness is fierce and violent; and without the right help, boys can get lost and end up living what Thoreau called "lives of quiet desperation."[2]

When Richard first came to see me (Stephen) in my counseling practice, he was thirty-five. He'd been married for eight years and had two kids, a boy (five) and a girl (two). After settling in, I asked him what had brought him to see me. He said he was "overwhelmed."

"My boss is on me at work, my wife says she is 'lonely,' and my kids are more an irritation than enjoyable. I don't feel like myself. It's like I'm just going through the motions."

I asked him, "What would it feel like to be yourself?"

"More passionate. More free. More engaged."

"When was the last time you remember feeling like this?"

Richard paused for a long time, his fingers raking the arms of the chair, his eyes staring at his tan loafers. "I don't really know. I used to like playing baseball when I was a boy."

"I sure would like to know more about that. Can you tell me about it?"

Richard's face began to shine as he told his story. "I lived all year for summer. I couldn't wait until school ended and baseball season began. My dad coached my team, and we would get out in the backyard every night after dinner and play catch 'til it got so dark that we couldn't see the ball."

"Sounds amazing. When did you stop playing?" I asked.

"When I was seven or eight."

"What made you stop?"

"My dad left."

As we talked that day, Richard laid out for me a story I had heard dozens of times from dozens of men. The story of a man whose heart had been wounded. The story of a man who had lost his way. For Richard, the assault on his heart started with his parents' divorce when he was eight. His dad moved in with another woman, and his mother slipped into a decade-long depression. The eldest boy of three children, Richard was left to manage the broken pieces as best he could. When he graduated from high school, he escaped to college and tried to figure things out on his own the best he could.

In college, he followed the conventional path and got a business degree for its "practicality," even though he "really loved history." He also met his wife, Becky, at college, and they started dating. After graduation, they broke up for a while, got back together, and then got married. Before long, Becky gave birth to their first child, Zach, and then Amy. Richard got a promotion at work. They bought a house.

All along the way, Richard was doing what he knew best—getting by. His life was full of chores, duties, and responsibilities. To anyone looking at him from the outside, Richard was okay, but inside he was lost, confused, and increasingly hopeless.

Like a lot of guys, Richard had never really found his way through the wilderness. He'd gotten turned around and had few landmarks by which to regain his bearings. In his father's absence, he had grown up without a clan; without wise, loving, and intentional guides; without appropriate challenges and initiations; and without memorable celebrations.

For boys to be successful, they need to be part of something bigger than themselves. They need help in recognizing their gifts and limitations (and what to do with both). They need guidance through the trials. They need the tender hand of discipline and the strong presence of love.

Without much help, boys grow physically—they get bigger, taller, and older. Through their interactions with the surrounding world, they grow mentally and socially. They learn reading, writing, and arithmetic. They gain savvy, know-how, and street smarts. Yet all this can occur without the boy ever making it through the wilderness to become an authentic man. If his heart is not addressed, he is left to wander the wasteland of his own self-absorption and immaturity, incapable of entering the promised land of true masculinity. Boys need to be vaccinated with values, mentored in morality, and steered in their spirituality.

More than anything else, a boy needs to have his heart nourished. He needs to be emotionally equipped and spiritually directed. He needs to have the fire in his belly stoked. In order to love a boy well, we must consider his character (so we can call out its nobler aspects), understand our role (as parents and caregivers) in his life, and help him find his way on the well-worn path through the wilderness of boyhood to the land of authentic masculinity. We need to help him get connected to his heart.

What do we mean by "heart"? When we talk about the heart, we're talking about much more than emotions. We're talking about the core being of a boy—the feelings, needs, desires, longings, and hopes that are bound up inside each boy.[3] A boy's heart is the essence of who he is created to be.

In the next four chapters, we will look at what it means to nurture the heart of a boy, from four different perspectives.

In these chapters, we paint the heart of a boy with a broad brush. Because every boy is a unique creation, we cannot (nor should we) give a "magic pill" prescription for engaging a boy's heart. In describing the heartbeat of a boy, we've tried to bring clarity to the big picture, but it's up to you to determine to what extent—and how—these ideas can be applied to your own boy.

Because so much of a boy's heart is seen through the window of his physical and social development, it might be helpful to refer back to part 1, "The Way of a Boy," to refamiliarize yourself with the different stages of a boy's maturation (Explorer, Lover, Individual, Wanderer, and Warrior). As with your boy's progress through the developmental stages, his heart will mature at its own pace. Some boys seem wise beyond their years; others are late bloomers. Some boys are tender; others are fierce. Some boys are courageous; others are cautious. It's our task as parents, educators, coaches, mentors, youth workers, counselors, and adult leaders to recognize the unique heart of each boy and encourage him to live from the depth and breadth of it.

CHAPTER 10

𝔑oble 𝔠reatures: 𝔑urturing a 𝔅oy's 𝔥eart

What are little boys made of, made of?
What are little boys made of?
Snips and snails and puppy-dog tails;
That's what little boys are made of, made of.

This familiar Mother Goose nursery rhyme, dating back to the early nineteenth century, gives one perspective on the heart of a boy. Attributed to the pen of Robert Southey (1774–1843), an English poet and historian who became poet laureate of Britain in 1813, this little verse captures the truth of a boy's earthiness and constant motion. So, boys are squirmy and grimy—true enough, but there

197

is much more we need to understand about boys if we are to love them well. Southey knew this, too, and what many people don't know is that his poem continues for quite a few more stanzas.

(Stanza 4):
What are young men made of, made of?
What are young men made of?
Sighs and leers and crocodile tears;
That's what young men are made of.
(Stanza 6):
What are our sailors made of, made of?
What are our sailors made of?
Pitch and tar, pig-tail and scar;
That's what our sailors are made of.
(Stanza 7):
What are our soldiers made of, made of?
What are our soldiers made of?
Pipeclay and drill, the foeman to kill;
That's what our soldiers are made of.[1]

Southey sketches a pretty good illustration of the growing heart of a boy. Boys are made to be wild, sensitive, strong, and courageous. The heart of a boy is wrapped around the ambivalences of mystery and knowing; of play and mastery; of autonomy and dependence; of creativity and destruction.

When considering the word *heart*, it is helpful to think of it as the ancient Hebrews did. To the Jews, the word for heart, *leb*, means "the seat of the senses, affections, and emotions."[2] The heart is the root of feeling, thought, memory, resolution, courage, passion, and action, all rolled into one. The heart is the center of "will and purpose; intellect and wisdom." It's the root of life.[3]

The ancient Greeks had similar ideas about the heart. Like the ancient Jews, the Greeks were a deeply religious and spiritual people.

NOBLE CREATURES: NURTURING A BOY'S HEART

For them, the heart was the center and basis of all spiritual life. They thought of the heart as "the fountain and seat of the thoughts, passions, desires, appetites, affections, purposes, [and] endeavors."[4]

Clearly, the concept of "the heart" is much broader than feelings (though emotions are certainly part of it). In these chapters, when we refer to the heart of a boy, we are talking about his entire inner being and how he is created to be.

It might be helpful to think of boys in terms of young lion cubs—noble princes of the wild. If they're not nurtured and guided by the pride, they will become rogues and die of hunger or disease. If they are captured and caged, they become tame, lazy, and unpredictable. Each boy needs to be taught how to live from his heart, and in order for us to do this, as adult caregivers, we must do three essential things:

- We must *see* him.
- We must *name* him.
- We must *draw him out*.

What It Means to *See* Him

To love a boy well, we must become a *student* of him. To *see* him, we must observe him, consider him, perceive him, and learn him. This involves lots of listening, patience, and attentiveness. The nature of *seeing* combines three elements: (1) a curiosity about who he is, (2) an appreciation for who he is, and (3) a vision for who he will become.

I (David) met with a ninth-grade boy who had been given the assignment of studying an animal of his choice for thirty-six hours. During that time he had to document every activity, except for when he himself was sleeping. Toby chose his family's golden retriever, Hoss. He watched the dog eat in the morning and recorded his observations. He charted how many times Hoss went to his water bowl, how long he chewed a tennis ball, when he barked—and at whom—when and where he relieved himself, and how he responded to human contact. Based on his observations, Toby had to answer a series of questions about the dog, and he made a number of assumptions based on his observations.

Later, Toby and I had a hilarious conversation about the assignment. He said, "You can't imagine how much I learned about Hoss just by having to watch the guy day in and day out. My dog has a great life. He naps all the time, eats, and plays a little. People pay attention to him, love all over him, and then he sleeps some more."

Toby came by the information solely by becoming a student of Hoss. Such is our task as parents and caregivers when it comes to the boys we love. We don't need to keep a scientific log on our boys, but we do need to pay attention to the mundane details of their lives. We need to listen well to what's said and not said. We need to linger with them long enough to study them and to hear from them (even if they aren't saying much). We need to listen for what they're saying about themselves when they tell stories—and discern what they're not saying as well. We need to watch them when they interact with their peers, and gather feedback from other adults who care for them.

We need to be curious about what makes them tick. Here are some "seeing" questions to ask yourself about your boy:

- What does he love to do?
- What is he afraid of?
- With whom does he spend time, and whom does he avoid?
- What is he like when you're not around?
- How does he perform for coaches and teachers?

- What is his favorite cereal?
- Who are his three best friends?
- Who is his favorite comic book hero, and why?
- When he is disappointed, what does he do?
- How well can he celebrate his own victories? What about the victories of others?
- Is he empathetic?
- What are his favorite, and least favorite, television shows, types of cars, and music?
- What state or country does he want to visit?
- What really makes him mad?
- How does he hold his pencil?
- What does he like on his pizza?
- How does he relate to God?

You need to see how your boy is uniquely made—both the good and the bad; the strengths and the weaknesses; the interests and the disinterests. Imagine where these characteristics will take him if they are not developed or refined. To *see* your boy is to also have a vision of who he is becoming and where he may end up if he follows the way of his heart. Having a vision helps us to structure a boy's life according to his design. Boys are so full of life that it's hard to know what to do with them sometimes. However, when we have a vision of who they are, and who they are becoming, we can engage with them and lead them toward the path they are to follow in their lives. The vision we hold for our boys becomes the compass that keeps them on track.

What It Means to *Name* Him

Another significant way to nurture a boy's heart is to name him. We're not talking about the blend of consonants and vowels you use to call him to dinner. We're referring to the authority you have in his life to declare the truth *about* him, *to* him, and *for* him.

To *name* someone means that we have a profound and intimate relationship with him. Nicknames are a great example of the power of names. They are most often terms of endearment used by close family or friends (or by admirers). Though I (Stephen) have successfully avoided being called "Steve" throughout my life, I have picked up a handful of different nicknames over the years. Growing up, I was "Hot Potato" to my family. In high school, I was "Stevo" to my closest friends. When we're alone, my wife calls me "Ginkers." (Don't ask.) And one of my closest friends has a list of names for me including "Stevie J," "Holiday Inn," "Doc Holiday," and "Stevie Guitar James," depending on what we are talking about. (Thank you, Chip.) I remember—and respond to—each of these names because they carry weight and affection. They mean that I am known and matter deeply to someone. If I took the time to tell you all the stories behind the names, you would see how each one fits me very specifically.

If you have *seen* your boy well (been curious about him, developed an appreciation of his uniqueness, and gained a vision for him), it's likely that you will be motivated to *speak* what you have seen. This is the process of *naming*. If it's accurate, the way we *name* a boy has an association with his identity, his reputation, his promise, and his glory. To name someone means that we have *read* him and have been provoked to move *toward* him.[5]

The power of naming also has a downside. It can have an element of warning, crying out, or rebuking. Just as naming has the power to bless, it also has the power to curse. To be "called a name" is usually uncomplimentary and frequently abusive. A famous quote about propaganda from the late 1930s sums it up this way:

Bad names have played a tremendously powerful role in the history of the world and in our own individual development. They have ruined reputations, stirred men and women to outstanding accomplishments, sent others to prison cells, and made men mad enough to enter battle and slaughter their fellowmen. They have been and are applied to other people, groups, gangs, tribes, colleges, political parties, neighborhoods, states, sections of the country, nations, and races.[6]

When this type of "bad naming" is applied to a boy, the effect on his heart can be devastating. We all know the saying, "Sticks and stones may break my bones, but words will never hurt me." And we all know that this is a lie. Sticks and stones can certainly break your bones, but it's the words that can scar your heart.

Dan and I (Stephen) met for coffee several times at the church where I'm a pastor. He and I are about the same age, and during our times together we talked about everything from work to family to faith. One day, we got onto the subject of Little League baseball, and Dan told me that he had been an all-star when he was growing up. I was impressed because I had never been very good at baseball.

I asked him, "Did you go on to play in high school?"

"Not much. I quit after my freshman year." He shrugged as the delight washed from his face.

"Really? Why did you quit?"

Dan went on to tell me how his love for baseball and his gift for the game had faded when he was fourteen. The summer before he started high school, he had tried out for and made a very competitive travel baseball team. He played second base and batted second in the lineup. He described himself as a reliable hitter. "I almost always got on base, either with a base hit or by drawing a walk."

When school started, Dan worked hard to get ready for the high school team. He wasn't a big kid, and he knew he had to give it his all if he wanted to make the team. When tryouts came for the high school team, Dan was ready. He had lifted weights all fall and had worked with a private hitting coach to fine-tune his swing.

On the last day of tryouts, the coach called all the players together to announce the names of the boys who had made the team. First, he called the varsity players. It was mostly juniors and seniors, so Dan wasn't surprised when he didn't hear his name. Then the coach began to call the names for the boys who had made the junior varsity squad. Dan's heart was in this throat. When he heard his name called, he was overwhelmed with joy.

When the team broke at the end of practice, Dan took off his cleats and went back into the school to get a book he had forgotten for his homework. When he got back to the locker room, everybody was gone. He sat down on a bench in the far corner to put on some shoes and gather the rest of his stuff before going to meet his mom in the parking lot. The coaches came in through a side door and sat down in the opposite corner of the locker room just outside the coach's office. From where they were sitting they couldn't see Dan, but he could hear them talking about the team. Dan was too nervous to speak up and let his presence be known, so he just froze, not making a sound.

The two coaches were talking about the JV players and the promising potential for the ball club for the next few years.

"This must be the best group of underclassmen we've ever seen," the assistant coach said.

"Absolutely!" the head coach exclaimed.

They then began to talk through each player on the roster. When they got to Dan, his heart was pounding so hard he could barely focus on what they were saying. "Danny, he's a good player," the head coach said, "but he'll never have the frame to make it at the varsity level."

"Yeah, he's just too small. He can't hack it," the assistant coach agreed.

Dan's heart fell and shattered. He sat for several more minutes, choking back his tears, until the coaches finished their conversation, turned out the lights, and left the locker room.

As Dan finished telling his story, his eyes were wet. "I've never talked about that before."

"What happened?" I asked him.

"I quit. When the next week rolled around, I didn't show up for practice," Dan said. "I told the other guys on the team that I had to get an after-school job to help out my mom. I told my mom that I didn't want to play because it took so much time. I just gave up the dream."

Dan was named that day. And the name stuck. As he and I talked over coffee, twenty years after the fact, we discussed how much of his life was still defined by his JV coach's assessment: "He can't hack it." Work. Family. Friends. In many ways, Dan has been trying his whole life to prove to that coach that he has what it takes.

Bad or negative naming can cause great shame in the heart of a boy. The invisible wounds of a misspoken name can be carried for a lifetime. When a boy is on the receiving end of negative naming, it causes great harm and exposes deep shame. Because it hurts so deeply and feels so shameful, a boy will often end up training himself to despise his emotions. He writes off the pain as evidence that he is "too sensitive," and he believes that the shame he is experiencing is somehow his own fault. *I must be broken if I feel this way.*

What It Means to *Draw Him Out*

Along with being *seen* and being *named*, the heart of a boy needs to be *drawn out*. He needs to be challenged, invited, coaxed, and directed toward authenticity, integrity, and intimacy.

Unlike a boy's physiology, which develops toward manhood whether or not he (or we) wants it to, his heart will not find its own way. As we mentioned in our previous book *How to Hit a Curveball, Grill the Perfect Steak, and Become a Real Man,*

> No guy makes it past seventeen or eighteen without receiving his fair share of dings to his manhood—and that's if he is lucky. By the time most guys get their driver's license, they have already experienced enough emotional and spiritual fender benders that their hearts are dented and their self-image is scratched for years to come. . . .
>
> Heartache is not terribly diverse, but it's certainly widespread. As counselors, we've heard thousands of sad stories from men. Every man loses his innocence at some point—some suddenly, and others more gradually.
>
> Sadly, these assaults on the masculine heart result in far more than adolescent angst. When a guy's heart has been wounded, the results are significant: Self-protection, distrust of others, suspicion of God, and a fervent reliance on the four horsemen of self-sufficiency: training, talent, intellect, and willpower.[7]

Boys learn from an early age how to contain their hearts and disguise who they really are—yet they desperately want to be known. The rub is that they are afraid to reveal their hearts to those who might judge or reject them. Erwin McManus articulates this well in his book *Soul Cravings*: "We're all struggling to figure ourselves out. We're afraid to expose our souls to those who might judge us, and at the same time we desperately need help to guide us on this journey. If we're not careful, we might find ourselves with everything the world has to offer and later find we have lost ourselves in the clutter."[8]

Though McManus is talking about people in general, he might as well be addressing the hearts of boys. Boys need guidance in their heart's quest for authentic manhood. It is our responsibility as parents and caregivers to confront their ambivalence and draw them out.

In Hebrew, the word that means "to draw" is *hiphil*. Curiously, the same word can also be translated "to be saved," which highlights an interesting truth: The work of drawing a boy out is the work of saving him. If a boy's heart is not drawn out—that is to say, called to its fullest and most genuine expression—it will be lost under the rubble of shattered dreams and disappointments, which are regular occurrences in life.

Far too often, we circumvent a boy's heart (not to mention our own) in order to protect him from the pain of life. Instead of teaching him how to engage with his losses (and thus gain wisdom, nobility, and integrity as a man), we teach him to suppress his pain and strive not to lose. But unless we give a boy permission to live *with* and *from* his heart, all our "strategies for success" will be meaningless. The truth is, a boy can do everything right and follow all the rules, but if his heart's not in it, his life will be aimless and ultimately meaningless. Like smoke rising from a fire being blown by the wind, he will become a thin vapor. A boy must be engaged with and directed in an ongoing and intimate relationship with himself, with others, and with God. It's our job to draw him out and help him to keep his heart.

What It Means to Keep His Heart

In order for a boy to keep his heart, he needs to know what he is feeling, what he needs, what he desires, what he longs for, and where he needs to place his hope. It's our responsibility to know that he can't figure this out on his own. He needs our help to put into words the experiences of his heart. Learning to *live fully* cannot be accomplished alone. It takes root and takes shape in relationships.[9] To keep his heart as he journeys toward manhood, a boy needs to be *guided by his dreams, helped in his ambivalence, engaged on his own terms,* and *assisted in answering the biggest question of all.*

A BOY NEEDS TO BE GUIDED BY HIS DREAMS.

Dr. Chip Dodd, a good friend of ours, has two sons who are now nearly grown. Starting when his boys were still little, he sought to ingrain two key ideas into their hearts:

- "Climb the mountain of your dreams."
- "Hold the flag brave and true."

Though, at first blush, these statements seem almost nonsensical, Chip was deliberately calling to the hearts of his boys. He was daring them to dream, drawing out their sense of nobility, passion, hope, creativity, desire, justice, imagination, and adventure—qualities that are at the core of every boy. Chip taught his sons that their dreams are important and that the standards and values that guide their lives are worth fighting for.

Of course, Chip was also setting his sons up for some serious heartache—because most of our lives don't turn out the way we planned. And on the battlefield of life, the guy flying the standard is the only one on the field without a weapon—in other words, he's a big target. But Chip understood that living from the heart is a decision we have to make on behalf of our sons. If the boys we love are going to keep their hearts, they will become targets of cynicism and sarcasm. They will be scorned for hoping, and daring to reach out, and being guided by the vision of who they are meant to be. And they will be ridiculed for having dreams that seem silly, unrealistic, idealistic, impractical, and unlikely.

Too often, we want to shield our boys from disappointment, discouragement, and dejection. And though, on the surface, we say it's for their own good, deep down we realize that we're trying to protect our own hearts from the pain of watching someone we love suffer the grief of living in a broken and painful world. We dampen their hopes and dreams, and we temper our honesty with them, to avoid *our own* disappointment. We help them set "realistic" goals, so they won't have to struggle or be disappointed by grasping for—and missing—the brass ring. But what we're really trying to avoid is the experience of our own powerlessness as we watch our boys grapple with failure, frustration, and pain. We don't fan the flames of their hearts because we aren't willing (or we're not equipped) to be there with them when they crash and burn.

In our attempts to protect our boys from despair and heartache, we often turn our relationships with them away from intimacy and toward instruction. Intimacy and instruction are very different things. Intimacy is about *being with, knowing,* and *experiencing* another person. Instruction is about *performing, doing,* and *mastering.* To *be* in relationship with a boy in the midst of life's ups and downs is vastly different from teaching him *about* life.

A boy's *ability* and *willingness* to know himself, and to be known by others in the midst of relationship, are essential if he is going to make it to manhood without losing his heart. A boy needs to be asked questions like, What are you feeling? What do you need? What are your dreams? He needs us to honor the words that come from his heart—even if we disagree with them or they scare us or we think they're silly. He needs help with putting his dreams into words. He needs for us to buy into his dreams and to invest our own hearts in them—even when we doubt them or think they're doomed to fail. And we must be willing to hurt and to grieve with him when he does fail.

A great example of the contrast between *being* and *teaching* can be seen in the 2006 Academy Award–winning dramatic comedy *Little Miss Sunshine*. It's the story of a dysfunctional family's trek to a girl's beauty pageant for the youngest child, Olive. As they are traveling together in their Volkswagen microbus, the Hoovers come to discover more about themselves and about how to love one another well.

One lead character in the movie is the Hoovers' teenage son, Dwayne. Dwayne's dream is to fly jets. He is extremely disciplined and committed to his dream, so much so that he exercises fanatically and has taken a nine-month vow of silence (communicating only by writing on a pad of paper). The story turns when Olive, trying to pass time on the eight-hundred-mile journey, starts giving Dwayne eye tests that she's picked up along the way.

Olive: Okay, I'm gonna test if you're color-blind. What letter is in the circle?

She holds up a chart with a green circle. Inside the circle in a mosaic pattern is a bright red letter *A*. Dwayne makes a gesture indicating "there's nothing there."

Olive: No, inside the circle! Right there!

Dwayne shakes his head again. Olive glances at Uncle Frank.

Olive: It's an *A*! Can't you see it?! It's red! See? Right there!

Dwayne takes the chart and stares at it.

Frank: You can't see the *A*? It's bright red. Can you see the difference between the green and the red?

Dwayne shakes his head desperately. Frank turns away.

Frank: Oh, man.

Dwayne looks at him, pulls out his pad, and writes: "What?"

Frank doesn't say anything. Dwayne points violently at the pad. Frank looks at him.

Frank (quietly): Dwayne, I think you might be color-blind.

Dwayne doesn't understand. He points at the pad again: "What?"

Frank: You can't fly jets if you're color-blind.

Dwayne starts to panic. He starts hitting the window and the seat in front of him, banging violently on the ceiling, and then he tries to open the door. When the van stops, Dwayne tears free and races down a hill into the desert, where he begins to scream, curse, and shriek like a wild animal. His dream is over. His hopes are shattered. His family is at a loss for what to do. Dwayne's dad, Richard, glances at Sheryl, Dwayne's mom, and points to his watch.

Sheryl: Let's give him a second.

Finally, Sheryl approaches Dwayne.

Sheryl: Dwayne? Honey? I'm sorry.

Dwayne: I'm not going.

Sheryl: Dwayne . . .

Dwayne: I'm not! I don't care! I'm not getting in that bus again.

The conversation grows heated. Dwayne and his mom exchange a few words as she tries to convince him to get back in the microbus so they won't be late for the beauty pageant. Finally, she gives up and climbs the hill back to the rest of the family. After some arguing between the mother and father, Olive descends the hill to be with her brother. When she gets to him, she squats down beside her brother, and without saying a word, she puts her head on his shoulder and rests there with him in his grief. After a moment, Dwayne responds kindly.

Dwayne: Okay. Let's go.

The two make their way up the rocky slope, back to the family and the van.[10]

Olive gives us a great picture of how to love a boy. They need to be loved unconditionally. Their dreams need to be encouraged, invested in, and lifted up. And when their dreams are lost or damaged (as they ultimately will be), they need our presence—not our solutions; they need our care—not our instruction; and, in time, they need our encouragement to get back up and dream again.

A BOY NEEDS TO BE HELPED IN HIS AMBIVALENCE.

At almost every turn in their development, boys experience deep conflict between their tenderness and their strength. Many boys are confused and disoriented by the conflict between their sensitivity and their aggression. It is our role as guides in their lives to help them find harmony between their softness and their passion.

Harper sat in my (David's) office a week after what he called "the most humiliating moment in my life." His sixth-grade class was reading aloud *Bridge to Terabithia*—taking turns, each reading three paragraphs, working their way up and down the rows.

The novel is the story of a lonely boy and girl, Jess and Leslie, who create a magical forest kingdom called Terabithia, and when Harper's parents had read the story at home with him a year earlier, he'd had a strong, emotional reaction to the tragic ending. As the reading progressed in the classroom, he hoped he wouldn't have a similar response. But as his turn to read drew near, he realized he would have to read the part where Jess discovers the death of his best friend, Leslie. Harper felt the tears welling up in his eyes. He became so distracted with fighting them back that the teacher had to call his name twice to let him know it was his turn to read. He started into the first sentence, but his voice cracked and his vision blurred so that he could barely see the words.

The entire class turned in their desks to see if he was indeed about to cry. He started into the second sentence and made it almost to the end of the paragraph before his voice cracked again and he could feel his breathing change. He stood and ran to the front of the room to ask permission to go to the bathroom, but it was too late. By the time he reached the door, he could hear two boys snickering under their breath: "Sissy."

Harper's situation is not unusual. By middle school, most boys have trained themselves to be ashamed of their feelings; and by the beginning of high school, many boys have lost their sensitivity altogether—effectively erecting a wall around their hearts.

Boys need our help and support to give them the courage to *feel* their feelings and to learn how to express their emotions well. They need to see that emotions are not unmasculine. It is our role as caregivers to nurture and protect the emotional lives of our boys so that they can be as caring as they are strong.

In their book *Raising Cain*, Dan Kindlon and Michael Thompson say that we must "give boys permission to have an internal life."[11]

> [They need] approval for the full range of human emotions, and help in developing an emotional vocabulary so that they may better understand themselves and communicate more effectively with others.
>
> The simple idea here is that you consciously speak to a boy's internal life all the time, whether he is aware of it or not. You respect it, you take it into account, you make reference to it, you share your own. . . . If you act as if your son *has* an internal life . . . soon he will take it into account.[12]

We cannot emphasize this enough: Boys need a model of manhood that includes emotional expression and deep male friendships. Boys will see many stoic, unemotional, guarded men, and they will try to emulate them. Most men we encounter in our counseling practices are lonely and haven't had a close male friend since high school or college. They were never taught how to develop and maintain authentic male friendships.

We must show our boys that authentic manhood can be expressed in diverse ways. They need to see that there are many ways to be brave; many ways to be caring and compassionate; many ways to be adventurous and creative; many ways to be strong. We must "celebrate the natural creativity and risk taking of boys, their energy, their boldness. We need to praise the artist and the entertainer, the missionary and the athlete, the soldier and the male nurse, the store owner and the round-the-world sailor, the teacher and the CEO. There are many ways for a boy to make a contribution in this life."[13]

Boys need to be encouraged to initiate friendships, and they need to be equipped to maintain them. They need to be taught how to manage the conflict that is embedded in male relationships. Learning how to relate well to other boys is just as important as learning how to relate to girls.

Along with encouraging tenderness, we need to nurture their emotional and spiritual strength. One way of bridging the gap between tenderness and strength, write Kindlon and Thompson, is by helping our boys understand that "emotional courage is courage, and that courage and empathy are the sources of real strength in life."[14]

> Popular movies aimed at boys seem to prize only
> one kind of courage: standing up to a physically
> larger opponent. The willingness to fight an enemy,
> to outwit a dinosaur, to defeat an alien monster, to
> look into the eye of a villain with a gun, is the media's
> definition of male courage. . . .
>
> Boys need models of emotional courage in their
> own lives, not just in the media. We need to recog-
> nize and identify for them emotional courage in the
> lives of [people around us]. . . . We need to provide

boys models of male heroism that go beyond the
muscular, the self-absorbed, and the simplistically
heroic. Many adults display emotional courage in
their work or personal lives, but rarely do we allow
our children to witness our private moments of conscience or bravery. . . . Boys can and will respond to
the complexity of real courage.[15]

If our boys are going to live with emotional strength, we must
consistently confront their passivity. The problem is that our culture has grown accustomed to male passivity. In their book *The
Silence of Adam*, Dr. Larry Crabb, Don Hudson, and Al Andrews
address the reality that many men have become flaccid in the face
of the world's chaos. Using the ancient story of Adam and Eve as
a lens on masculinity, the authors give a path for reclaiming the
full potential of manhood. Using Adam as the masculine archetype, they also address the common passivity of men: "Adam,
then, was a silent man, a passive man. Like many men in history, he was physically present but emotionally absent. He fades
into the background of the story rather than standing front and
center on the stage. . . . He was passive. He chose silence and was
absent."[16]

This kind of passivity in boys (and in men) is dangerous. When
boys can't or don't express their hearts with courage and empathy,
it comes out in other ways: in aggression, depression, or isolation. The result of their passivity is defensiveness and emotional
elusiveness. When faced with the chaos of life (school, competition, hormones, sports, academics, family, friends, girls, future,
hobbies), many boys shut down, become angry, or both. We must
teach the boys we love to face their everyday challenges courageously if we hope for them to fight against the evil, cruelty, and
chaos of this world.

A BOY NEEDS TO BE ENGAGED ON HIS OWN TERMS.

Is relating with boys hard? You betcha. Boys can be a royal pain. They are often hardheaded, inarticulate, and clueless. When we ask them to share with us (even the smallest parts of themselves) they become annoyed. When they need to cry, they get angry. When we tell them that they have done something wrong, they defend themselves to the bitter end. What's the deal?

When it comes to tender emotions, boys get scared. They're frightened by sensitivity because they don't know what to do with it (whether it's their own feelings or the feelings of others). So they need for us to read between the lines and break the code. This is part of *seeing* them and *drawing them out*, and it requires presence, persistence, and patience, if we're to do it well. Every boy has great potential for emotional health; but he can't get there on his own. Unless we patiently coach him, nurture him, and draw him out, he's likely to get stuck and become stilted. The key to constructive engagement with a boy can be found in four *P*s: *presence, persistence, patience*, and *picking your spots*.

Be present. When a boy is eight years old or younger, he is still tender and growing in his emotional vocabulary. He hasn't yet been shaped (or misshaped) by the culture's harsh messages about how men are to behave. The hormones haven't kicked in yet, his feelings are more pure, and he is freer to express his emotions authentically and accurately. During these years we need to be present to our boys, to linger with them. Parents need to spend large chunks of time talking and reading to them (our boys need to hear our words), building with puzzles and Legos and whatever else is at hand (our boys need our participation and our time), and playing games (boys need to play for play's sake—and so do parents). Just hanging out with a young boy sets a tone for relationship and comfort in each other's presence.

Be persistent. Things change when a boy enters the Individual stage (around age nine). Many boys begin to act disinterested in family life. Read between the lines and break the code: It's mostly an act. Family is still the primary influence at this stage. But by the age of nine or ten, many boys begin to channel their primary feelings (such as hurt, loneliness, fear, shame, guilt, and sadness) into anger. They will start to talk less about what they're feeling and also cry less often. Instead, they will hide in their rooms, kick, yell, pick fights, or brood. They'll start to give a series of one-word answers, regardless of the question. As parents and caregivers, we can't give up on them. They need for us to be persistent with them. This is a time for gentle, loving, firm, and consistent boundaries and expectations. This is a time when we need to help our boys connect with their primary feelings and name them accurately, so they can process them successfully.

Sometimes it's more than appropriate to push a boy to work through his emotions with you, not letting him off the hook with one-word answers. Call it like you see it: "Son, you're stuck. You are obviously feeling something very strongly and for some reason you either can't or won't talk about what that is. You want to be left alone, and I'm all for giving you your space, but I'm also interested in helping you grow into a man who understands what he feels and can call it what it is."

A dad I (David) respect uses a strategy he calls "get a Coke." It's a catchphrase he first employed with his son at age nine. His son had been in a long season of being angry at 90 percent of what came his way, yet when his parents asked what was going on, he would simply respond, "Nothing." One day, his dad said to him, "Why don't you get a Coke out of the fridge and meet me on the back porch." When the two met out back, the dad announced in a strong but loving way that the son could exit the conversation as soon as he gave a real answer—something besides "nothing."

He told his son they could sit on the porch and sip their Cokes and look at each other until midnight, if that's what it took, but he cared too much about him to let him stay stuck with unexplored and unexpressed emotions. This tuned-in dad has used the same strategy with his son in all sorts of situations, including turning off the motor on the family boat and sitting in the middle of a lake until his son was ready to talk. His son now smiles when he hears "get a Coke." He knows exactly what's required of him.

Be patient. Once a boy hits the Wanderer stage (during his teenage years), persistence becomes more difficult, because boys tend to spend a lot of time and energy pushing adults away. He'll be resistant, sometimes disrespectful, and disinterested. Much of his behavior will say, "Get away from me." Again we need to read between the lines and break the code. By their behavior, adolescent boys are asking two important questions: "Am I loved?" and "Are you interested in me?" They will at times act extremely unlovable just to test how unconditional your love really is. This is a time for patience (and consistency). You may need to see a bunch of dumb Adam Sandler movies, go to some obnoxious concerts with him, and listen to lousy music in the car. Your willingness to meet your boy where he is—instead of demanding that he step outside his boyhood and meet you in your tidy adult world—will carry the day. There's no question; parenting an adolescent boy requires great presence, dogged persistence, and a large dose of patience.

Pick your spots. Parenting boys in transition is a little bit like learning to line dance. There's a lot of stepping in and stepping out. To do this well, you have to learn to pick your spots. For example, bedtime is often a great time to *step in*. Boys are more vulnerable at bedtime; their emotional defenses are down, and it's a great time to engage them.

If your boy has been irritable since the moment he got in the car after school; if his attitude is, "I had a lousy day, and I don't want to talk about it," then your first task is to honor his boundaries. This is a time to *step out*. It is rarely ever a good idea to pester a boy with questions when he obviously doesn't want to talk. (It just shuts him down and teaches him that he can't trust you.) Give him some space; let him ride home in silence (or with loud, blaring music, if you can tolerate it), and then wait him out. If you give him some time to work his way through his own emotions, he may come back to you and be ready to talk.

If he stays somewhat withdrawn (or grumpy or irritable) for the remainder of the day, we recommend that you go in at bedtime, sit down on the edge of his bed, and gently make yourself available to him. (Here's where presence, persistence, and patience come in.) You could say something like this: "I know from what you said when you got in the car this afternoon that you had a lousy day, and I just want you to know that I'm here if you need me. If it would feel helpful to talk, I'd love to be available to you. If not, just know I'm in your corner. I love you, and I believe in you." Then shut up! This is called *stepping in*.

He may not take you up on your offer, but chances are good that he will. Just knowing that you respect him enough not to push him farther than he wants to go will likely free him up to confide in you. This feeling of safety, combined with the vulnerability that comes just before rest, is the perfect recipe for openness when it comes to boys. Sometimes, just a gentle prompt is enough to open him up and get him talking. If he's really hurting, he may cry and need you just to sit with him—not to fix anything or offer advice, but just to sit with him in his pain. (Again, presence, persistence, and patience.)

Knowing when to step in and when to step out requires that we be good students of the boys we love. We need to study them closely enough that we get fairly good at predicting their next steps. With presence, persistence, and patience, we can become pretty proficient at knowing when they need us to talk and when they need us to listen; when they want us to offer advice or share stories from our own lives, and when they want us to be quiet and just be with them; when they want us to crowd them, and when they want us to leave them alone.

If a boy doesn't want to talk, it's time to step out. This is particularly hard for moms. When you know your son is hurting, everything in you wants to stay and ask questions . . . and ask more questions . . . and then more questions.

Moms are great at asking questions. They're also pretty good at emotionally nagging their sons. Moms will pursue a boy to the ends of the earth, believing that's what makes him feel loved. There's no question that pursuing a boy makes him feel cared for and a priority. But when it comes to *adolescent* boys, they can start to feel violated. There's an alarm that goes off in a teenage boy's mind when his mom starts asking questions. It sounds something like this: *Be careful, bro. Give her too much information, and she'll be all in your business. And if you start telling her stuff, she'll start asking more and more questions. And if you get emotional . . . well, it's all over then. She'll be all over you then.*

Moms, when you won't step out, your son begins to fear that anything he says can and will be used against him. He knows that answering your questions will elongate the process, and he's afraid that he'll never escape you.

For dads, the challenge often involves *stepping in*. We don't have a lot of trouble stepping out. Our challenge is to engage with our boys when we know they're struggling—and then to wait them out. For most dads, it's the sitting, listening, and waiting that gets us. Too often, we defer to our wives as "the emotional lifeguard," who will jump in when the kids are struggling. But a boy desperately needs to feel pursued by his father. He needs to know that his dad believes he is capable of navigating things on his own.

Men tend to be fixers and doers. We are focused on analysis and solutions. We often talk too much about our own experiences and how we "solved" the problem ourselves (which is just a roundabout way of giving advice). But we need to understand that we disempower our boys when we rush in and start handing out advice. When we offer solutions instead of support, or advice instead of a listening ear, here's what we communicate to our sons: *You're not quite capable of figuring things out on your own, son, so let me tell you what you need to do.*

Now, men, hear us clearly: Our boys need for us to step in, not step out. And just because we sometimes overstep doesn't mean we shouldn't step at all. Our boys need to hear us tell stories from our own experiences—but not just all our successes and victories. They need to hear us talk about where we struggled and where we failed. And every story doesn't have to have a victorious, tied-up-with-a-bow ending. We set our boys up for feelings of failure, inadequacy, and incompetence when we present ourselves as always having a solution and always overcoming our fear, shame, confusion, or sadness. Life just isn't that neat and tidy—and we know that. But if we present it that way, we leave our boys feeling as if they'll never measure up and never get a handle on things.

A BOY NEEDS TO BE ASSISTED IN ANSWERING THE BIGGEST QUESTION OF ALL.

Most boys begin to doubt themselves as they make their way toward manhood. They come to realize that they aren't action-adventure heroes or the second coming of Michael Jordan, Brett Favre, or Willie Mays. Most boys are average height, awkward with girls, unexceptional athletes, socially anxious, and physically scared. But when they compare themselves to the narrow and extreme definition of masculinity that prevails in our culture, they come to the inevitable conclusion that they don't have what it takes and don't measure up. To compensate, they learn to fake it.

No matter their skill set, creativity, intellect, personality, or athletic ability, boys cannot escape the shame and self-doubt that comes with being a boy. This shame is hard to bear and can be even harder to articulate. Throughout their lives, boys (and men) have certain questions stirring in their hearts:

- "Do I have what it takes?"
- "Am I the real deal?"
- "Do I matter?"

Rarely do we, as the adults in our boys' lives, hear these questions spoken out loud. Instead, they ask them in subtle and quiet ways (or in ways that are not quite as subtle or quiet). They will show up in their behavior; they will surface in their responses; they will be hiding underneath some other questions; and on occasion, we'll get a modified version of the *real* question being asked. Most of the time, we'll be digging and searching and reading into what's *not* being said.

When we speak to our boys, we must be careful to not use our words to destroy the relationship. We must speak in ways that create bridges to their hearts, so that they feel safe enough to bring their hearts to us. With boys, most rebellion and trouble stem from one of two sources: an impaired expression of what is going on emotionally inside their hearts or an immature attempt to answer their heart's core questions. When boys can't articulate what's really going on in their hearts, or when they come up empty on their core questions, they often resort to behavior that can be completely irrational.

- "I just failed this test." *I will steal this CD.*
- "I got cut from the basketball team." *I will pick a fight.*
- "My dad is never at home." *I will have sex with this girl.*
- "My girlfriend cheated on me." *I will key the teacher's car.*
- "I don't have any friends." *I will act like a freak.*
- "My grandma just died." *I will get drunk this weekend.*

Discipline and a Boy's Heart

Boys will get in trouble; it's just part of growing up. When they do, what they need is discipline that is clear and consistent (not shaming and aggressive). This discipline must come from a framework of maturity, wisdom, and love.

We must use discipline to build character and conscience, not merely to manufacture compliant behavior and obedience. True obedience is a by-product of love, not fear. For obedience to be authentic, it must be grounded in trust and loyalty—as a response to trust, not as a reaction to the threat of harm. When a boy believes that we have *his* best interests in mind, he is more likely to obey than if he is motivated by fear. Discipline through manipulation or fear will ultimately bury a boy's heart in shame, and eventually he will feel that he has no choice but to rebel in order to be himself.

Boys need the strong hand of love and the tender hand of discipline. The best discipline combines both tenderness and strength. For a boy to become a man of courage and sensitivity, he must be disciplined with love and respect. If he is shamed, punitively demeaned, frightened, or raged at, he will learn to distrust authority, deny his sensitive nature, rest in passivity, or dissent.

Discipline is more closely related to teaching than it is to punishment. Think of Jesus and his disciples. He taught them mostly by example, action, and gentle correction. Only occasionally did he rebuke them. To discipline the boys we love, we need to lead them by modeling truth, justice, love, honor, mercy, compassion, passion, risk, hope, and faith.

The book of Proverbs says, "Direct your children onto the right path, and when they are older, they will not leave it."[17] This is not (despite what we wish) a warranty for a boy's happiness. It does not mean, "If you do all the right things as a parent, your son will be happy when he grows up." It does not mean that there is a simple formula for success.

Because every boy is different, each one requires that we take a unique approach toward guiding him. Any great teacher will tell you that it's foolish to instruct a quiet, reserved, or shy boy the same way you would discipline an outgoing, rambunctious, or aggressive boy. To nurture and discipline a boy effectively, we must see his unique heart and adapt our approach.

Nurturing boys requires that our discipline be geared toward lovingly unveiling their strength and courage, according to how these characteristics are uniquely present. Whenever we discipline boys, we must do so in a way that addresses them as the unique, noble creatures they truly are—in ways that honor them and their masculinity. By disciplining our boys in ways that do not shame them, we honor their desire for strength, reinforce their sensitivity, and encourage them toward valor. If our boys are to stand a fair chance at life, they need to enter manhood believing that they are good men. If they don't, they will be starting out behind the eight ball.

Putting the Principles into Practice

Most of us expected that parenting boys would require a lot of physical energy, but who knew that boys could require so much emotionally? Weren't we taught to believe that kind of work was reserved for adolescent girls? With boys, it can be exhausting to study them, name them, draw them out, step in and out at the appropriate times, and be present, persistent, and patient. Here are some suggestions for making the emotional load a bit lighter.

TIP 1: **Read about him.** We strongly recommend *The Way of the Wild Heart: A Map for the Masculine Journey,* by John Eldredge (Nelson, 2006).

TIP 2: **Practice on other kids.** Train yourself in the art of reading between the lines. Watch movies such as *A Perfect World, October Sky,* and *Simon Birch.* Make a list of questions that the boys are asking within those stories.

TIP 3: **Meet him on his turf.** Choose one area of your son's interest and spend an extended amount of time with him engaged in that activity this week.

TIP 4: **Take account.** Grade yourself (A–F) on your skill at "stepping in" and "stepping out." Now ask your spouse to grade you. Track your progress in this area over a nine-week grading period.

TIP 5: **Practice curiosity.** Fill a jar with questions that you can pass around the dinner table to spark conversation. Let every family member take a turn. Create a dinnertime ritual, or schedule it periodically for a weekend morning pancake breakfast.

TIP 6: **Tell a tale.** Use mealtimes to share stories with your boy. Introduce complex themes from your own experience (such as conflict with coworkers, friends who might divorce, or issues of illness and death) and get his perspective. Expand the conversation to include stories from your boy's life (such as conflict with friends, competition among his peers, or issues of body image).

Keep in mind that his intellect and spiritual competency are expanding, and use that to your advantage.

TIP 7: **Catch him with his guard down.** Go into his room at bedtime and take advantage of the opportunity to talk and listen to him while his emotional defenses are down. Use this opportunity to draw him out, build him up, encourage him, and let him know that you love him, respect him, admire him, and support him.

TIP 8: **Require him to use his words.** Don't let him off the hook with the whole "boys will be boys" line of thinking. Anger and aggression may be the primary ways he channels his emotions, but encourage him to work out the intensity of his emotions through some productive, physical outlet, and later help him learn how to use his words to name his emotions.

TIP 9: **Show physical affection.** Boys of all ages need to be touched in ways that are affirming, tender, and kind. They need hugs. Kisses goodnight. Rubbing their hair. Pats on the head. High fives. Secret handshakes. Hands on their shoulders. Arms around their backs. Boys need to be wrestled with, certainly, but they also need to be cuddled (when they will let you) and lovingly, physically engaged. They need to be affirmed with our words, but they also need the tactile experience of being affirmed with our touch.

TIP 10: **Teach him to manage his emotions.** At different stages in his development, help him make lists of ways to constructively release his anger and aggression. That way, when he's in the middle of the intensity (and can't think clearly), he can simply refer to the list of ideas he came up with at an earlier point. Having a list also makes it easier for you to redirect him toward something constructive when you are feeling a lot of emotion yourself. Here's a list that a nine-year-old came up with and posted on the inside of his closet door:

When I feel really angry, I can . . .
Go shoot hoops
Do push-ups or sit-ups
Beat a tree with a plastic bat
Throw a tennis ball up against the garage door over and over
Run around the house
Go to the basement and scream
Practice chin-ups

Once I don't feel so angry and have calmed down, I can . . .
Write in my journal
Talk to my mom or dad
Call my friend, Josh, and tell him what happened

CHAPTER 11

A Boy and His Mother

As I (David) write this, I am holed up at a coffeehouse in my neighborhood. At the table next to me are a mother and her son. It's Sunday morning, and the two are just hanging out. The boy looks about fourteen. He has on track pants, Nikes, and a black polo shirt with the collar turned up. He is wearing sunglasses (indoors—and it's dark in here). I couldn't even begin to describe his hair to you. I couldn't do it justice. The mom has purchased a lot of food. (Smart mom! The more courses you serve a boy, the longer you can hold him captive.) They are talking . . . well, she is doing most of the talking (he's mostly grunting), but he's chipping in occasionally. This is not a place where any of his buddies would likely hang out, so she's removed the risk of his being seen eating out with Mommy.

I want to applaud her. Actually, I want to say, "Hang in there, Mom. He'll be normal here in a few years. Just hang on."

This snapshot of the relationship between mother and son gives us a picture of the central role a mother plays in the life of a boy. Boys learn their earliest lessons about tenderness, mercy, care, and love from their mothers. In this chapter, we will identify two important roles that a mother plays in the life of her boy—an anchor of security and a mirror to his masculinity—and provide some touchstones that she can use to gauge the quality of her relationship with her son as he completes his journey to manhood.

An Anchor of Security

According to William Pollack, author of *Real Boys*, "Far from making boys weaker, the love of a mother can and does actually make boys stronger, emotionally and psychologically."[1] Mothers play a significant role in the lives of boys by providing an anchor of security. In our chaotic, cruel, and complicated world, a mother can be a loving and encouraging refuge for a boy.

When boys are young, they waffle between two worlds. They are wild and wired for adventure and exploration, *and* they need adults who will keep them safe and secure.

I (Stephen) remember my son Teddy when he was just learning to walk. We would take him along with our other kids to the playground a couple of blocks from home, and he would wander away from my wife across the playground, toward the swings. Every few yards, he would look back over his shoulder at Heather with a look that said, "Can I go on? Are you watching? Am I safe?" Sometimes, he would come back and hug her and then move away again.

Now, take this image and jump ahead eighteen years to when he goes off to college—he'll do much the same thing. He'll go away to school and be a big man on campus; and then every few weekends, he'll come back for some home-cooked meals and to be taken care of again.

Much of the self-respect and confidence a boy has when he enters manhood comes from the quality of his home life growing up. Mothers play a vital role in this process. They give boys a sense of acceptance and significance that can only come from a mother. A solid and affectionate relationship with his mother gives a boy the platform of emotional intimacy, relational empathy, and sensitivity he needs to develop mature and secure relationships as an adult.

Even more, a boy's relationship with his mother is largely responsible for shaping his view of femininity. Will he respect women? Will he honor them? Will he use his strength for their good? Will he be able and willing to share his tenderness with them? A mother is an influential guide when it comes to teaching a boy about women . . . and about his own masculinity, too.

A Mirror to Masculinity

In the most basic ways, a boy is unlike his mother. Not only are they separated by age, but there's also a chasm between the sexes. But it's precisely these differences that make a mother's role in the life of her son so important. Far from making a boy into a "sissy" or a "momma's boy," a loving mother actually plays a vital role in guiding him into the fullness of his masculinity. She gives him a reflection of the impact of his strength and the power of his tenderness. In many ways, a mother teaches her son things about his masculinity that he could never learn from his father, because a boy gets a real sense of who he is as a man in contrast to the opposite sex. It's a mother's job to help her son accept himself as a man, without shame or fear. If she is willing to champion his journey through boyhood, he will gain his independence and realize his strength. He will know that perhaps his greatest strength comes from his sensitivity and compassion.

A mother is a boy's first and most intimate encounter with the opposite sex. Thus she bears an enormous responsibility to teach her son how a woman feels cared for, enjoyed, protected, honored, respected, and cherished. We've all heard about how a boy tends to marry some version of his mother; well, there's some truth to that, so it's vital that a mom be well connected with her own femininity. Being the mother of a son requires a woman to reconcile her feelings about men and masculinity. Statistics tell us that four in ten females are abused before the age of eighteen. This means that almost half of all women have experienced some form of harm, most often in their relationships with men. This harm can't help but shape a woman's perceptions and ideas about men. Though a mother has enormous opportunities to bless her son, she also possesses the power to curse him. Following are three stereotypes of mothers that we hear about frequently with the men and boys we counsel: the *man hater*, the *mother hen*, and the *overly bonded mother*.

THE MAN HATER

Sadly, many women carry emotional, psychological, and spiritual wounds that were inflicted by men. Any woman who has not experienced the healthy use of a man's strength, or who has learned not to trust the strength and power of men, will inevitably subvert her son and teach him to be ashamed of his masculinity.

She will send him messages about his manliness that in effect will emotionally, psychologically, and spiritually neuter him.

We can't count the number of men we've seen in our counseling offices who carry complex and debilitating shame that was given to them by mothers who fundamentally distrusted men. Many of these mothers had been sexually, physically, or emotionally abused or harassed by men (either while growing up or in adulthood). Even more of these mothers were women who were emotionally or physically abandoned by a passive or absent father or husband. Others had not been abused or abandoned, but they were in troubled marriages.

Though no one can hold a mother responsible for the wounds she bears from her own experience, for her son's sake she must come to terms with her contempt for men and the shame she feels about her own femininity. Women who carry contempt for their husbands, ex-husbands, fathers, or other men often transfer their unhappiness to their sons. For instance, the more disappointing a woman's marriage, the more negative she is toward her son—who consequently is more disrespectful toward his mother.

Healing these wounds and resolving the resulting contempt and resentment are imperative for a woman who wants to mother her son well. Mothers must learn to parent from within their own giftedness, as loving and compassionate women who are willing to trust and empower the strength of men. If they don't, they will surely parent from their woundedness and inevitably pass that wounding on to their sons.

THE MOTHER HEN

We all know mothers like this. The overprotective, hovering, Purell-squirting, "Baby don't climb so high," anxious type. This is the mom who follows her son everywhere, making sure nothing goes wrong. She triple checks his homework to make sure he gets good grades. She handpicks his friends by setting up playdates with boys that are "good for him," and she surely doesn't let him eat worms. She rushes onto the soccer field when her son gets pushed down. And when he starts dating, she is certain that no girl is good enough for her little boy.

Now, to some degree, every mother has a natural instinct to protect her children. The trick for moms of boys is to foster a balance between his desire for adventure, exploration, and separation and her desire for a healthy, nurturing, and safe environment—without erecting barriers to her son's ability to assert himself as an individual.

This type of neurotic parenting rarely stops when a boy goes to grade school or junior high. And the mother who guarded her son from bullies, ran interference with difficult teachers, and never let her son get a mosquito bite is the same mother who can't let go when her son heads off to college. After college, she's happy to let him live at home, and she'll be certain to tell his wife how to cook his favorite meal and how he likes his clothes ironed. The mother hen needs to check in her own heart to see if she is protecting her son because there's a legitimate and justified concern for his safety, or because she's reacting out of her own anxiety and fear.

THE OVERLY BONDED MOTHER

Perhaps the most significant type of problem mother is the one who is overly bonded emotionally and psychologically with her son. An overly bonded mother regularly sleeps with her son until he is well past two or three. As he gets older, she often insists that he listen to her problems. She makes him carry her emotional burdens. She is in constant physical contact with her son—always touching him, stroking his head, neatening his hair, and kissing his cheek. She requires him to spend much of his time with her.

Usually this type of overly bonded mother/son relationship is found in families where the mother is unhappily married, divorced, or unwed (though not always). These moms often develop an emotional codependence with their sons—when one is unhappy, the other will be upset too. In the worst cases, this is called emotional incest.

The more a mother sees her son as her "Little Prince," the less room he has to be himself—a boy. As he enters his adolescence, and his needs for independence increase, he remains overly bonded emotionally to his mother, even though he may want to date and be with girls his own age. This emotional tug-of-war creates psychological chaos for a boy, and it produces massive amounts of shame in his heart. A boy trapped in this kind of mother/son relationship has little concept of who he is. He feels like an adult and a child at the same time; he feels that he is his mother's emotional partner and his father's rival. Many boys live with this inner turmoil, and their lives may make little sense—except when they try to fulfill their mother's fantasies.

Cutting the Apron Strings

If you are a woman reading this, we encourage you to spend some time thinking about your experience with the men in your life, both past and present. If necessary, consult with a trusted source (a counselor, pastor, or mentor) and evaluate your feelings, so as not to allow the harmful experiences you've had with men spill over into the parenting of your son. Ask yourself how you define masculinity. Do you view it as lazy? Do you see men as workaholics? Do you see them as people not to trust? Do you see them as people who won't come through for you? Do you see them as people to correct or control?

Also, pay close attention to your relationship with your son's father. If you're married, be attuned to the interactions between you and your husband that play out in front of your son. How you view your son's father and how you dialogue and interact with him will shape your son more than you can know. If you're a single mother, or a mom whose husband isn't well invested in parenting or isn't respectful of you as a person, you'll want to make certain your son is exposed to other men who treat women with respect and dignity. He needs to see couples who interact in positive and healthy ways. Remember, most boys are visual and experiential learners. They need to see life played out in front of them. We can't just give them information.

Even when a mother is emotionally, psychologically, and spiritually healthy (she isn't overly bonded, a man hater, or a mother hen), she may struggle with letting go when her son begins to exercise his independence. Whether it's simple things with a young boy, such as picking out his own clothes, dressing himself, or making his own meals or snacks; or more complicated things like dating, working after school, choosing a college, or moving away from home, many mothers experience their boy's desire to handle things himself as rejection.

A powerful paradox of motherhood is that if you do your job well, your son will leave you completely.[2] As boys mature, mothers must learn to strike a balance between supporting their sons and letting them stand on their own two feet. When a mother can't fully release her son, she creates needless power struggles—especially during adolescence, which is difficult enough for mothers and sons without complicating it.

The best way for a mother to nurture the heart of her son

is to develop a relationship with him from an early age that is grounded in mutual respect. This means she must show him that she respects his individuality, his feelings, his strengths, and his needs—especially when she doesn't agree with him.

Mothers need to show respect for themselves, too. It's never okay for a boy to dishonor his mother and treat her disrespectfully. Boys need limits, especially the limit of respecting authority if they are to mature into capable, wise, and loving men. Mutual respect between mother and son lays the groundwork for the boy to later have fulfilling relationships with his wife and daughters, and it ensures a long, fruitful, and appropriate relationship between mother and son.

Mothers and Sons: Age by Age

No matter what, a son needs his mother's unconditional love and respect. A boy also needs the freedom to begin his own journey through life. No matter how old or young a boy is, the image of his mother is stamped on his heart. When a mother engages her son's heart well, she prepares him to stride confidently and courageously into manhood. Let's take a look at the unique relationship between a mother and son at each stage of his development.

MOTHERING THE EXPLORER AND THE LOVER

For a long season at the beginning of a boy's life, Mom is the center of his universe, the safest place on earth. When he is at his most vulnerable—whether he's sad, hurt, scared, or angry—he'll bring his feelings to Mom. She gets the best and worst of who he is.

When boys are Explorers and Lovers, their moms are like home

STEPHEN JAMES | DAVID THOMAS

plate—the place they are always moving toward and where they want to land. Even as Explorers move back and forth in search of independence, they always come back to home plate. From the earliest moments of a boy's life, his mom provides the essentials he needs for living. This starts from conception, carries straight through delivery, and proceeds right into the earliest days of his life outside the womb.

I (David) remember standing witness to my wife during her first pregnancy and delivery, thinking that the most I was needed for was to drive her to the hospital, bring her ice chips, say, "Breathe, push, breathe," and change some diapers. Now, of course I contributed a lot more than that, but the essentials for living were all met through my wife's being. She carried our children, delivered our children, and for a year after they came on the scene, her body was their primary source of nutrition. She fed 'em; I burped 'em. She soothed 'em; I changed the poop. And though I've become more involved with my kids as they have grown, Connie still plays the central role in how they understand the world.

Perhaps the most important thing a mom can do to nurture her son is to be aware of his emotional development. Unless she's attentive to this specific area, it's likely that her son's heart will begin to harden. Research shows that mothers of infant boys are far less likely to interact with their sons when they exhibit unhappy emotions compared with mothers of girls.[3] William Pollack, the author of *Real Boys*, concludes from this study that "these mothers were concerned that if they let a boy express too much grief, pain, or vulnerability, somehow he would become something less than a 'real,' fully functioning boy, in accordance with our society's rigid code."[4] These kinds of interactions actually move boys away from experiencing a broad range of emotions toward a narrow window of what is emotionally socially acceptable.

Boys learn from an early age (at home and in the world) that certain feelings are off-limits to them. But if a boy is to achieve the full expression of his masculine potential, he will need the broadest range of emotions available. As primary caregivers, moms are on the front lines of helping their boys become all they can be. By showing a boy tenderness and emotional empathy and allowing him to express the fullness of his heart, a mom can help guide him toward an emotionally rich and well-rounded expression of his masculinity (instead of instilling shame in him for feeling hurt or unhappy).

A mother can help her son connect with his heart during the first third of his boyhood by talking with him about his feelings. She might say things like, "What's going on, buddy? Are you having trouble with your blocks? You look angry that they keep falling over. I bet that makes you sad, too." This type of emotional dialogue helps a boy stay connected with the fullness of his heart, even as the world around him is trying to squash his heart and teach him to compartmentalize his feelings. It's important for a mother to be very expressive when she interacts with her son. And she needs to help him navigate his unhappy emotions (sadness, hurt, loneliness, guilt, and shame), even if she is intimidated by their intensity.

MOTHERING THE INDIVIDUAL

As a boy moves through the Individual stage, his mother continues to play an important role in terms of his emotional, spiritual, and relational development. In fact, his increasing emotional and spiritual competency opens up opportunities for her to expand her role of teaching, modeling, and nurturing.

Parents need to focus on character development issues during the Individual years, because once this brief season ends, they will no longer play the most central and influential role in their son's life. Before a boy steps into his teenage years, he needs to have a handle on key character traits such as compassion, honesty, self-control, discernment, respect for self and others, personal responsibility, the courage to do what is right, and the strength to stand up for personal convictions. It's while a boy is an Individual that his parents can help build the foundation of moral values that will shape his self-image, actions, and worldview.

Because a boy's mother is often the one most connected with him during this time, she has a unique opportunity to teach him about character and about developing and maintaining relationships. Because women think in relational terms, it's often natural for them to impart to their sons the idea of compassion or empathy, which helps boys understand how others see and experience life. A mother can promote compassion by helping her son consider how others might feel or what they might be thinking in a particular situation. For example, if a boy says something cutting or critical about another child (which Individuals often do), his mom can help him develop empathy by saying, "How do you think Corry feels about what you just said? If he had said the same thing to you, how would you feel?"

As experiential learners, boys develop compassion and empathy by practicing kindness and showing care and concern for others. Moms need to emphasize how important this is and affirm their sons when they see them being compassionate or giving to others. "Andy, I saw how you got up from the table to get your sister a new fork when hers fell on the floor. That's so cool. You're really a compassionate and thoughtful young man."

Individuals will find their relationships with peers becoming more and more complicated. Boys in this age group are often obsessed with competing with one another and their rank in the pecking order. They will experience hurt and betrayal more frequently, and they'll be tempted to hide and isolate themselves. When boys learn to be compassionate for their friends, family members, and others, they have a tool that can balance their competitive drive. Compassion allows a boy to be happy and excited—rather than angry and jealous—at another person's success and achievement.

MOTHERING THE WANDERER

Remember what we said earlier about a mom being the safest place on earth for a boy? Unfortunately, this safety has a downside. It's called the "rubber band phenomenon." Because a boy feels so safe with his mom, he instinctively believes she will never abandon him—no matter what he says or does. Therefore, he starts to believe that he can push against his mom emotionally and stretch her out as far as he wants, because she will always bounce right back to being that same place of safety. He will be his most tender and his most punishing with her. (As we said before, a mom gets her son's best and worst—and it's during this season of life that she's most likely to get the worst of who he is.)

Often, the worse a boy feels about himself, or the more complicated things get in terms of his other relationships, the more his mom will become the target of his wrath. How's that for fair? And if that's not bad enough, it's during this stage that she'll have to start letting him go. *Ouch!*

At some point between the Individual stage and the Wanderer stage, depending on how a boy is progressing through his developmental journey, he will begin to psychologically individuate and separate out from his mother. It's an important part of his masculine journey. In order to move fully into the world of masculinity, he must leave the world of femininity. He will begin to pull away, share less, and become more argumentative.

A number of factors—such as birth order—can affect the process of separating out. If he's your firstborn (or oldest male), this will be the first experience of separation for both of you—and it can feel both foreign and confusing. If he's your second son (or further down the line), it's typically easier, simply because you've seen the process played out with his older brother(s) and have a sense of what's coming. If he's the last born or last son, you may struggle with letting go for the last time, and this might complicate the journey for both of you.

Temperament also plays a role. Some boys come out of the womb more self-determined and challenging than others. The nature of your relationship—whether it has been close or distant, peaceful or full of conflict—will affect the journey as well.

Transitions also play a role in separating out. For example, if your family has recently been through a separation or divorce, it can seem confusing for your son to separate out, because it can feel as if he's abandoning you. You may also struggle with releasing him because you are working through (or not working through) your own feelings of loneliness and abandonment.

We have worked with some young men who were in the process of separating out when they lost their fathers to death. Some boys, under these circumstances, will attempt to resist separating out, feeling obligated to take care of their widowed mothers. If you have unique circumstances, such as death or divorce, it might be helpful to engage the assistance of a therapist to aid in the transition and help facilitate dialogue between you and your son.

Regardless of the circumstances, try to not take your son's separating out personally. Separation feels very personal, but it's a universal journey and one that is vital to his graduating into manhood.

Mothers of Wanderers need to be creative. Our friends and colleagues Melissa Trevathan and Sissy Goff wrote a book on adolescence called *The Back Door to Your Teen's Heart*. It opens with these words: "To the degree that kids can predict you, they'll dismiss you." Thus, one of your primary objectives with a Wanderer is to be as unpredictable as possible. Being unpredictable requires creativity and thought.

You will need to be creative about staying connected with him. One mother I (Stephen) know made spaghetti and meatballs one summer evening for dinner. She served her husband and two sons (ages twelve and fifteen) on the patio behind their house. Halfway through dinner, she picked up a handful of spaghetti and threw it at her eldest son. Then she took a meatball and chucked it at his younger brother. Both boys were so amazed that they just sat there, stunned. Their mother took that opportunity to launch salad at them, using her fork as a catapult. When she told me the story later, she said that her family had never laughed so hard for so long. She said that none of her sons' friends believed them when the boys told them what had happened. This mother was neither predictable nor dismissed. She was a hero.

MOTHERING THE WARRIOR

The Warrior stage is the season in a boy's development when his mom can make a date with him for coffee and actually linger with him for an extended period of time. By this point in his journey, he's fine with being seen with his mom, and he has evolved into a creature that seems normal again. One mom, who was talking recently about her nineteen-year-old son, said, "Why in the world kids don't go away to college at thirteen and come home at eighteen is beyond me. By the time he was ready to leave home at eighteen, I had enjoyed him so much that all I could do was weep when he left. I have missed him and found myself longing for breaks when he comes home."

A mother's role at this stage is to be that safe harbor again that a boy can come home to—both physically and emotionally. (Remember the toddler on the playground? Here's the theme of safety showing up again.) Warrior boys who are off at college, or in the service, or starting their life's work, need a safe place to call home. They need to be able to talk about and process what it's like to be out in the world. They need a place of reprieve, where they can talk about the dangerous things they've encountered, test new ideas against the old tried and true, and express their sense of accomplishment and hope. Warriors need a place to come for a home-cooked meal, bring their dirty laundry, and remember all that is familiar and safe to them—not a place that they use merely as a restaurant and a Laundromat, but a place where people love them and receive them in whatever condition they're in.

The mother of a Warrior will do a lot of listening at this stage. She will listen to her son dream about his future and who he sees himself becoming. She'll listen to him talk about his hopes and his fears. She'll listen to him talk about a girl he loves. And while she is listening, she will need to wait for him to invite her input (as opposed to shelling out her advice at will). Moms of Warriors need to listen to their own hearts and be attentive to their own difficulty in letting their sons go as they take their final steps into manhood.

Putting the Principles into Practice

Mothering a boy is one of the most challenging and rewarding journeys a woman can take. Few relationships will prove to be more rewarding and more complicated. It will require things of you that mothering a daughter will never require. Try these ideas for navigating the journey.

TIP 1: Soak it up while he's young. Enjoy your son while he's so into you. Take lots of pictures and video of the two of you together. Once he starts to pull away, you'll need both to remind you of who he was and who he will become.

TIP 2: Don't panic. Toward the end of the Individual stage and the beginning of the Wanderer stage, wear a rubber band around your wrist to remind yourself of what's happening. If necessary, take it off and fire it at him when he's at his worst.

TIP 3: Mum's the word. A close relationship with a teenage boy can feel shaky. Parents are most successful when they understand why their sons are reluctant to open up to them, and when they work hard to develop an environment in which teens feel that it's safe to talk about themselves. It's imperative—*imperative!*—that you keep your son's confidence and that you honor his privacy. Moms, this means you can't talk about your son's secrets with your friends. When a mother shows her son that she can keep his disclosures to herself, he'll see that he can trust her.

TIP 4: Kidnap him. One way for moms to connect with their boys (especially boys fourteen and under) is to take them on errands in the car. You will have him captive. Try to incorporate something fun—like getting ice cream or a hamburger—while you're out.

TIP 5: Be unpredictable. Play practical jokes on him. Put Vaseline on his doorknob (or, better yet, his toilet seat), short sheet his bed, hide behind a corner and jump out to startle him, set his clock an hour earlier after he goes to bed . . . you get the idea. As he gets deeper into adolescence, you must learn to handle him with humor.

If you meet his intensity and sullenness with your own frustration, it's a recipe for a perfect storm. We often encourage moms to turn on the radio in the car when he's being a total poop and just sing.

TIP 6: **Remember, it's not about you.** Moms, keep in mind that you are preparing your son for his relationship with his future wife. You are preparing him in some practical ways (by not raising a slob) and some emotional ways (by not coddling him; by allowing him to individuate). You are also preparing yourself by having a positive and healthy relationship with your son, so that his wife will be the kind of woman with whom you will want to spend some time.

TIP 7: **Check your heart.** If you recognize that you're carrying contempt toward men in your heart (for whatever reason), find a constructive way to deal with it—for the good of your son.

TIP 8: **Stay available to him.** Some mothers, absorbing cultural messages about "real masculinity," believe they should push their sons away emotionally, often as early as the age of two or three. A boy needs a connection with his mother all the way through adolescence. Moms, you need to be sensitive about invading your son's privacy, but separating from him prematurely will do him more harm than good.

TIP 9: **Set aside a weekend a year for a mother/son getaway.** A few weeks before your trip, ask him to help plan what you will do throughout the weekend.

TIP 10: **Respect him.** Even the most skilled conversationalist can't force a teenage boy to communicate when he doesn't want to. But once he does begin to open up, talk with him in ways that encourage the conversation.

It's important that you respect your son's independent ideas. A boy is far less likely to give his opinion when mom (or dad, for that matter) regularly disagrees with him or criticizes him. That doesn't mean you have to agree with everything he says, but please respect his right to be different (even when his ideas seem immature). When you talk with your teenage son, try to let him lead the conversation. And don't offer advice unless he asks for it.

CHAPTER 12

A Boy and His Father

For Christmas one year, "St. Nick" brought my (Stephen's) four kids a play set . . . except he really didn't bring the play set, he brought a picture of a play set along with a letter that explained that the equipment was too big to fit on his sleigh and he would have it delivered in a few weeks by his elves. The kids were excited. They pored over the picture and studied the letter—and my seven-year-old verified its authenticity. Then, one day in mid-January, a giant box truck pulled up outside our house, and two burly men, who looked liked they hadn't showered in a few days, unloaded six large boxes into our backyard. By large, I mean *gargantuan*. In each box were hundreds . . . no, thousands . . . no, millions of pieces—boards and screws and nuts and bolts and washers and a slide and swings and a rope ladder and a bell and a rock-climbing wall and . . .

For weeks, the boxes sat in our backyard. The kids would climb on them, and I would try to convince them that climbing on the boxes was just as much fun as having the actual play set. Eight weeks later, after much begging and cajoling, I caved in and began the process of erecting the playground. But like every other home improvement project I have ever attempted, this construction venture turned into a much bigger job than I had anticipated. Like the time my wife and I had the idea to put new cabinets in our kitchen. . . .

The guy at Home Depot had said, "This isn't that hard. I think you and your wife could do this yourselves in a couple of weekends." Right. The first weekend came, and we ripped out our old cabinets to find that our drywall was covered in mold and the framing lumber was rotten with termites that spread to the floorboards and the subfloor. Before we knew it, we'd gotten a total kitchen remodel and were several thousand dollars poorer.

Well, this playground was kind of that way. What started with a "simple" play set installation ended in a total backyard landscaping project: new planters, moving old vegetation, planting new bushes, and tilling up the entire yard to prep it for sod.

So there I was with a rear-tine power tiller (the big kind), ankle deep in topsoil, churning up my backyard. My wife and kids came out to watch the spectacle of Dad wrestling with a power tool. After some time, three of the kids got bored and went off to play with the dog. However, one of my sons, Henry, stayed with me. As I worked with the tiller, he proceeded to follow right behind me with his toy lawn mower—step for step, stride for stride. When I stopped to clean out the tiller's tines, Henry stopped and fiddled with his toy mower. When I backed up to turn the tiller,

Henry matched my movements. He shadowed me for more than an hour with a serious look of concentration and determination. This glimpse of my afternoon with Henry is a clear image of the powerful role a father plays in the life of his son and how a boy looks to his father to get his bearings, inspiration, and identity.

Men, we all intuitively know that being a dad is a really big deal. It's the most significant thing a man could ever do. There's no bigger title a man will wear than "Daddy"—not CEO, not president, not all-star, not hero. As a father, a man has the tremendous power to bless or curse his son. The quality of relationship a boy has with his dad will directly affect the rest of his life—from how he relates to God, to how he will relate to his future wife, to how he will one day parent his own sons. A son's connection to his father is one of the most defining experiences in a boy's life, but being a father to a boy is not an easy relationship to establish, grow, or maintain.

Unlike mothers, who are physically connected with their sons from conception, fathers must bond with their sons through relationship, ritual, and experience. While in the womb, babies receive high levels of hormones from their mothers that chemically bond the two together. Dads have no such connection.*

If the difficulty for moms with sons comes in parenting a creature so different, for fathers the challenge lies in their boys' "sameness." Sons have the capacity to expose the chinks in a man's masculinity—forcing the father to face himself. Through his sons, a father reconnects with his own experience of being a boy (and a son himself). When looking at his son, a dad often sees himself (sometimes missing his son altogether).

---

* Though we recognize that the idea of chemical bonding does not apply to stepsons or boys who have been adopted, we're simply trying to show how a boy's relationship with his mom is typically far easier to establish and nurture than his relationship with his dad.

A father is the cornerstone of a boy's life. It would be hard to overstate the importance of a father in the life of his son. Reams of research have documented the positive effects of involved fathers in their children's lives. Here is just a sample of the evidence:

> Children in father-absent homes are five times more likely to be poor. In 2002, 7.8 percent of children in married-couple families were living in poverty, compared to 38.4 percent of children in female-householder families.[1]

> Children who live apart from their fathers are more likely to be diagnosed with asthma and experience an asthma-related emergency, even after taking into account demographic and socioeconomic conditions.[2]

> Compared to living with both parents, living in a single-parent home doubles the risk that a child will suffer physical, emotional, or educational neglect.[3]

> When a father is involved in his children's education, the kids are more likely to get As, enjoy school, participate in extracurricular activities, and are less likely to repeat a grade level.[4]

> Sixty-three percent of youth suicides are from fatherless homes.[5]

> Eighty-five percent of all children that exhibit behavioral disorders come from fatherless homes.[6]

Without a dad, kids suffer. Sadly, the state of fatherhood in our culture is bleak, and this doesn't bode well for our boys. Without a dad who is engaged in his life, a boy is likely to perpetuate this sad state of affairs.

A Brief History of Daddydom

In order for a father to nurture the heart of his son on his heroic journey through boyhood, he must first be present. That seems obvious, but too many fathers are out of the picture—emotionally, spiritually, or physically. Too many dads, because of their own emotional isolation, psychological underdevelopment, and spiritual immaturity, are AWOL. Frank Pittman summarizes the cultural shift in fatherhood over the last two centuries in a 1993 *Psychology Today* article:

> For a couple of hundred years now, each generation
> of fathers has passed on less and less to his sons—
> not just less power but less wisdom. And less love.
> We finally reached a point where many fathers were
> largely irrelevant in the lives of their sons.[7]

That's a strong statement, but we happen to agree with it. Fathers are less relevant, have less authority, and are less involved than ever before.

About the time of the first Industrial Revolution (ca. 1760–1830), what we think about fathers in our society began to change considerably. The Industrial Revolution marked a fundamental shift in human social history. The effects spread first throughout Western Europe and North America, eventually affecting most of the world. The impact of these changes on society was enormous.

Almost every aspect of life was influenced—from how we got our food, to how we learned, to how we got our clothes, to how we raised our children.

As the economy shifted from primarily agrarian to industrial, from rural to urban, somebody had to leave the farm and go to work—and that was usually Dad. As fathers began traveling to the city for work, their families were lucky to see them during the week. (Some would be absent from home for long stretches, only to show up on weekends or for a few days a month.) Even when the entire family would relocate to the city (to be closer to the factory), the father was away from home all day, working, instead of working around the farm as he once did. As a result, Pittman argues, "masculinity ceased to be defined in terms of domestic involvement."[8]

As fatherhood became less relational, it began to be measured in terms of provision. Because these absentee (or simply, employed) dads were no longer around to teach their sons and relate to their sons, they became primarily providers. Fathers had to find other ways to become involved when they were home. Along with being providers, fathers became disciplinarians ("Wait till your father gets home!") and spectators ("Show Daddy what you did today."). A father's place in the family was now determined by his status and economic prowess, not by the character of his heart. Dad had left to "conquer the world"; he was no longer home to lead his family.[9]

As fathers focused more and more on earning money, nurturing children became the work of women—and "boys began to grow up without fathers."[10] Not much has changed socially and economically in the last 150 years. The children of our generation still grow up with the idea that a father's place is at work, and that they should not want or expect anything more from him. The problem is that kids do want and expect more. Emotionally, spiritually, and psychologically, when a boy craves his father and his father has to leave the family to provide, the boy begins to think that something is wrong with him. He tells himself, *I shouldn't feel this way. If this is the way that it is supposed to be, I shouldn't hurt so bad, or want my dad so much. Something must be wrong with me.* This experience is one root of toxic shame in a boy's life. And it is often from this place that boys make vows not to feel, not to want, not to need, and not to be as emotionally present as they could be.

I (Stephen) was talking with a man named Braden in my office one day about his relationship with his father and how it affected his increasingly difficult relationship with his own sons. Braden shared with me that his dad had rarely, if ever, come to his high school basketball games. "And when he did come, he spent most of his time talking with his customers."

"What was that like for you?" I asked. "What do you think about that? What do you feel?"

"Well, I'm not that upset," Braden said. "I wish my dad would have made it to more of my games, but he was busy providing for the family. He owned his own insurance agency, and like he said a thousand times, if he wasn't working, we wouldn't eat."

"That really sucks for you—that your dad didn't have a way to be present at your games. I know how important basketball was for you," I said.

"It wasn't so bad," Braden responded. "I mean, of course it used to bother me . . . make me sad. I really wanted my dad to be around. But he was a great provider, and he always asked about my games. He wanted to know every detail."

"I'm glad for that. I'm glad that he was interested in you. And yet, I still wonder if you know what happened to those feelings?"

"Well, I remember thinking to myself around sixth or seventh grade, *I can't let this . . . dad not being at my games . . . bother me anymore.* It was really affecting how I played. I was always watching the stands to see if he was there. I remember saying to myself, *I'm a baby for wanting my dad so much. I just need to grow up.*"

"That's a really profound vow you took, not to have feelings about your father's absence," I said. "It sounds like you really shamed yourself for missing your dad. Is that what you think about your own sons when they want you around? Do you think they should just grow up?"

"No, of course not. I should be there for them." Braden was emphatic about his love for his sons. "My dad was great, but I want to do this better than my father. I should be able to figure this out. I just have trouble connecting with them. Especially as they are getting older."

"Do you think the vows you made about *not* feeling about your father keep you from connecting with your sons?" I asked. "It sounds as if, in order for you not to feel about how much you needed your dad, you walled off part of your heart—the part that deals with being a man and having more tender emotions. What do you do with your sadness and disappointment and loneliness now?"

"I just push it away."

As a gender, men struggle with staying present—be it emotionally or physically—with themselves and with their families. I've had countless conversations, like this one with Braden, about how men, in the shame of their own heartache, shut off their hearts in order to cope with the pain of their fathers' absence. And David has had many more exchanges with boys about the same thing, trying to help them stay open to their hearts while they struggle to become men.

Most boys (and many men) search for their absent fathers. He's the one who can provide the emotional and spiritual nurturing, modeling, and blessing they need if they are to make it successfully to manhood. Many boys are hungry for a father. They go through their childhood and adolescence waiting for a man to invest in them, and bless them, and tell them that they have what it takes. Boys act out, get into trouble, get hurt, hurt themselves, and compete with other boys, all in an effort to get a man's attention. Boys desperately need the help of a man in becoming men themselves. The problem is that, most often, the men in their lives are just as lost as the boys they are trying to connect with.

Unpack Your Bags

For a dad to nurture the heart of his son on his heroic journey through boyhood, he must clearly understand where his concept of masculinity comes from. A father must ask himself, *Where did I learn what it means to be a 'real man'?* A dad must recognize how his own ideas of masculinity were shaped. From his own father? his mother? a mentor? a grandparent? *Die Hard* movies? Whatever a dad *thinks* a "real man" is will have an impact on his son. Are real men athletic? successful? smart? good looking? confident? unemotional? If a father doesn't consider himself a "real man," he will likely be unable to give his son what the boy needs to finish the journey into manhood with his heart intact.

The problem is threefold:

- Most dads don't ever stop to ask these questions.
- The questions aren't easy to answer.
- All kinds of definitions are floating around about what it means to be a "real man."

To engage the heart of a boy, a father must first engage his own heart—especially as it pertains to his relationship with his own father. Dads must come to terms with what their fathers did well and what they struggled with—and how these things play themselves out in the next generation. For instance, men whose fathers were absent (either emotionally or physically) will often become absent to their own sons. Men whose fathers misused power and authority or were abusive in their efforts to control, train, or discipline them will often parent their children the same way. At the very least, they will have to come to terms with how their fathers shaped their ideas of manhood. No matter how you slice it, a man's relationship with his own father goes a long way toward defining his masculinity and shaping his relationship with his sons.

Monkey See, Monkey Do

So much of fathering sons has to do with modeling what it looks like to be an authentic and complete man. Boys need to see that men are strong, courageous, sensitive, spiritual, disciplined, relational, teachable, compassionate, etc. Boys look to their dads to be what Ken Canfield calls "reference points."[11] Because boys are experiential learners, a dad's actions will speak louder than his words. Boys need to see their dads living well in all areas of life. Fathers need to order their lives in such a way that they are purposefully walking in a direction that they want their sons to follow.

A boy needs his father to set an example of how to be in relationship. Sons need a picture of what it looks like to be a husband, a father, a friend, an employee, and a leader. When a man takes the effort to build strong relationships that his son can observe, he lays the groundwork for his son to do the same when he grows up.

Dads need to make conversation with their sons a priority. Remember, boys learn by example, experience, and practice. Dads need to listen to their sons' stories before giving them advice. They need to pay attention to their sons' hearts—and listen first before making their own opinions known. Dads need to dispense with the lectures and respect and honor their sons enough to open the door to dialogue. Too often, when fathers talk to their sons, it's a monologue—which, to boys, sounds like "yada, yada, yada" after a while. Dads need to be open to receiving feedback, even if it's negative. And it's important that dads be the ones to take the initiative in rebuilding relationships when fractures occur. When we have the courage to admit that we're wrong and seek forgiveness, we set a powerful example of authentic masculinity for our sons.

Dads need to model for their sons appropriate, responsible, and healthy ways of expressing their emotions. Boys need to *see* and *hear* how to identify, resolve, and express a full range of emotions—joy, sorrow, anger, disappointment, awe, remorse, anticipation, hope, affection, desire, fear, and so on. Boys need to learn how to express their strong feelings, such as anger and shame, as well as more tender emotions, such as sadness, affection, and loneliness. This is a challenging aspect of parenting for most dads, because they may not have learned from their own fathers how to handle their emotions. Many men efface their emotional selves, and consequently their boys grow up with unhealthy ideas about how to process their feelings. Boys need to learn that emotions are an essential part of developing and maintaining healthy relationships. They need to know that *feeling* is not a dangerous sign of weakness, but a natural part of life. They need to see that feelings are a vital part of the lives of strong and courageous men.

Boys Need a Champion

Because all boys struggle with the same core question, Do I have what it takes? they need to experience their father's passionate support for them. A boy needs for his dad to participate in his activities and cheer him on—whether it's competitive or non-competitive. Whatever a boy is into (sports, music, art, cooking, mountain biking, skateboarding, etc.), he needs his father's support, encouragement, enthusiasm, involvement, affirmation, acceptance, and participation. Boys and dads need to experience life together. This can be particularly difficult if a father and son have different interests, passions, and hobbies, but as fathers we need to make the effort to support our sons in all their endeavors. That's part of our role, and our boys need that from us.

Boys need for their dads to be verbally and physically affectionate with them. Boys whose dads are loving are more likely to develop a deep sense of self-worth. Boys of every age need their father's hugs and kisses—and they need them a lot. Boys also need their father's words of affirmation. Dads need to tell their sons multiple times a day how much they love them. Every boy needs his dad to affirm what is good about his character and his behavior. He needs to hear that his father is proud of him.

Part of being a boy's champion is considering his future and moving to name him, prepare him, and encourage him toward who he was made to be. Every boy needs a man to pay attention to him and study him and know how he is wired. A boy needs a father figure who considers what makes him tick, and how his particular makeup will affect his life as an adult. A boy needs a dad who is looking ahead for him, mindful of his tomorrows. A boy needs a dad who is willing to call him out when he is living contrary to his unique design. For example, a dad could say, "Son, I have noticed that you and your friends have been really pushing the envelope with your attitude toward your coach lately. I want to remind you that you are a leader and that those boys will follow you. I also want to remind you that you are usually very respectful, and that if you have a problem with your coach, you need to address him directly. I can help you with this if you want help, because confronting an adult can be really scary, but I expect you to be true to yourself."

Yoda Dad

The role of spiritual guide is an important part a father can play in nurturing the heart of his son. Boys need guidance and inspiration that reaches far beyond Sunday school, church attendance, or youth group. They need someone like Yoda— that little green guy from *Star Wars*—who will impart wisdom, challenge their assumptions, and guide them toward the truth. Even though Yoda was pudgy, old, and kind of weird looking, he played a central role in helping Luke Skywalker find his way and become a man. Yoda acts as a sounding board for Luke, taking more of a Socratic approach to teaching rather than preaching or evangelizing.

As our sons look to us for spiritual guidance, we dads need to *show* them what it looks like to have a vital relationship with God. They need to *see* us grappling with the concepts of surrender, gratitude, and mystery. They need to see us working out and celebrating our relationship with God.

A boy needs to learn from his father how to recover when life throws him a curveball or when things don't go his way. He needs to learn what it means to "live a life that looks out beyond himself."[12] This outward focus runs contrary to a boy's natural instinct for self-protection and looking inward. Teaching a boy how to look beyond himself is part of the process of drawing him out, urging him forward, and guiding him toward wisdom, nobility, integrity, and strength.

Many boys think of faith as feminine. A father's strong example as a spiritual guide will clear a path for his son to gain an understanding and appreciation for prayer and other spiritual disciplines. Many fathers are passive or absent in this area, and thus their boys grow up without a masculine model of spirituality—a model that is passionate, contemplative, strong, tender, courageous, and humble.

Fathers can also teach their sons about authentic spiritual expression by initiating and modeling acts of service. Remember, boys need memorable *experiences* in service to others. Fathers should give their sons as many experiences as possible to serve others—everything from soup kitchens, to Habitat for Humanity building projects, to missions trips abroad, to raising money for needy organizations, to simple service projects at church or in the community.

Fathers and Sons: Age by Age

A boy needs to know his father's love by experiencing his emotional presence, his modeling, advocacy, and spiritual guidance. Regardless of whether he is two or twenty-two, a boy needs for his dad to walk beside him on his journey. When a father engages with his son's heart, he helps his son engage with his own heart, too, which enables him to live without the levels of shame that drive so many men. This constructive engagement looks different at the various stages of a boy's development. In this section, we offer some specific ways in which fathers can engage with their sons along the journey from boyhood to manhood.

FATHERING THE EXPLORER

Boys in the Explorer stage need to feel a man's physical presence. They need a man to hug them, to hold them, to kiss them, and to cuddle them for long periods of time. And of course they need a man to wrestle with them. They need to experience the tender side of masculinity, which builds a sense of safety, security, and comfort and also prepares them for dealing with members of the fairer sex; but they also desperately need to wrestle, so they can begin to feel and test their emerging strength. (Wrestling is also a constructive, relational outlet for some of their boundless energy.)

After I (David) spoke to a group of educators recently, I was approached by a male teacher who had two Explorers of his own. He told me that he had recruited a group of dads of Explorers to join him on Saturday mornings in the school gym. There they dragged out all the wrestling mats used by the school's wrestling team and created a wide open space for the dads and boys to wrestle, romp, and play. What a great example of constructively engaging with young boys!

Explorers also need to feel a man's presence and strength in support of their mothers. When a father supports a boy's mother, he lays a foundation and sets an example for how the boy will interact with and respect (or disrespect) his mother. As we've mentioned, a boy will push against his mother throughout his childhood as he tries to individuate into being a man. Boys need the example and input of their fathers to help them separate out with respect and without undermining their mother's position of authority. A boy should never be allowed to disrespect or demean his mother. Fathers play the most important role in curtailing this behavior. In doing so, they model something important for boys in terms of the relationship between men and women or a husband and wife.

FATHERING THE LOVER

As an Explorer evolves into a Lover, it's easier to see his likes and dislikes, his strengths and weaknesses, and his passions and desires. As these aspects of his personality emerge (and they will continue to emerge and evolve as he matures), a boy needs his father to help him identify and explore these areas. A boy will try out various expressions of his personality in the Lover stage. As he is exploring his options, his dad needs to watch and listen for what he enjoys. As much as possible, at this stage of his development, new experiences should center on exposure and enjoyment, not on competition. This is not to say that boys can't compete. They will and should. But before the age of eight or nine, a boy's primary agenda should still be about having fun, exploring, developing, and mastering. If his sense of pleasure and acceptance is connected to competition too early in life, it may derail much of his development. We've worked with plenty of boys and men who were coached at an early age around themes of winning and losing. These boys who were pressured to perform often formulated distorted ideas about their abilities and gifts that were difficult (and sometimes nearly impossible) to reverse. For younger boys (boys not yet in puberty), the vast majority of coaching should be geared toward skill acquisition, physical and motor-skill advancement, and character development. At the Lover stage, a coach's or instructor's primary objective should be to promote fun. They need to keep in mind that boys who have not yet reached puberty lack the emotional maturity to handle intense competition. Practices and games should be geared around maximum enjoyment and learning how to play.

Coaches aren't the only ones who need to get this message. Some dads who decide against coaching on the field end up coaching from the sidelines. They stand behind the chain-link fence, or courtside, screaming instruction and criticism. I (David) once urged a dad, following a tearful conversation with his eight-year-old son, to write the following words on his hand with a Sharpie before his son's next game: "My job is to SHUT UP and ENJOY my son!"

A Lover needs to be enjoyed for who he is. If your son's wiring is identical to yours, let him become his own man. If his wiring is different from yours, discover, celebrate, and enjoy exactly how he was made, rather than try to bend him into more of who he is not.

Lovers want to be enjoyed, and they also need their fathers to engage with them. As with Explorers, engagement comes through physical contact and connection. But Lovers also need to feel their father's emotional presence. Fathers can engage with their sons by being involved in things they like to do. Start a project with your son—who cares if you finish it?

The Lover stage is a key opportunity for fathers to teach their sons how to connect with their heart. We've said it before, but it bears repeating: Boys need to *see* that emotions belong in the life of a man. And they need to learn how to identify, resolve, and express their emotions. If a dad doesn't know how to do this himself (and many men don't), he needs to learn how so he can pass that wisdom on to his son. If that's the situation you find yourself in, let us encourage you to get plugged into a men's group, or see a counselor, or go on a men's retreat (like the ones offered by John Eldredge at his Ransomed Heart Boot Camps). Whatever you do, find a way to learn how to be emotionally present with yourself and your son. (Your wife will appreciate it too.) If you don't, your son will grow up missing a vital skill he needs to successfully navigate his relationships. We strongly believe that every man who wants to love his sons well should be regularly engaged in experiences that develop, promote, and encourage strong emotional connections.

FATHERING THE INDIVIDUAL

In fathering the Individual, we need to expand our repertoire. We must continue to be present with our sons, both physically and emotionally, and continue enjoying them and engaging with them, but in this next season we must also be intentional about validating them. Boys at this stage need to know that they are a force to be reckoned with. It's our job as fathers to call out a boy's strength. Boys feel their own strength when they push against Mom's and Dad's. Dads, when you play games with your son, you may need to let him win some of the time. Men can be so ridiculously competitive that at times they're even willing to squash their own sons. But it's more important for your boy to be able to test his mettle against you than for you to assert your dominance. At the same time, boys at this stage know when you're not giving your best effort, so you can't dog it too much; but neither do you have to play as if you're the defending world champion.

Dads need to call out specific strengths they see in their Individuals—and not just physical or athletic strengths, but also emotional, spiritual, artistic, and relational strengths. Create opportunities where your boy can utilize his entire palette of strengths. Draw attention to his strengths and affirm and validate them. At the Individual stage, there is no such thing as a boy thinking too highly of himself. He needs to know that you see his strengths and value them.

One thing in particular that dads must look for, underline, and validate in their boys is when they show emotional vulnerability. For example, if your boy comes to you for help with a particular challenge he is facing with a peer, a teacher, or a coach, in addition to listening to him and allowing him to discover his own solutions, be sure to recognize and affirm his willingness to be open about his struggles. That kind of positive reinforcement will help him stay in touch with his emotions, and it will keep the lines of communication open between you and him. Similarly, these kinds of interactions create opportunities for you to recognize and affirm your boy's strength and creativity—especially if you're careful not to solve his problems for him or offer unsolicited advice.

FATHERING THE WANDERER

Fathering the Wanderer takes creativity and wisdom. The phrase "being wise as a serpent" certainly applies to the challenge of parenting adolescent boys. Boys in this stage will likely want to hang out with their buddies, do their own thing (sports or other interests), or pursue girls. Notice that none of these categories involves Dad. It takes some ingenuity for a father to engage with a Wanderer. He'll need to figure out ways to get time with his son and think about places to go with him that will pique the boy's interest. During this season, he needs to continue to validate his boy's strength and call out his courage.

Wanderers are likely to resist opportunities to be with their dads, so dads need to release their sons to other trustworthy adults who can come alongside them in ways they won't resist. If your son is at this stage, help him find a mentor or other guide— and when he finds one, encourage these relationships.

Mentors are adults who are interested in and compatible with a particular boy. They must be interested in the boy's life and check in with him regularly—see how he's doing academically, emotionally, and relationally. Mentors can offer help in areas where the boy is open to it. But most importantly, a mentor is devoted to the boy's well-being. Even if a Wanderer has two loving parents, a mentor can become a surrogate parent during this stage (which is often defined by a boy's strained relationship with his parents). A mentor can become a voice of guidance to which a boy is willing to listen. And with boys who are having real difficulty with their parents during this stage, a mentor can be one of the few adults he will go to for direction, help, and encouragement.

FATHERING THE WARRIOR

Fathering boys gets much easier as they enter the Warrior stage. Dads must keep in mind that relationship in this stage in particular is more about quality than quantity. You can plan a weekend to go see him at college, but you must be willing to access only pockets of that time. Let him go about his life, but grab him for coffee or dinner or to shoot some hoops. Dads, this is a time for fitting into your boy's life, rather than the other way around. And during those times when you're together, keep calling him out and validating the man he is becoming.

In many ways, a father's role in his son's life will shift in the Warrior stage. He will still be Dad, but he will be less of an instructor and more of a comrade. At this stage, father and son are relating more as peers, even as the father continues to empower his son with words that speak to his abilities and strengths. For example, I (David) have every letter my dad wrote to me in college. I feasted on his words of validation and support. A friend and colleague of mine lost his dad as a young adult, but he can recite from memory a letter his dad wrote to him validating his strength and affirming how he saw him. So, dads, even when you have less access to your son at this stage of his life, you can still write to him, encourage him, and affirm him.

Putting the Principles into Practice

We met a guy who has a side business filming individuals in their last season of life. These people create a video saying anything they want to say to the people they are leaving behind. Many have been diagnosed with a terminal illness and have only months or weeks left to live. The videographer told us he has yet to meet a man in the last moments of his life who cared at all about what he had done vocationally. These men wanted only to speak to their children. There's no other role than that of a father that bears this responsibility and allows a man to so directly put his handprint on the life of another person. Wrestle well with your calling as a father, and consider these ideas as you do.

TIP 1: **Pass on a legacy.** Throughout your son's development, ask yourself what your own father gave to you that you loved—and then do the same things for your son. Then ask yourself what you *didn't* get from your dad that you wanted and needed, and give those things to your son as well.

TIP 2: **Don't go it alone.** Find a community of other men and boys to plug into (whether it's with sports, Scouting, church, backpacking, model train group, or whatever). Boys need to see their dads interacting with other men, as well as have other men in their lives. Take your son with you hunting or golfing with your buddies. Have him spend time with you at your office. Put him in situations where he sees you interacting in relationships with other men.

TIP 3: **Reach out often.** It's important for a boy to know that his dad is thinking about him. For example, if you leave for work before he gets up, leave him a note on the kitchen table. If he takes his lunch to school, put a note in his lunchbox. If he's old enough to have a cell phone, send him a text message of affirmation or encouragement during the day.

TIP 4: Have a ritual. Dads can develop regular rituals with their boys. For example, let Mom sleep in on the weekends and do Saturday morning pancakes. Or take an after-dinner walk with your son.

TIP 5: Fire up the grill for him and his buddies. One way to be with your son is to serve him. Ask him to invite his friends over, and grill steaks for them. This will create a chance for you to hang out on the fringes of your son's life as well as observe his relationships with other boys.

TIP 6: Hit the road, Jack! Remember that boys love adventure. So surprise your boy by picking him up from school one Friday at noon (on a weekend when he doesn't have much else going on). Throw him in the car, hand him a map, and say, "Where do you want to go?" (Be sure to take into account his personal life and what plans he may have.) Spend the weekend exploring the back roads or a city or town you've never been to.

TIP 7: Shoot something. Whether you own guns or not, you can take your son out shooting. Go to the gun range, or hire a firearms instructor for half a day and spend time shooting with your son. Boys need to be given opportunities to feel their own strength and power. Nothing says *power* like firing a weapon. If firearms aren't your thing, get a bow and arrow or a slingshot.

TIP 8: Take him into the wild. Go camping. It can be difficult for fathers and sons to bond during the transition into the teenage years. But if you take him into the woods where there are no televisions, video games, or iPods, you can spend some good time together.

TIP 9: Pump some iron. Set up a regular time to take your boy to the gym or the YMCA to work out. Lift weights, stretch, do the treadmills. Besides getting some time with your son, you will also get the exercise you need.

TIP 10: Give him a pocketknife. The gift of a pocketknife says to a boy, "You are on your way." Be sure to teach him how, when, and why to use the knife.

CHAPTER 13

Rituals, Ceremonies, and Rites of Passage

I (Stephen) got to know Marcel well when he joined a men's group I lead. He was a successful plastic surgeon in his mid-fifties, but his marriage was hanging on by a thread, he was bored with his work, and from what I could tell, he was on the verge of depression. But that's not what struck me the most about him. What stood out with Marcel was how unmanly he was. Not unmanly in a feminine way, but in a childish way. There was something distinctly boyish about Marcel. He was not immature, per se. It was more like he was unhardened by life—kind of still wide-eyed and exuberant.

Over the weeks and months that the group met, I came to discover that Marcel's seeming innocence had less to do with purity and far more to do with the absence of his father. Shortly after Marcel turned fourteen, his dad had died in a violent car wreck when another driver ran a red light. It was a Sunday morning, and Marcel's dad was on his way to the market to get some cream for his coffee. He died three days later in the hospital.

Obviously, Marcel was never the same. He remembered his dad—a minister of a small church—as a kind and gentle man who loved people. One of Marcel's favorite memories was going with his dad to visit parishioners in the hospital.

As Marcel began to take responsibility for his stressed marriage and address his dejected mood, he realized that much of the turmoil came from the shame that surrounded his masculinity. After being challenged by men in the group to come to grips with how his father's death had affected him, Marcel said one night through tears, "I guess I never learned what it means to be a man. My dad died when a boy needs a dad the most—when *I* needed him most." What Marcel came to realize was that he was still grieving because he had never gotten to say good-bye to his father (his mother had thought he was too young to visit his father in the hospital before he died), and he had never been initiated into manhood. At the urging of the group, Marcel made a plan to accomplish both of these things.

Growing up in Southern California, Marcel had gone to Yosemite National Park with his family for several vacations. (Some of his most vivid memories of his father were from these vacations.) Marcel remembered his father hiking the back side of Half Dome—a gigantic granite mountain in Yosemite Valley. Possibly Yosemite's most familiar sight, along with El Capitan, the magnificent granite dome rises to an elevation of 8,836 feet, close to 4,800 feet above the valley floor. Marcel recalled thinking that his father was so manly for being able to climb such a big mountain, and he remembered his father promising to make the hike with him when he was older. As a boy, Marcel was too young to climb it; as an adult, he was ready for the challenge.

On the last night of every group I lead, I conduct a ceremony in which each group member brings an icon that speaks to what the group experience meant for him. Marcel brought a stack of picture frames, one for each group member. In the frame was a photocopy of an old photograph of Yosemite. On the back of each image, Marcel had handwritten an invitation to join him on a trip to Yosemite. The goal was twofold: to say good-bye to his father, and to hike Half Dome to symbolically reclaim his masculinity.

Marcel had discovered the basic necessity of the male heart for initiation, rites of passage, and rituals. His father had never initiated him into manhood. Other than his graduations from college and medical school, he'd had few rites of passage. And his life was devoid of any meaningful rituals.

We cannot emphasize enough how significant these rites and rituals are in the lives of boys (and men). As experiential, spatial, and tactile learners, boys need events and ceremonies to help mark significant moments and transitions in their lives. Culturally, we recognize the importance of these markers and incorporate them into our lives. For example, think of all the pomp and circumstance that goes along with graduations and commencements, marriage ceremonies, oaths of office, and funeral services. Or the National Anthem at sporting events, or throwing out the ceremonial first pitch at baseball games. The spiritual core of a boy's heart longs for these types of "Ebenezers" or stones of remembrance.[1]

An Aimless World

In our postmodern culture of rapid change and global transformation, boys are wrestling with questions of identity, morality,

STEPHEN JAMES | DAVID THOMAS

and belonging. In a world that is rooted in relativism like never before, there is seemingly little truth to which we can anchor a boy's heart. As Richard Rohr points out, it is only our Western culture that has "deemed it unnecessary to 'initiate' young men. Otherwise, culture after culture felt that if the young man were not introduced to 'the mysteries,' he would not know what to do with his pain and would almost always abuse his power."[2]

Though many ancient, indigenous, and tribal cultures cling tightly to rites of manhood and ceremonies of initiation, we have largely left our boys to find the truth for themselves. There is little to guide boys in our society and still less to tell them they have what it takes. Rohr continues, "For rites of passage, we've moved toward the only collective agreed-upons we have: sports, education, work, Boy Scouts, and war. Coaches and drill sergeants, smoking and driving, money and merit badges, graduation and girlfriends have become our only mentors and rites of passage."[3]

If we don't create rites of passage for our boys, they will find their own. If we don't mark their passage into the fellowship of men, they will create experiences that make them feel like the men they long to become. A rite of passage for a boy can be anything from smoking pot to sleeping with a girl to racing drunk or breaking the law in some way. The rise of inner-city gangs in our culture is a direct result of the absence of fathers and the resulting failure to properly initiate boys into men. Gangs have all the central components of initiation: Boys are ushered into a male community around a common ideology for the sake of something larger than themselves. Tragically, the common threads of this community are violence, confrontation, and abuse.

For many boys, life will eventually initiate them, but it is often too late or too imperceptible to have any real meaning. When boys are initiated by happenstance, they rarely comprehend the sacred significance of the moment, and thus it has little impact. Without initiation, boys become disillusioned, dissatisfied, and disenchanted. They have nothing greater than themselves to be a part of—they lack a moral and spiritual identity—and they have no greater story to guide them. They become what Henri Nouwen calls "nuclear man," living in "a dislocated world . . . without meaningful connections to his past and future."[4] Without initiation, boys are groping for direction, but without meaning or purpose. Ultimately, an uninitiated boy lives isolated and disconnected from himself, from others, and from the world. "An uninitiated man," writes Richard Rohr, "must take personal responsibility for creating all the patterns and making all the connections—if there are any. It is an unwhole, incoherent, and finally unsafe world. No wonder the typical young man in our non-mythic culture spends so much time posturing, climbing, and overcompensating. In his heart he knows it is all not true—and therefore not sacred."[5]

That's why initiation is so fundamental to the heart of a boy. It introduces him to manhood. By providing rites of passage and rituals for boys, we create a memorial process that helps them grow into mature men. A boy who has been initiated is connected to something bigger than himself, and he grows up knowing that life has meaning. Rohr concludes, "A truly initiated man . . . lives inside a sacred universe of meaning. Even the seemingly absurd, even the pain has meaning."[6]

Say "Hello" to Manhood

Initiation is more about providing boys a compass of sacred meaning—a way to find true north—than it is about specific moral principles. Ritual is more experiential than directly instructive. Rituals give boys an inner GPS that will help guide them on their journey to manhood when they're confused or grow deaf or insensitive to the voices around them. That's why rituals and rites of passage (as opposed to lectures about "doing life better") are so central to the process of becoming a man. Rituals, rites of passage, and initiations reach deep into the heart of a boy and touch what theologians call the *Imago Dei*—Latin for "image of God"—the part of our humanity that bears the mark of God and speaks to our "inherent value independent of [our] utility or function."[7]

For initiation to be valuable, it must be costly. For a boy who has been tested by the furnace of life and made it through, life seems different. He finds himself connected to something greater than himself, for he has faced himself and seen that life is not only about him. In the process of initiation, the shell of his boyhood dies, and what emerges is the heart of a man connected to God. Initiation, at its core, is both painful and spiritual. It is more about revealing God's character than it is about revealing the boy's character. Through initiation, a boy becomes connected to those who have gone before him, and he will be connected to those who come after. When a boy belongs to something bigger than himself, he feels larger than life.

Think of a young man joining the Marine Corps. Once he makes it through boot camp, he will always be a Marine. Remember the Marine motto, Semper Fidelis, which means "always faithful." Joining the military has served as a rite of initiation for generations of men. It teaches self-discipline for the sake of the common good; it requires sacrifice for something larger than oneself; it imparts values such as honor, heritage, and tradition. Initiation rites define courage, heroism, and fidelity for a boy. It shows him what is worth suffering for and what is truly glorious to die for. It shows a boy what matters most. (And it's not him.)

Richard Rohr, in his excellent essay titled "Boys to Men:

Rediscovering Rites of Passage for Our Time," identifies five essential truths that "male initiation must communicate . . . to the young man." They are worth repeating here:

Life Is Hard

If you can be convinced of this early in life and not waste time trying to avoid it or making it easy for yourself, you will, ironically, have much less useless suffering in the long run. Because we avoid the legitimate pain of being human, we bring upon ourselves much longer, meaningless, and desperate pain.

You Are Going to Die

The certainty and reality of one's own death must be made very real. The young man must live as one who has already died "the first death" and is not protecting himself from the second. This is seen in the traditional Christian baptismal teaching: "Do you not know that you who were baptized were baptized into the dying of Christ?" (Romans 6:3). One's death must be ritualized through trials, facing loss and one's fear of loss, and [the] symbolic drowning of the baptized. Now, we are unpracticed and unprepared for loss of any kind. . . .

You Are Not That Important

Cosmic and personal humility is of central importance for truth and happiness in this world. The initiate must be rightly situated in a world that demands respect from him, or he will have an inflated/deflated sense of himself that will need continual reassurance. This is almost the complete contrary of the postmodern "I am special" button. Littleness is nothing to be denied or disguised, but gives a basis for all community, family, and service.

You Are Not in Control

The illusion of control must be surrendered by a deep experience of one's own powerlessness. Usually only suffering accomplishes this task, especially unjust suffering and things that one cannot change. Reality and God are in control, and we will normally not accept this until led to the limits of our own resources.

Your Life Is Not about You

This is the essential and summary experience. You must know that you are a part of something and somebody much bigger than yourself. Your life is not about you, it is about God. Henceforward, the entire human experience takes on a dramatically different character. We call it holiness.[8]

Initiation shows a boy what is wonderful and beautiful about life. We will offer some specific ideas for initiation rituals later in the chapter, but here is a framework to guide your thinking:

- Initiation is primarily spiritual. Boys are looking for a spiritual experience, and they desire something that moves them deep in their hearts.
- Initiation must be defined corporately and be rooted in tradition. It must be something that a boy's family, "tribe," or community sees as admirable and positive; something that is worth trusting in; something that has stood the test of time.

- Initiation can never be about proving oneself—it's always about discovering oneself. It helps a boy answer the question of, Who am I? Initiation helps him understand himself and come to terms with the role he plays in the larger story evolving around him. Every boy longs to know who he is, to be initiated into a group, and to experience a sense of belonging and purpose.

- Initiation cannot be spontaneous; a boy must prepare for it and look forward to it—and the longer the better. Boys don't choose to be initiated; it is something the older generation passes down to the younger as part of the family tradition. It's best when governed by older men who are significant to the boy and who deeply love and respect him. One warning here: Dads can only give to their sons what they themselves have received. For example, if a boy's father lacks a significant spiritual connection to God born through hardship, struggle, and deliverance, he cannot meaningfully initiate his son.

- Initiation should be mysterious. Though a boy should expect it, he doesn't need to know what is going to happen. Richard Rohr suggests, "Don't tell them a lot beforehand, except what they need to bring and who will be there."[9] In the same vein, initiation rites are not to be talked about much afterward or the symbolism explained.

- Initiation cannot be rushed—it has to be at the right time. A boy needs to be old enough to grasp what is happening. That means he needs to be at least in the Individual stage, but more likely in the Wanderer stage.

- Initiation cannot be easy, flaccid, or hollow. It must have some element of suffering attached to it (something that a boy must struggle through). Historically, these rites of passage have required feats of strength, endurance, and

bravery—such as swimming across a river, spending a
night in the jungle alone, or running great distances—
something that reveals *to the boy* his ability to test himself
and gives him a deeper sense of who he is; something to
strengthen his connection to his spiritual core (the image
of God).

"Celebrate Good Times, Come On!"

One significant part of initiation that we need to acknowledge is
the power of celebration. A great picture of this is the Jewish tradition of Bar Mitzvah. This ritual celebrates the end of one stage in
the life of a boy and acknowledges the beginning of another. It not
only marks the boy's passage into manhood; it also celebrates it.

In considering this kind of experience for a boy, here's one
thing to keep in mind: Make certain to keep your son's interests
at the center of the celebration. You don't want to put so much
emphasis on a theme, or the event itself, that you miss who *he* is
or what *he* loves. Make sure the nature of the celebration matches
the nature of the boy.

For example, I (David) had an opportunity to be a part of a celebration for a young man named Jeff, who was an Eagle Scout and
loved the outdoors. He had a long history of camping and backpacking. With this passion in mind, on Jeff's thirteenth birthday, his dad simply told him that he wanted to borrow him for a
Saturday morning to hike and then take him to lunch. Without
his son being aware, he sent a letter to six men who had played
a significant role in Jeff's life and asked them to show up on this
particular morning to speak to him about some specific parts of
the journey to becoming a man and to speak blessing over him.

When we arrived early that morning, Jeff's dad had mapped

out a particular trail, and he stationed us throughout the woods at points along the way. Jeff arrived shortly after and began hiking with his dad.

When they had walked a short distance into the woods, they came across one of Jeff's grandfathers, resting on the side of the path. After Jeff's dad explained to Jeff what he had planned, he left him with his grandfather, and the two of them walked for a while as the grandfather spoke about his own life, his journey of becoming a man, and the things he loved about his grandson. Jeff was then handed off to a family friend who had known him and loved him since he was a toddler. This man walked with Jeff for a while, and they talked about what it means to become a man.

For Jeff, it was one surprise after another for a couple of hours. He hiked through the woods and met up with one man after another who loved him. In the course of the day, more stories were told, more information was shared, and more memories were made. The morning ended as Jeff arrived with his uncle at a lodge where his mom, his aunt, one of his elementary school teachers, and other women who loved him had gathered to share a meal and celebrate his becoming a man. We sat around and told more stories, gave him some gifts, and shared in his milestone. This ceremony was a beautiful picture of the blessing that comes from celebrating the boys we love in ways that mark their evolution and draw attention to the men they are becoming.

Another young man I love experienced the divorce of his parents at a young age. His mom, a wise and committed parent, understood that there were limitations to what she could offer her son, and that it was important for him to experience strong male community. Throughout his development, she put her son in the way of opportunities to experience risk, purpose, and belonging. For his thirteenth birthday, she gathered a group of men who love her son and have played a role of significance in his life for a steak dinner in her home. She prepared a beautiful meal, including some of the boy's favorite foods, and then slipped out of the house to allow us men to speak into his life and usher him deeper into the sacred community of men.

The young man's grandfather was present at the dinner, and every man in the room wept as this grandfather spoke blessing over his grandson and recounted the events on the day he was born. Other men spoke to the boy's strength, courage, and bravery, as well as his compassion, humility and tenderness. It was a rich time of celebration and blessing.

You might be wondering . . .

Can women be a part of these initiation events? The answer is yes and no. No, in that a portion of this ritual needs to take place only in the company of men. Welcoming a boy into male community can only be accomplished by men. As they speak freely and openly about becoming a man, the boy will feel the presence of masculine strength around him as the ritual unfolds.

Yes, women can participate in some portion of the ceremony, if so desired, and you can be creative about how this can happen. For example, in the hiking ceremony, Jeff hiked only in the company of men, but the meal was shared in the company of women who loved him as well. Their absence on the hike spoke to how parts of the journey can only be taken in the company of men. Their presence for the meal spoke to the vital role that women had played (and would continue to play) in his masculine journey.

What is the ideal age for boys to experience initiation? There's no magic number here. A number of individuals who have pioneered this movement suggest somewhere between the ages of thirteen and sixteen. We would agree because of the significant development shifts taking place during those years, which demand attention and care. There's a physical, intellectual, sexual, and spiritual awakening taking place during the Wanderer years that creates rich opportunities for boys to be addressed and nurtured strongly.

However, depending on transitions that may have taken place in a boy's life, he may need initiation of some kind prior to age thirteen or after age sixteen. After a painful loss, such as a death in the family or divorce, we have encouraged parents to consider some kind of ritual or ceremony to mark the end of a painful journey, acknowledge what was lost, affirm what has been endured, and initiate the beginning of a new season.

It's equally important that we not stop celebrating our sons after they graduate into adulthood. We know a father who created a ritual with both his sons shortly before they became husbands and fathers. These ceremonies addressed the sacred life stages they were entering and affirmed how these young men would now exercise their power in the context of marriage and parenting.

How do you create rituals if you have multiples? As fathers of twin boys, this is something we both continue to wrestle with. Quite simply, there's no easy answer. An ideal scenario would be for each boy to experience his own rite of passage, celebrating his particular passions and gifts. It's not at all uncommon for multiples to have different interests, temperaments, and strengths. Creating ceremonies for each individual not only allows you to uniquely design them, but it also counters the obvious ongoing challenge of having multiples—namely, finding individual time to attend to their individual needs. With that said, it would be common for a number of the same men to be involved in both (or all) ceremonies. Inviting them for multiple initiations in a short span of time may not be logistically possible. There's also the issue of who goes first—and how to keep two ceremonies a surprise, should you choose to do so.

Multiples can still be addressed and celebrated uniquely within the same ceremony, as long as the logistics and creative components are well thought through, and both (or all) boys are given the proper attention.

An End, a Beginning, and a Middle

Initiation rituals can be a tricky and confusing time for boys, because most rites of passage mark the ending of something familiar and the beginning of something unknown. They bring closure to an important part of a man's life (his boyhood), while at the same time initiating him into the start of something new (manhood). Arnold Van Gennep, the anthropologist who coined the phrase *rites of passage* in the early twentieth century, described this journey from boyhood to manhood as having three parts:

- rites of separation
- transition rites
- rites of incorporation (or re-entry)[10]

Van Gennep describes a kind of sacred "neutral zone," in which the person in transition "wavers between two worlds"—in our case, between the worlds of boyhood and manhood. "This symbolic and spatial area of transition may be found in more or less pronounced form in all the ceremonies [that] accompany the passage from one social . . . position to another."[11]

Building on Van Gennep's observations, Brad Griffin, assistant director of the Center for Youth and Family Ministry at Fuller

Theological Seminary, writes, "Navigating that change is much like negotiating the way across the in-between space from a familiar land to a foreign land. In a very real way, a person emerges as someone 'new' once they cross the boundary out of the transitional territory and into a newly defined space."[12] Thus, as a boy moves through the sacred neutral zone of transition during an initiation ceremony or other rite of passage, he emerges as something new and different—a man.

Often called the *liminal* stage (from a Latin root meaning "threshold" or "doorway"), this middle ground or neutral zone is a crucial part of the initiation process. If our boys are to be initiated well into manhood, we must try to create a secure middle space for them to pass through. The challenge, in our contemporary culture, is that we must work around, work with, or work through the culturally contrived threshold of middle school and high school. For many boys during these years, it's like they're trapped in a holding pattern with nowhere to land. They are living between two sovereign territories, boyhood and manhood, and yet don't exist fully in either one.

In this environment, creating a secure space for boys while they complete their transition means that we must help them *see* themselves, *know* themselves, and *love* themselves. We need to repeatedly reinforce their identity. A boy's sense of personal identity will suffer most during these times of limbo (a word from the same root as *liminal*), between the already and the not yet.

One way in which we can help a boy to *see*, *know*, and *love* himself is by illuminating his story. We can help a boy keep tabs on himself by recounting the stories of his life, remembering them on his behalf, and retelling them with enthusiasm. This can be as simple as talking about how he learned to walk, or remembering his first hit in Little League or how he loved spending time with his grandfather before he died.

Telling stories should be commonplace, and it can also be ceremonial. For example, my (Stephen's) wife's family has the tradition of telling each child's birth story every year on that person's birthday. Heather brought this custom into our family, and she has expanded it by creating a birthday tree each year for our children. This small, metal tree, adorned with pictures of the child from the previous year, sits on our dining room table during the weeks before and after each child's birthday.

When the process of storytelling becomes ritualized, so that a boy's story is canonized in his heart, he carries with him into adulthood an awareness and appreciation of his story and where it might take him.

Putting the Principles into Practice

Celebrating and initiating your son may be one of the most lasting and influential gifts you give him. Study him throughout his development to identify times when he needs a community of adults who love him to speak blessing over him and honor how he is progressing and growing. Here are some practices to consider as you structure these pivotal experiences.

TIP 1: **Stoke the wildness of his heart.** Remember, boys are meant to be nurtured toward being Warriors. As John Eldredge points out in *Wild at Heart*, we need to give up making young men "good boys" and recognize that boys were created with a "desperate desire for a battle to fight, an adventure to live, and a beauty to rescue."[13] Their initiations, rites of passages, and rituals of celebration need to reflect this wildness.

TIP 2: Keep his stories alive. Make a list of the key stories and scenes in your boy's life. When was he born? Where? Where has he lived? What was his first haircut like? What was his first day of school like? What key events (happy and sad) have marked his life? How have his faith and spirituality developed? What men does he admire and look up to? What have been his victories? What have been his defeats?

TIP 3: Don't use the cookie cutter. When creating rituals or rites of passage for a boy, remember that you must consider his unique bent. There is no one-size-fits-all ceremony. Each event should be tailored toward your son's heart. If he isn't into the outdoors, it's not a good idea to build a weekend around hiking and camping. If he's an artist, taking him to a museum and setting up an art studio in the basement may be more in line.

TIP 4: Nothing is more scary and stressful for a boy than having the world revolve around him. It's imperative that we help the boys we love not be the center of their own stories. They need to know that there is a God who is bigger than they are—and he's in charge, so they don't have to be. As caregivers, we must develop our own relationships with God, so that we have something to give to the boys we love.

TIP 5: Involve older men in his initiation. Only older men can effectively initiate younger men into manhood. Fathers are too emotionally tied to their sons to do the job alone. They need the help of other men.

TIP 6: Read some books that help you think about the practice of initiation. We recommend *Raising a Modern-Day Knight* by Robert Lewis (Tyndale, 1997), and *Adam's Return: The Five Promises of Male Initiation* by

Richard Rohr. These books offer ideas about the importance of initiation, as well as suggest and outline ceremonies that you can adapt for your own use.

TIP 7: Open the windows for him. Times of transition in a boy's life are great moments for initiation rituals and rites of passage. It's at these obvious moments that we can help him make the transition by underlining it with a ritual or a celebration. Here's a brief list of key times of transition:

- Grade school to middle school
- Middle school to high school
- When he begins to shave
- When he gets his driver's license
- When he begins dating
- High school to college
- College to work

TIP 8: Give him a gift. Commemorate a boy's initiation with an icon, token, or gift. Gifts with meaning that are geared toward the individual boy provide the greatest impact. Some examples are a knife, watch, compass, rifle, journal, plaque, or a Bible.

TIP 9: Affirm him with words. Boys can never receive enough affirmation from their dads. When you design an initiation ceremony, plan to have each participant speak words of affirmation, give blessings, or offer prayers for your boy. You may want to consider having each adult tell your boy why he is special and encourage him for his journey ahead.

TIP 10: Let the mystery reign. One common mistake when it comes to rites of passage is wanting to talk about it afterward. One word of advice: Don't. Much of the power of a rite of passage has to be figured out by the boy himself. If he wants to talk with you about it, he'll come and ask. If he doesn't, respect him enough to let it be.

CHAPTER 14

Sailing for Home

*Max stepped into his private boat and waved good-bye
and sailed back over a year and in and out of weeks
and through a day and into the night of his very own
room where he found his supper waiting for him.*

MAURICE SENDAK, *Where the Wild Things Are*

At the end of *Where the Wild Things Are*, Max, the boy hero,
looks sad as he climbs aboard his ship and sets sail for home.
After a long return voyage, he makes it back to his room—where
his supper awaits him—and back to the safety, comfort, and
happiness of his mother's love. His emotions are passionate,
full, and rich—they shift from moment to moment. At home, in
relationship with his mother, Max seems more controlled by his
feelings than in control of them. But when he enters the realm of
his imagination—the land of the wild things—his feelings drive
a powerful and vivid creativity. Sendak's portrayal of Max is a
great picture of the way, the mind, and the heart of a boy. As with

Max, for most boys, the journey toward manhood is marked with ambivalence, conflict, loss, and celebration.

As a boy makes his way from childhood to manhood, he is never quite sure if he wants to continue forward or go back a few steps to where it is safe and comfortable. His drive toward being a man is guided by his own double-mindedness that says, "I want to be a man" and "I love being a boy." In many ways, this uncertainty sets a boy up to doubt himself, second-guess his identity, and distrust his power. This is understandable, of course, because the world is laced with complex relationships that any child is ill equipped to navigate. A boy's ambivalence about who he is (boy or man) and whether he measures up is fertile soil for a conflict with power.

Boys grapple with power on two fronts: externally and internally. They wrestle with external forces that bridle (and often criticize) the activity and impulsiveness that is so much a part of their minds, bodies, and hearts. The first point of conflict is usually in relationships, specifically with the adults a boy must encounter on his journey to manhood. Whether it's a coach, youth worker, mentor, teacher, or parent, everywhere a boy turns he hears another adult who says, "Do this" or "Don't do that" or "Try harder." Even when boys need adult intervention (which they do frequently), it clarifies where they lack the power and authority they crave (even though they are not ready to handle it).

Similarly, boys struggle with external power that comes in the form of rules, structures, and restrictions. In the West, most boys grow up in a culture that deters them from being boys. In school, they're asked to sit still. In church, they can't be noisy. At home, they're required to be neat. But at their core, boys are not calm, quiet, or neat. As they face the world, they are told more often than not that who they are is not who they need to be.

Either through stubbornness, toughness, bravery, cunning,

grace, or luck, a few boys realize their authority in spite of all the external forces, but most boys lose their wild, passionate edge and grow up to be nice, neutered, and numb.

Boys also struggle with power internally. Much of the time, when boys are in conflict with the external world, they are also in conflict with themselves. Physiologically, boys have no control over the hormones that are surging through their bodies, causing acne, BO, and mood swings, among other things. Psychologically, boys have a strong drive for autonomy from authority and an intense desire for camaraderie with peers. Emotionally, boys develop much more slowly than girls and are often underdeveloped in significant areas at the same age. Spiritually, boys have a hard time negotiating the complex combination of sensitivity and passion that makes up a vibrant spiritual life.

Though there may be little we can do to defuse these power struggles in our boys' lives, there are ways we can nurture them so that they can make it successfully across the badlands of boyhood and be prepared to sail wholeheartedly in the rough seas of manhood.

There is a verse of Hebrew poetry from the prophet Zephaniah that paints a picture of our three-part responsibility as parents, teachers, coaches, and leaders to guide, protect, and bless our boys.

> *The LORD your God is with you,*
> *he is mighty to save.*
> *He will take great delight in you,*
> *he will quiet you with his love,*
> *he will rejoice over you with singing.*[1]

Though this verse is in reference to God, the poetic imagery also provides a picture for what it means for us to be a positive presence in the life of a boy—with our *presence, strength, wisdom, comfort, pleasure,* and *affection.*

PRESENCE

The first line of the poem makes it clear that everything good comes from *presence.* Just as God is with us, we must be present and available to our boys. Though they need to take the journey to manhood for themselves, they don't have to go it alone. Boys need loving adults nearby to guide them and direct them. If we are consistent, loving, and authentic, we will gain their trust and earn the right to whisper direction in their ears along the way. As caring men and women, our presence in their lives becomes a reference point for boys on their journeys. Through our relationship with them, our love for them, and our desire for them to succeed, we become guiding forces as they find their way, not only through boyhood, but also through the rest of life.

STRENGTH AND WISDOM

Another thing we see in this poem is the mighty *strength* of God. While boys are making their way toward becoming men, they must have a secure shelter from the storms of life. Part of being present for them is offering our strength, so that we can bear the weight of life on their behalf while they learn to stand. With strength must come *wisdom,* and it is through our strength and wisdom as adults that we can guard the hearts of boys. Adults have a responsibility to shelter boys as we guide them through the course of life's difficulties.

COMFORT

Boys also need our *comfort*. Though it may break our hearts, our strength is limited and our wisdom is incomplete; we cannot always be there to protect our boys from life. But often, in terms of their own growth and maturation, it's better for them to suffer. When life delivers its cruel blows, boys need the mercy that only someone who has known sorrow can provide. We can help our boys by consoling them. We can, as Zephaniah suggests, quiet them with our love and rejoice over them with singing—like a lullaby. And when there is nothing left to say, we can hold them and be with them.

PLEASURE AND AFFECTION

Along with our presence, strength, wisdom, and comfort comes the opportunity to confirm our *pleasure* and *affection* with our boys. Perhaps more than anything, they need to know and trust that we have faith in who they are and that we find joy in their masculinity. They need to know that we believe they have what it takes. They need to experience our joy and delight in them. In their hearts, they need to know that we will celebrate who they are, regardless of what they do.

God is portrayed in this poem as a kind of warrior-lover. What a bizarre paradox, don't you think? Can't you just see an armor-clad soldier holding a baby and singing a lullaby? Well, it is in this paradox of strength and mercy that we are called to love our boys.

Whether you are a mother, father, grandparent, teacher, church worker, mentor, volunteer, uncle, friend, or neighbor, know that a boy needs you. Thank you for hoping for him enough to invest the time it took to read this book. You must care deeply for him. Good for you, and great for him to have you!

We hope that you will move from here with greater confidence about what it means to nurture the boy in your life; with greater passion to walk with him on his journey toward authentic manhood; and with greater wisdom to guide him well, all along the way. And when it is time for him to take that final step out of boyhood into the country of men, may you have the courage to let him go, so that he can live as fully as he was created to be, with confidence, character, and compassion.

Hot Topics

SPANKING AND DISCIPLINE

Few topics are as emotionally charged, polarizing, and likely to be controversial as that of spanking. With that in mind, we're simply going to suggest some ideas for you to consider in choosing a form of discipline, and you can decide which side you're on.

1. Boys are naturally aggressive. They don't need any help in being more that way.
2. Always discipline to build character, not simply to punish behavior.
3. Avoid disciplining in anger, whether physically or verbally. Anger creates opportunity for harm, both physical and emotional. It also models a response that isn't useful. At its core, anger breeds a lack of self-control. Boys benefit from being sent to their rooms and waiting while you formulate a consequence that's not steeped in anger.
4. Try to make the punishment fit the crime. We realize this isn't always possible, but most of the time it is. Greater learning takes place when kids experience natural consequences.
5. To have the most impact, discipline should be consistent and administered with as little emotion as possible. Screaming or yelling doesn't create greater impact for learning with kids; it only makes the adult look more out of control.
6. A fantastic guide for disciple is the Love and Logic series by Jim Fay, Foster Cline, and others. They have books and resources for parenting kids as young as six months all the way through adolescence. Their philosophy is extremely honoring to children, and their techniques are highly effective when utilized consistently. Go to www.loveandlogic.com to explore their resources.

SCREEN TIME

Visual stimulants in the media don't help to develop the *limbic* and *neocortical* areas of the brain. The limbic area is the emotive center of the brain, and the neocortical area (or cerebral cortex) controls intellectual functioning and creativity. Too much media exposure actually handicaps the development of these two areas of the brain (playing off their weaknesses) and thus doesn't benefit boys emotionally or physically. Here's what you can do:

1. *Monitor media input.* Limit daily consumption of TV, computer, and video games. A boy should never engage in more virtual reality than real activity; he should never spend more time watching sports than playing them; nor should he spend more time playing video games than playing with friends.
2. *Monitor MySpace, Facebook, and other online communication* until your son understands the dangers. Demand to know his password, and let him know that you can (and will) check his history at any time.
3. *Model healthy limits.* Your words and standards will carry more weight if you practice what you preach and limit the amount of time you watch TV or spend on the computer. Also, your kids notice the kinds of movies and shows you watch, so model responsibility there as well.
4. *Use media to your advantage.* Pick movies and programs that contain topics you want to discuss with your son (money, sex, drugs, family, friends, etc.), and use them to engage in conversation. (See Michael Gurian's book *What Stories Does My Son Need?*)

SENSITIVE OR INTUITIVE BOYS

Some boys have a broad emotional range. They don't meet the criteria of the typical boy, who is emotionally illiterate, hard to read, and even harder to engage.

A certain percentage of boys are uniquely wired with a well-developed emotional vocabulary, high intuition, and deep feelings. We often describe them as "sensitive boys."

Sensitive boys will potentially spend a portion of their development feeling different and at times isolated. They will have a sense that "something is wrong with me." As early as stage one (Explorer), girls will often gravitate toward intuitive boys. They find them easier to relate with; more on par with their emotional and relational skills; and typically less aggressive, impulsive, loud, and boisterous.

An intuitive boy may feel somewhat isolated from his male peers and may grow into an awareness that his "wiring" is somewhat different from that of other boys. Such a boy needs particular attention from the adults around him. He needs to hear that his uniqueness is a gift, not a weakness. We can tell him, "You have a strength that a lot of boys don't have." With very young boys, we might couch it in terms of a "special power" (like X-ray vision); with older boys, we frame it as a "gifting" or a "strength." We might say, "This won't mean much to you now, but when you become an adult man, your gift will bless your wife and children."

These boys also need specific validation from the men in their lives, and they need to be introduced to men who are similarly gifted. They need to see how this gift resides in the lives of grown men. Expose them to men in their sphere of influence, as well as to characters in literature and film.

A number of parents with sensitive sons start to question their boy's sexuality and wonder if he is gay. Such questions won't serve your son well. Sensitivity doesn't equal homosexuality. It just means he's sensitive.

Our role as caregivers of intuitive boys is to read between the lines, listen, and watch with even greater curiosity and greater persistence. We may never encounter the type of resistance we experience with more emotionally stilted boys, but sensitive boys may require us to listen and linger for extended periods of time. We should also be attentive and aware that many of these boys can be more vulnerable to experiencing symptoms of anxiety and depression. They simply feel all things deeply. The impact of the bruises and scrapes of life can cut deeper with this type of young man. Intuitive boys need to keep company with adults who will hear them out, and they desperately need to seek out male peers with similar wiring, who can normalize their experience and provide camaraderie. Intuitive young men will typically find their own way to each other by stage five (Warrior) and into adulthood, but earlier in their development they may need help finding like-minded friends.

COMPETITION AND RELATIONSHIP

We've already discussed the emergence of competition and the role it plays in a boy's life at the Individual stage and beyond. As boys become consumed with their rank in the pecking order, the heavy reliance on one-upmanship and dominance in male conversations at this stage makes it difficult for them to express their emotions of fear, sadness, or confusion. What they more often experience in relating with their male peers is a lack of safety in being vulnerable. When the cultural norm says that expressing these emotions looks weak, boys can easily feel they have no options, and thus go underground with their emotions in an effort to "save face" or appear in control.

Out of this phenomenon, boys can begin to adopt relational styles that are void of collaboration or encouragement. Boys with this deficit look like ball hogs on the court, know-it-alls in the classroom, and cocky and unreachable jerks in relationships with peers. Left unchecked, these same impulses can evolve into narcissism in marriage and ruthless and inflexible behavior in the workplace. Boys who have learned to subvert their emotions and play the one-upmanship game tend to have few male relationships of any depth and are absent of accountability. They play to win and for no other reason. They thrive on bringing recognition to themselves and are willing to function at another's expense, regardless of the outcome.

In their relationships with women, men with this relational pattern go in and out of relationships, feeling disinterested once they've "won her over" or "accomplished the quest." Once competition isn't a factor, they don't have a sense of maintaining a relationship.

In their relationships with other men, they don't have a sense of how to negotiate, compromise, or collaborate. They are typically only comfortable when in a position of dominance. They make lousy team players and terrible coworkers.

Our role with boys who display these characteristics is to call out the deficits and create (or force, if necessary) opportunities for them to develop different patterns of relating. They may need to take a season or a semester off from competitive opportunities and only engage in activities that involve service and the development of humility, servant leadership, and collaboration.

I (David) once worked with a young man who fit this profile to a T. For a four-game stretch, I encouraged his parents to partner with their son's coach to have him benched and to serve in the role of team manager. Rather than playing, he filled water bottles, handed towels to his teammates, and cleaned up equipment after practice. His parents went along with it, but he was absolutely furious about the arrangement. During the first two games, he complained, argued, and performed his tasks with sarcasm and a lack of commitment to the role. His coach approached him after the second game to inform him that this shift in roles was about developing his character, and because the coach saw no evidence that it was working, he would extend the experiment for two more games beyond the original four. His message was simple and clear: "All the adults in your life care more about you becoming a team player in the game of life than we do about facilitating your becoming a ball hog in the game of life. Until you get on board with us, we'll elongate the process until you develop the necessary skills."

TALKING WITH BOYS ABOUT SEX

Here are some pointers for parents on how to talk with boys about sex and relationships.

1. *Take the initiative.* Teaching boys about sex means a loving, consistent, and steady flow of information that should begin as early as possible. For example, when teaching an Explorer about his body, use the correct names for his body parts. As a boy matures, his parents should continue his education by gradually including more and more information, until he understands the subject well.

2. *Explore your own attitudes.* If it is hard for you to talk with your son about sex, it will be hard for him to talk with you. If you are very uncomfortable with the subject, read some books and discuss your feelings with a trusted friend, relative, physician, pastor, or counselor. The more you examine the subject, the more confident you'll feel discussing it. Boys who feel they can talk with their parents about sex are less likely to engage in high-risk behavior as teens than kids who do not feel they can talk with their parents about the subject.

3. *Offer accurate, age-appropriate information.* Talk about sex in a way that fits your boy's age and stage of development. This means anticipating the next stage of development too. Boys can get frightened and confused by the sudden changes their bodies begin to go through as they reach puberty. To alleviate anxiety, talk with your son not only about his current stage of development but also about the next stage to come. This also means talking with him about girls.

4. *Cover more than sex.* In addition to telling a boy about the biological specifics of puberty, parents need to discuss

dating with him as well. Boys need to understand that relationships with girls can be very emotionally powerful. By discussing this aspect of a sexual relationship with your son, he will be better informed to make decisions later on and more likely to resist peer pressure.

5. *Talk with boys specifically about girls.* Boys need to be as informed about female sexual development as they are about their own sexual development. If they only hear about themselves, they only have half the equation.

DATING

By the time a boy hits the end of the Individual stage or the beginning of the Wanderer stage, he will likely begin to express some interest in dating. There are several things to keep in mind in terms of boys and dating.

1. There is no magic age. Girls mature faster than boys. A boy is ready when he can articulate a plan for handling the situations that are of concern to his parents.

2. Every bit as important as knowing your son's friends and their parents is knowing the girls he is interested in and their parents. Insist that your son bring a girl home for dinner before they go on a date, and make sure he introduces himself to her family as well. Don't give in on this issue. Show an interest in whom he is dating, even if you don't approve of everything about her or them as a couple. Showing interest doesn't necessarily equate with giving permission.

3. Encourage the girl's father (either through a phone conversation or in person) to get to know your son. Hear his expectations clearly regarding your son's spending time with his daughter.

4. You wouldn't ask a toddler to do multiplication and division, so don't expect your Individual or Wanderer son to know what to do with a girl when it comes to dating. Keep in mind what is taking place developmentally with him. Let this help you set limits *and* provide opportunities. (Don't turn him loose to be influenced primarily by his peers, and don't eliminate opportunities for him to fail).

5. He needs education in terms of the way girls think, how they interpret things differently, and also how some girls gravitate toward manipulation as a pattern of relating. Use

role-playing with him as a tool, and involve other individuals to whom he might be more willing to listen on this topic (a youth director at church who works with girls, an aunt, a family friend with a college-age daughter whom you trust, etc.).

6. He needs strong information about physical boundaries and sexual experimentation, as well as how to respect his own body and hers, and that no means *no* when spoken by a girl (regardless of his interpretation).

7. Remember that although it's normal for him to express an interest in dating and to have experience with dating, it should never preclude his having and maintaining relationships with his male peers. If he becomes obsessed with a single, female relationship at the expense of his relationships with his male peers, you have reason to be concerned. Talk to him about maintaining a healthy balance, and don't be afraid to limit the number of dates he can have in a month, how much he can talk to the girl on the phone or on MySpace or Facebook, or how often he can text, IM, or e-mail her each week.

MASTURBATION

I (David) once met with a guy whose (single) mother, when he was fourteen, showed him a diagram of an erect penis, as part of her teaching him about his physical development, and told him two things. The first was, "Don't touch it." The second was, "If you do, you'll get genital warts." That's how this mother chose to handle the topic of masturbation.

We'd recommend a slightly different approach. When dealing with boys and masturbation, the first thing we emphasize is *normalizing* the behavior. A boy needs to know that it's normal to want to pleasure himself, and it's normal to masturbate. However, we tell them, just because it's normal, stimulating, and arousing doesn't make it beneficial.

When talking to boys about this topic, we like to introduce the psychological principles discovered by Ivan Pavlov in his experiments with dogs. No doubt you're familiar with Pavlov's dogs and how he eventually trained them to salivate merely by ringing a bell. Boys need to understand that if they train themselves to need pornography or some other kind of visual stimulation to experience arousal, and then pleasure themselves through masturbation, they are locking in a neurological response every bit as predictable and powerful as Pavlov created by ringing a bell and feeding his dogs. They can also lock in a connection between getting an erection and immediately masturbating, and with quickly ejaculating in response to physical touch.

We tell boys that God built in a solution to the physical buildup they feel that drives a desire to want to masturbate. This natural solution is called a nocturnal emission or wet dream. (Moms: Considering you've never been a guy, it's good for you to know that this is a legitimate physical reality. We won't get into the physiology of it right now, but you can trust what we say.) The male body is designed to rid itself naturally when a buildup takes place, but when we introduce masturbation into the equation, we confuse the body's natural rhythm of buildup and release. It's as if we trick the body into believing it needs to relieve itself more frequently.

As with the use of pornography, a long-term pattern of masturbation makes it more difficult for a man to experience a healthy sexual relationship with a woman. He has basically trained his body and mind to need sex for one reason only—physical release—and as a primary means of pleasure centering on himself. Sex was designed for mutual pleasure between two consenting adults in the context of marriage. It was never intended for solo gratification.

Because of the stigma surrounding masturbation in segments of our society, the experience is often followed by emotions of guilt and shame.

As counselors, our experience over the years has been that guys are more likely to modify their behavior when straightforward, documented, scientific data is presented to them, rather than a lot of guilt, shame, and condemnation.

BOYS AND MONEY

The statistics are staggering.

Nineteen percent of Americans between the ages of eighteen and twenty-four declared bankruptcy in 2001, according to a widely cited article from *USA Today*.

The fastest-growing group of bankruptcy filers are twenty-five years of age or younger, according to a 2002 study by the Senate Committee on Banking, Housing, and Urban Affairs.

According to the JumpStart Coalition for Personal Financial Literacy, students entering college are offered an average of eight credit cards during their *first week* of school. More than 80 percent of undergraduates have at least one credit card, and nearly half of college graduates carry four or more credit cards. According to the Department of Education, the average balance carried by these students is more than three thousand dollars.

The 2007 Financial Literacy Challenge found that 62 percent of the high school seniors they surveyed failed a basic financial skills test (down from 65.5 percent in 2004).

According to a 2003 Visa USA survey, nearly half of college-age adults (49 percent) said they believe they are more likely to become millionaires by starring in a reality TV series than by learning how to budget and save wisely (36 percent). The same survey found that 83 percent of adults are unaware of the resources available to help them teach children practical money skills.

We have a responsibility to educate our boys in terms of money, economic realities, and stewardship. Many parents aren't aware of the number of resources available to inform and educate boys about these concepts. A number of these resources are formatted in a faith context to include the concepts of stewardship and tithing.

One example is the series of financial teaching tools for kids and teens from best-selling author and financial expert Dave Ramsey (www.daveramsey.com):

Financial Peace Jr.: Teaching Kids about Money! (Lampo, 2003)
Financial Peace for the Next Generation (Lampo, 2003)
Foundations in Personal Finance (Lampo, 2008)

This is one area in which, as caregivers, we can really help boys prepare for adulthood. Teaching them from an early age (around five or six) how to manage money wisely (giving, saving, spending) will help them avoid future pain and shame in adulthood.

SUBSTANCE ABUSE

Boys today are more at risk to abuse drugs and alcohol than at any other time in history. Addictive substances are more available and more prevalent as a socially acceptable experience among adolescents than ever before. The typical adult or parental response is to try to restrict exposure or access to these things, but we'd like to invite you to consider responding in a different way. Consider a paradigm shift from one of restricting his access or opportunity to one of diminishing his hunger for experimentation.

We believe boys experiment primarily for one of four reasons (or a combination):

- A hunger for power or risk
- A desire for purpose or to have a sense of belonging
- As a way of experiencing initiation
- As a means of escaping their current emotional reality

Aside from frank, direct, and accurate information about substance abuse, we believe the antidote to these four reasons include the following:

- Creating opportunity and outlets for boys to experience acceptable risks
- Providing outlets where boys experience purpose
- Providing outlets for healthy connection that nurtures a sense of belonging
- Initiating boys (as outlined in chapter 13)
- Raising emotionally healthy and resilient boys

Our objective as parents and caregivers is not to rein our boys in more (although they need healthy and consistent boundaries, expectations, and consequences), but actually to release them to more opportunities and healthier options.

We've found three common denominators in the young men we've worked with who either chose not to experiment with substances at all, or who did so for only a short amount of time:

- A strong family
- A strong community of peers and adults who are invested in him
- A strong faith

Although there is no certain way to keep boys from experimenting with tobacco, alcohol, drugs, and other mood-altering substances, we can do our best to guard them from the dangers inherent in these risky behaviors.

BOYS AND PORNOGRAPHY

It may be hard for some parents to believe, but pornography is a real problem for boys. For many boys, seeing it, having it, or distributing it is a rite of passage. Sexually explicit images satisfy their curiosity, give them a taste of forbidden fruit, and answer some of their questions. Sadly, however, peer pressure convinces boys that unless they know about sex or are sexually active, they're missing out on something.

Talking to boys about pornography is just as important as talking to them about alcohol, smoking, and drugs. It's imperative to talk with boys about pornography because of the relational damage it can do. Pornography is damaging to boys. Research shows that boys who look to pornography for sexual guidance and arousal are sexually immature, have terrible sexual experiences, and are often confused about sexual issues. It hinders normal sexual development and gives boys the wrong ideas about sex. Allowing pornography to teach boys about sex sets them up to be very confused and very selfish. It also sets the table for disappointing sexual relationships later in life. When considering how to protect boys from the effects of pornography, we need to address two central issues: *education* and *protection*.

Parental guidance—regardless of how difficult it is to muster the courage—is irreplaceable when it comes to pornography. Boys' actions and attitudes regarding pornography are strongly influenced by their parents' style of parenting. When parents educate their boys, and monitor and discipline their computer use, the boys are more likely to internalize their parents' values than when parents are neglectful or indulgent. Parents need to work to keep the communication lines open. When boys discover pornography, their parents need to temper their reactions.

Because pornography is so accessible and prevalent on the Internet, parents need to set up barriers to protect boys from the dangers of pornography. Here are some suggestions:

- Keep computers in family rooms or rooms that are highly visited.
- Install parental controls and filters that block categories or inappropriate Web sites a child can view.
- Use monitoring software that records or reports computer activity. (Parents should inform their son that monitoring is being used, unless they suspect he is involved in risky behavior.)
- Limit the amount of time a boy spends on the Internet.
- Regularly check the computer's history to see what sites your boy is visiting.

Source: *Monitor on Psychology*, November 2007.

HOMOSEXUALITY

Homosexuality is one of the more confusing issues we face as a culture. Most people don't fully understand the complexity of the matter. Like so many other difficult topics in our fast-food culture, the issue of homosexuality is often reduced to sound-bite–level analysis, typically divided into two camps: for and against. But like most things in life, it's not quite that simple. The truth is there are numerous viewpoints on homosexuality.

Some people see it as pure choice. (We'll call this the *moral* view.) Under the banner of *morality*, some people support and affirm homosexuality as a legitimate, chosen expression of human sexuality. Under the same banner, others see it as morally and biblically wrong.

Some people see homosexuality as a primarily scientific issue. (We'll call this the *biological* banner.*) One biological view, among several, says that it's an abnormality or deviance in human development. Another view argues that it's a difference but not a deviance.

A third view is the *psychological* perspective. Under this banner, some see homosexuality as a subcategory of sexual addiction; others see it as *paraphilial* (the psychological word for "false love"), akin to voyeurism, pedophilia, or fetishes.

The point is that, if you do a little research, it will not be hard to find credible, articulate, learned, compassionate, and sensible people who will argue sincerely from any one of these viewpoints, or still others.

Regardless of one's viewpoint on homosexuality, most people would agree that the statistical number of boys who grapple with this question is less than ten percent of the population (probably

---

* It's getting more and more difficult to deny that there are some biological influences to homosexuality. Some studies have put forward that there is a structural difference in the hypothalamus of the brain that influences sexual orientation. But there are also reputable studies that show there is a high degree of fluidity when it comes to sexuality. And it would be foolish for us to deny that psychological and emotional factors have some influence also. To what degree any of these contribute toward homosexuality, no one is sure, and we will have to wait and see. If your son is wrestling with this issue himself, know that in nearly every case this is not an issue of parenting.

closer to five percent), which is a minority, yes, but still a significant number of boys.

Typically, boys begin to have questions about their sexual orientation and how they will identify and express themselves sexually during the Wanderer stage. Some boys become aware of their lack of sexual attraction to girls, either with or without a sexual attraction to other males. Some boys go through a stage of sexual experimentation with other boys during adolescence, and some will identify themselves as "gay."

Tragically, adolescent boys who struggle with this issue are often exiled by their peers and condemned by their communities. It's likely that a boy in this situation will experience a sense of not fitting in. He will potentially struggle with depression, anxiety, substance abuse, or addiction as he tries to cope with the humiliation and fear that commonly accompany same-sex attraction or gender confusion. To make matters worse, teachers, mentors, and church leaders—out of their own fear and lack of understanding—often abandon these boys emotionally and spiritually.

With such a dire threat of isolation and condemnation hanging over his head, a boy struggling with homosexuality desperately needs guidance and care. It's essential that he receive help from a professional counselor who understands him and his parents, and who can guide them along the way.

For a number of parents, few things would be harder to hear from their son than, "I think I might be gay." But if a boy is courageous enough to come to his parents about this issue, or if they discover it in some other way, the parents must never withhold or withdraw affection, love, or resources from their son—no matter the parents' own fear or shame.

It's important that the boy be given a support system that is on his side and *for* him (counselors, spiritual mentors, coaches, family members). He needs to be directed toward one or two activities that he enjoys and excels in. This type of loving environment is essential in reinforcing his fundamental worth and in helping him construct a positive self-concept.

No matter what you believe about homosexuality (its causes and consequences), as far as the boy is concerned, if he expresses questions about his sexual identity, he needs as much support and love as he can possibly get. If the culture at large has trouble coming to grips with this issue, you can imagine how difficult it is for an adolescent boy to navigate his way in these murky waters.

ADD AND ADHD

If a boy is having a hard time at home or at school, his parents may worry that he has attention deficit disorder (ADD) or attention deficit hyperactivity disorder (ADHD). However, it's also possible, and probably more likely, that he's struggling with a learning disability, or maybe depression, anxiety, another psychological issue, or some family or school tension. Despite how often it seems we hear about ADD and ADHD, they are extremely uncommon disorders that affect only a small percentage of the population. (Estimates vary between 3 and 11 percent.) But because overdiagnosis and overmedication are common, a number of families have significant concerns when attention deficit shows up on the radar.

How do you know if a boy has ADD or ADHD? A boy *might* have ADD/ADHD if he has a majority of these symptoms:

- He has trouble paying attention and becomes easily distracted.
- You notice that he makes careless mistakes.
- When he is spoken to directly, he doesn't seem to hear.
- He struggles with following instructions.
- It is clear that he has trouble planning, organizing, and following through on assignments or activities.
- He avoids certain tasks or chores (or does them begrudgingly)—especially the ones requiring sustained mental focus.
- He is forgetful, or he frequently misplaces the things he needs for tasks or activities (homework assignments, books, etc.).
- When he is someplace where he has to sit still (such as in a restaurant, at church, or in school) he squirms in his chair or fidgets, gets up, runs around, or climbs.

- He acts like he is the Energizer bunny and can't stop moving.
- He seems to talk incessantly and to blurt out answers before questions have been completed (or he interrupts or intrudes on others' conversations and can't wait his turn).

A boy with a majority of these symptoms *might* have ADD/ADHD—or he might just be a boy. Many, many, many boys are diagnosed with attention deficit disorders they don't have. ADD and ADHD are real, and sadly there are many boys who would be helped greatly in their ability to manage daily life if they were treated for this significant brain malady, but not every active, mistake-prone, rowdy, squirrelly boy has ADD.

Making an accurate diagnosis, selecting proper treatment options, and deciding when to begin treatment are some of the greatest challenges in treating children. In determining whether a boy has ADD or ADHD, his parents and doctor must consider the following factors:

- Is he exhibiting normal, age-related development? (For instance, it's normal for a five-year-old boy not to sit still in church or in a restaurant.)
- What are realistic expectations of a boy's ability to pay attention, control his restlessness, and manage his impulses?
- Are the symptoms severe enough to impair the boy's normal life (and don't just make a parent's life or teacher's job difficult)?
- Are the symptoms frequent enough that they show up significantly in all areas, such as home, school, scouts, sports, etc.? A boy can't be ADD at school and not at soccer practice or fishing with his grandpa.

So what is ADD or ADHD?

We have to answer that question on two levels. The first level is diagnostically. The diagnosis of ADD and ADHD results from a cluster of specific, unwanted behavioral symptoms that co-occur with enough frequency and intensity to be deemed clinically significant. In this way, ADD and ADHD diagnoses are largely subjective and can only be made by a trained and licensed mental–health care provider— preferably a pediatric psychiatrist or child psychologist. (And be cautious of anyone who tries to diagnosis a boy who is not yet through kindergarten with ADD or ADHD. There is limited information supporting the validity of the diagnosis among preschool children.)

The second way to understand ADD and ADHD is as a medical brain dysfunction. As science teaches us more and more about the brain, we are learning that ADD and ADHD are actually medical brain disorders that have to do with the brain's neurotransmitters (the system that transfers information along the pathways of the brain and tells the body what to do). Research now suggests that ADD and ADHD are likely rooted in a problem with how the brain processes and holds on to information. The good news is that we are very close to being able to diagnose ADD and ADHD at the source with brain imaging technology instead of parsing symptoms. (In fact, many physicians won't diagnose ADD or ADHD without a brain scan.)

Here's the long and the short of it: If your boy has most of the symptoms listed above much of the time, you should arrange for him to visit a psychiatrist or psychologist.

FIVE WAYS TO HELP BOYS WITH ADD

1. *Set the right expectations at the right level.* Accept the fact that no boy is perfect. Realize that ADD or ADHD is not the end of the world. Boys with this disorder need parents who will see them as they are (limited in some ways and gifted in others). Parents need not hold on to Pollyanna ideals, but neither do they need to carry around resentment and pessimism. Every boy needs to feel accepted and supported for who he is. This is especially true for a boy with ADD. He needs to feel that his parents, teachers, coaches, and mentors have confidence in who he is.

2. *Provide more than medicine.* Certainly, many boys diagnosed with ADD or ADHD need medication to function well—but medicine is not the only thing that can make a big difference. Here are some other things he needs:
   - **Loving authority.** A boy's behavior is affected more by how we nurture his nature than by anything else. Boys with ADD need a supportive, loving, and consistent structure from those who have authority in their lives.
   - **Good diet.** We all need to watch what we eat, and boys with ADD need to steer clear of the types of foods that drive unwanted behavior, such as caffeine, sugar, and excessive carbohydrates.
   - **Plenty of rest.** One of the major contributors to ADD-like behavior is lack of sleep. Good sleep is food for the brain; without it, boys with ADD will really struggle.
   - **Daily exercise.** Exercise provides so many benefits for boys in general, and especially for boys with ADD. Having plenty of opportunities to move and exert themselves is essential for boys living with ADD.

3. *Discipline toward character.* For boys with ADD, it is easy to ignore their hearts while focusing on correcting their behavior. Let's face it, sometimes you just want a boy to "sit down and shut up." Though loving discipline alone won't cure ADD, without it a boy has little hope of succeeding in his childhood. A lot of people interchange the terms *discipline* and *punishment*, but the two concepts are very different. *Punishment* relies mostly on fear and shame to force the will of a child into an outcome. *Discipline* is focused on teaching and has a variety of characteristics, such as the following:

- **Curiosity** about the boy and the behavior in question. ("John, I noticed that you didn't put your dinner plate in the dishwasher after dinner.")
- **Explanations** of how the boy misbehaved. ("It's really helpful to the whole family when we each take responsibility for our own messes.")
- **Suggestions** for how the boy could do it differently the next time—because there will be a next time. ("How about next time, when you get up to leave the table, you take your plate with you.")
- **Logical consequences** that bring a measure of loss into the boy's life. ("Since you didn't take your dinner plate to the kitchen, you don't get to have dessert tonight.")
- **Redirection** of the boy's energy toward acceptable behavior. ("Instead of watching TV right now, why don't we go for a walk?")
- **Positive feedback** when the boy does something well. Especially with ADD boys, by rewarding positive behavior we help foster feelings of success and steer their motivation toward doing the right thing. ("I noticed how you put your shoes away when you came home from school. Great job!")

Punishment has its place, but only when a boy shows little effort or willingness to change within a framework of discipline. For example, punishment is warranted if a boy continues to tease or pick on another child despite being repeatedly instructed toward some other behavior. When a boy is being openly defiant, punishment is warranted. But we must be careful not to punish a child for behavior he is unable to control. When an ADD child fails to follow the rules or follow a command because he was distracted, he needs to be reminded, not punished. He needs logical consequences (at worst), not reprimands.

4. *Keep an eye on the horizon.* Boys with ADD need the adults in their lives to anticipate potentially difficult situations for them. For example, if you are taking a boy with ADD to church, it's probably a good idea to bring a bag of comics or a drawing pad, and to sit near the back of the sanctuary. Formulating a plan before you head into problematic environments will save everybody involved a lot of heartache. It also helps to talk with a boy before heading into a situation like this, letting him know what challenges he may face and some ways to navigate those. It's also good to let him know what will happen if he doesn't exhibit the appropriate behavior.

5. *Be consistent.* ADD kids must have consistency. A sudden change in the routine, or an interruption in the rhythm of things, can throw them for a loop. For boys in this category, it's best if the adults in their lives have as much of a routine as possible and set rules and consequences and stick to them. This means that parents of ADD boys must be on the same page with each other. When mom and dad present a united front, a boy knows exactly what to expect.

BRAVADO AND DEPRESSION

We feed boys all kinds of *cultural messages* about the emotional lives of men. In the movies, we've been doing this for decades. At one time, John Wayne was the standard; more recently, Keanu Reeves. In both cases, the picture is of stoic, detached men whose emotional repertoire ranges from anger to aggression, with nothing in between. These guys are also all about bravado. It's sort of a "kick butt and take names" mentality to living. These iconic figures shape the way our boys see masculinity and how it should look. Every time boys flip on the TV or go to the movies, these images are reinforced.

Boys are all about bravado. It's a way to hide their fear and insecurity. When a boy asks himself, "Am I enough?" or "Do I have what it takes?" and comes up with an answer of no, he'll sometimes go to great lengths to cover it up. It's one of the reasons we often miss the symptoms of depression in boys.

Our cultural definition of what depression looks like is based more on the symptoms that show up in adult women—symptoms such as extreme sadness, feeling lethargic and unmotivated, being teary and hopeless while feeling despair for periods of time. And though it's possible for depression to show itself that way in adolescent boys, it's more likely he'll express it through anger, volatility, and explosiveness. Depressed boys can become more risk seeking, dangerous, and destructive in their behavior.

Because anger is such a central and strong emotion in a lot of what boys do, we can easily misread, misinterpret, and mislabel depression in boys. We experience them as angry and destructive when they are actually sad and in pain. Anger is a derivative emotion. It always has its roots someplace else. Underneath the bravado, the bluster, and the fury is either fear, sadness, or disappointment, or some combination of the three.

If you see a consistent pattern of anger and aggression in your son that feels even slightly beyond the developmental norms we described in the first part of this book, consult with a therapist who specializes in boys and adolescent males. It may involve nothing more than some coaching on your part to aid your son's emotional development. However, he could be experiencing some early indicators of depression, and it would benefit him to explore this possibility early rather than waiting for it to evolve. Depression tends to exaggerate itself over time, and if depressive symptoms intersect with the biological and emotional shifts that occur during adolescence, the result can be an emotional tsunami that puts him at risk for self-harming behaviors.

EMOTIONAL LITERACY

Many boys are emotionally illiterate. They don't have the ability to read or understand their own emotions or those of others. In our book *"Yup." "Nope." "Maybe.": A Woman's Guide to Getting More out of the Language of Men*, we have an entire chapter devoted to this topic. Before we began writing that book, we sent out a mass e-mail to every woman we knew and asked each of them to send it out to every woman she knew, and so on. In return, we received an influx of questions that women have about men. There was no shortage of issues, but the one that showed up with the greatest frequency was some version of "why can't guys talk about what they feel?" We believe that a first response to this question centers on the issue of emotional literacy. And it's important to realize that literacy is a skill— one that boys simply don't have at the very beginning and one that many boys don't have strong ingredients for developing. But it *can* be learned. Unless there are pervasive developmental disorders at play, such as autism, Asperger's, or some kind of nonverbal learning disorder, boys can learn this skill. (Even *with* those disorders, which are extremely common among boys, certain parts of those skills can be acquired.)

We often encourage parents to imagine teaching emotional-literacy skills to boys in the same ways they might teach a child with dyslexia to read. Understand, first of all, that he will take to the process at a slower rate, and it will involve some studying on the part of the adult (which is what you're doing right now). You will also need to introduce, review, and reinforce these skills at a different pace than you would for an average to above-average reader. Furthermore, you can anticipate (as you would with a dyslexic reader) that he will be frustrated by your instruction as well as resist it. The bottom line is that it's just plain hard for him. He doesn't come by these skills naturally. Your instruction makes him want to bang his head on the table at times. He'd rather be playing video games or running wild outside. And his resistance will make you want to throw in the towel at times. But you've got to remember that having these skills is a foundational building block for his future. You may want to watch old episodes of *The Office* and pay particular attention to Dwight and Stanley. You'll get easily motivated.

As we've discussed throughout this book, you'll want to expose your boy to characters with a broad emotional range through books and film—men who have an emotional life. He'll also need to be exposed to men in his own world (dad, uncles, grandfathers, coaches, teachers, friends' dads, etc.) who have an ability to talk about how they feel.

He will also need experiences that require him to stretch emotionally and relationally in order to develop this skill set. Explore resources within your community that engage boys on this level and create opportunities for their emotional development.

BOYS AND SEXUAL ABUSE

There are no clear statistics of how many boys are sexually abused, but a pretty conservative estimate is that one out of six boys will be sexually abused before the age of sixteen. What does this statistic mean? It means that it's four-hundred times more likely that a boy will be sexually abused than have ADD.

Tragically, most boys will never tell anybody that they've been abused. Many experts believe that sexual abuse is the most under-reported form of child mistreatment, because of the secrecy and silence that often accompanies the abuse. As safe adults in the lives of boys, we can do the following to protect boys from abuse and to care for them if they have already been abused:

1. *Know what sexual abuse is.* Though there is no universal definition of child sexual abuse, the American Medical Association describes it like this: "A central characteristic of any abuse is the dominant position of an adult that allows him or her to force or coerce a child into sexual activity. Child sexual abuse may include fondling a child's genitals, masturbation, oral-genital contact, digital penetration, and vaginal and anal intercourse. Child sexual abuse is not solely restricted to physical contact; such abuse could include noncontact abuse, such as exposure, voyeurism, and child pornography."

2. *Know which boys are likely to be abused.* Boys of all races, cultures, or economic status are at "approximately equal risk for sexual victimization."

3. *Know who the abusers are.* Sexual abuse is far more likely to be perpetrated by someone a child knows (such as a parent, sibling, relative, babysitter, mentor, coach, pastor, or friend of the family) than by a stranger. Sometimes older children abuse younger children. Abusers can be women or men. Gay

or straight. Young or old. If you think you can spot an abuser, you're wrong. Abusers don't want to get caught, so they often tell the boy to keep the abuse a secret. They will even threaten him so he will keep the secret. When this happens, a boy feels trapped. Abusers may offer a boy presents, privileges, or other favors to try to get him to agree to the abuse. In this way, an abuser can maintain power over a boy and make the victim think the abuse was his own fault.

4. *Know what to do to prevent abuse.* Because the typical parental advice—"Don't talk to strangers"—doesn't apply to most cases of abuse, boys need to be taught appropriate boundaries. For example, they need to be free to express affection on their own terms. Don't make them hug and kiss relatives if they don't want to. Also, boys need to be confidently aware of their privacy regarding their own bodies. They need to know specifically that no one should touch the "private" parts of their body. They need to know that sexual advances from adults are wrong and against the law. Give your boys the self-confidence and inner strength they need to assert themselves against any adult who attempts to abuse them. Teach them to say no. Explain the importance of reporting abuse to you or another trusted adult. Parents need to have strong communication with their sons. Boys need to be encouraged to ask questions and talk about their experiences. This includes parents making an effort to know their son's friends and their families.

5. *Know the signs of sexual abuse.* Though there is no sure way to tell if a boy has been sexually abused, there are some things to look out for. Some boys show sharp changes in behavior or emotional symptoms. "Children who have been, or are being, abused will often be very confused and uncertain about what to do and who to tell. Some children may not realize what has been done to them is abuse." Any of the following may be a sign of sexual abuse:

- Brings up the subject of sexual abuse or drops hints, possibly testing your reaction
- Mentions that an adult has asked him or her to keep a secret
- Is secretive about relationships with older children or adults
- Shows sexually explicit behavior or uses sexual language inappropriate for his age
- Seems very withdrawn or depressed for no obvious reason
- Has physical complaints with no obvious explanation—for example, soreness or redness in the genital area
- Starts bed-wetting or has very disturbed sleep
- Refuses to go to school
- Behaves very aggressively
- Self-harms
- Becomes reluctant to be with particular adults, or to go to activities he or she previously enjoyed
- Seems very clingy
- Tries to avoid being left alone with an adult in the family
- Shows [new] fear of an adult or older child

6. *Know what to do if a boy you know tells you about abuse.*

- Believe him. It's rare that a child will lie about abuse.
- Don't freak out. If you are hysterical or become overly emotional in front of him, he will likely not talk to you.
- Let him talk. Listen carefully. Encourage him to talk about it with you, but don't force him to go into details if he doesn't want to. Don't pressure or prompt him by asking questions. Allow him to speak at his own pace.
- If a boy discloses abuse, make written notes unless you think that note taking will stop him from talking. In that case, write down what was said immediately after the

conversation. Make it clear that the abuser is the one to blame, and that the abuse is not the boy's fault.

- Protect and praise him. Emphasize that he's done the right thing by telling you. Reassure him that telling you was the best thing to do. Tell him he is safe now.
- Get professional help to deal with the situation. Call the police, talk to a pediatrician, or call the local child protective services department in your area.
- Get support for yourself. Talk to a trusted friend or relative about your own feelings, or get professional support to help you deal with your feelings if you need to.

7. *Know what to do if you think a boy is being abused.* If you have any concerns about a boy's safety, it's better to trust your instincts and take action.

- Provide an opportunity for the child to speak privately with you.
- Say in a calm, matter-of-fact manner something like this:
- "Is there something you want to tell me?"
- "Are you having a problem and need help?"
- "When something feels bad inside, it's okay to talk about it."

Don't promise the boy that you will keep his secrets; only promise that you will help him. It is better to call the police than not. If a boy is in danger, contact the police immediately. Many states require by law that certain professionals—such as school officials, counselors, doctors, dentists, police officers, day-care workers—report suspected child abuse. If you have questions, talk with one of these people.

Sources: American Psychological Association, "Understanding Child Sexual Abuse," http://www.apa .org/releases/sexabuse.
BBC, "Your Kids—Keeping Them Safe: Sexual Abuse," http://www.bbc.co.uk/parenting/your_kids/ safety_sexual.shtml.

SINGLE MOMS

Being a single mother of boys (or a married mom with a husband who isn't well invested in parenting) can be a journey long on challenge and short on reward. It doesn't have to be that way. It's important that you attend well to some unique circumstances and challenges that exist within your relationship with your son.

1. *Involve other men.* A boy needs the voice and presence of men in order to be ushered fully into manhood. Pull in any available family members who are appropriate role models and willing to be invested in your son's life (e.g., a grandfather, uncle, or college-age or young-adult cousin). Also solicit the help of scout leaders, coaches, male teachers, fathers of his friends, pastors, etc. Ask that they make a particular commitment to your son that involves being in relationship with him, showing him how to do a number of male-oriented tasks (see our book *How to Hit a Curveball, Grill the Perfect Steak, and Become a Real Man: Learning What Our Fathers Never Taught Us*), and talking with him about his physical, emotional, relational, and spiritual development.

2. *Anticipate confusion as he pulls away from you.* Allowing your son to separate out from you may feel disturbing and possibly even unrealistic. In an ideal world, he would begin to pull away from you and move toward his dad. If his dad isn't in the picture, or isn't invested in parenting, your son will feel the same urge to pull away from you but will have a sense of floating in the middle of nowhere with nothing and no one to move toward. It's important that you recognize that this is happening and involve other men to meet his needs.

3. *Allow him to gravitate toward men.* It's natural for a boy to need and crave male attention. If his father is not a man

you can respect, or someone who has hurt you in the past, it can be difficult to believe he's safe enough for your son to gravitate toward. But keep your own emotions in check. Men who make lousy husbands are capable of being great fathers. Allow your son to have his own journey with his dad. The more you stand in the way of that relationship, the more your son may resent you, both now and later.

4. *Don't coddle him.* Coddling doesn't help his masculine journey. It's normal for a mom to ache for her son when he's lacking something he so desperately needs. Often, moms will overcompensate for their boys because they feel sorry for them in ways that end up being a disservice to them down the road. It's okay (and even good) for you to acknowledge this loss and to state what you want for him, but don't placate him or let him off the hook with daily responsibilities and expectations. He still needs to be parented.

5. *Broaden your own perspective.* We'd highly recommend reading *To Own a Dragon: Reflections on Growing Up without a Father*, by Donald Miller and John MacMurray. The authors supply great insights (and hilarious stories) about a boy's journey while being raised by a single mom.

ACKNOWLEDGMENTS

We approached *Wild Things* with the hearts of teachers—with an eye turned toward helping parents, educators, coaches, mentors, youth workers, and anyone who has given themselves to the great and wonderful art of nurturing boys on their dangerous journey. Along the way, we became students who gleaned much from the wise men on whom we have leaned so heavily: Michael Gurian, William Pollack, Dan Kindlon, Michael Thompson, Richard Rohr, and John Eldredge—great teachers and writers all.

Between the two of us we have five sons (Stephen has three and David has two), and we wrote *Wild Things* with our boys in mind—trying to prepare a path for them to walk toward manhood. It's a rare sentence that in some way doesn't come from our passion for these great boys.

Similarly, we want to recognize the faithfulness of our wives, Heather and Connie, for facilitating the writing of this book. If *Wild Things* helps anyone, they get much of the credit, because their sacrifice was far greater than ours. We are also grateful for our former agent, Greg Daniel. Thank you for championing this project and running interference on our behalf. Thanks also to David Huffman, our current agent and manager. Thank you for casting a large vision on our behalf and then helping us figure out how it works day in and day out.

We get to work with quite possibly the best publishing house anywhere—Tyndale House Publishers. This is a group of people whose commitment to being lights in a dim world is inspirational. We want to thank the Beers Group at Tyndale for their continued support, effort, and encouragement, especially Ron Beers, Becky Nesbitt, Carol Traver, Kathy McClelland, Dave Lindstedt, and Vicky Lynch.

Thanks again to the great folks at Daystar Counseling Ministries, and for the many families who have shared their boys with us. Their voices are present throughout the chapters of this book, and it has been an honor to walk with each one.

Most importantly, we thank our heavenly Father. We are continually awed and grateful that he shows himself through us, and to us, as we write, speak, and sit with boys and men in our counseling practices.

RECOMMENDED RESOURCES

Ty Burr, *The Best Old Movies for Families: A Guide to Watching Together* (Anchor, 2007).

John Eldredge, *The Way of the Wild Heart: A Map for the Masculine Journey* (Thomas Nelson, 2006).

John Eldredge, *Wild at Heart: Discovering the Secret of a Man's Soul* (Thomas Nelson, 2001).

Michael Gurian, *Boys & Girls Learn Differently! A Guide for Teachers and Parents* (Jossey-Bass, 2001).

Michael Gurian, *A Fine Young Man: What Parents, Mentors, and Educators Can Do to Shape Adolescent Boys into Exceptional Men* (Tarcher/Putnam, 1998).

Michael Gurian, *The Good Son: Shaping the Moral Development of Our Boys and Young Men* (Tarcher/Putnam, 1999).

Michael Gurian, *The Wonder of Boys: What Parents, Mentors, and Educators Can Do to Shape Boys into Exceptional Men* (Tarcher/Putnam, 1996).

Michael Gurian and Kathy Stevens, *The Minds of Boys: Saving Our Sons from Falling Behind in School and Life* (Jossey-Bass, 2007).

Conn Iggulden and Hal Iggulden, *The Dangerous Book for Boys* (Collins, 2007).

Dan Kindlon and Michael Thompson, *Raising Cain: Protecting the Emotional Life of Boys* (Ballantine, 1999).

Robert Lewis, *Raising a Modern-Day Knight: A Father's Role in Guiding His Son to Authentic Manhood* (Tyndale, 2007, revised edition).

Richard Louv, *Last Child in the Woods: Saving Our Children from Nature-Deficit Disorder* (Algonquin, 2005).

Jane Nelsen, Cheryl Erwin, and Roslyn Ann Duffy, *Positive Discipline for Preschoolers*, third edition (Three Rivers, 2007).

William Pollack, *Real Boys: Rescuing Our Sons from the Myths of Boyhood* (Henry Holt, 1998).

Richard Rohr, *Adam's Return: The Five Promises of Male Initiation* (Crossroad, 2004).

Maurice Sendak, *Where the Wild Things Are* (HarperCollins, 1964).

NOTES

Introduction: "Wild Thing!"

1. Plato, *Laws* (Whitefish, MT: Kessinger Publishing, 2004), 370.

2. G. K. Chesterton, *The Autobiography of G. K. Chesterton* (San Francisco: Ignatius, 2006), 62.

3. Because God chose to illuminate himself through his relationship with his son, Jesus, we believe there is spiritual significance unique to sons, and a boy's relationship with his parents, and what that relationship can teach us about our relationship with our Father God. This is not to say that daughters are in any way less significant. The biblical imagery is simply different.

4. *Encarta World English Dictionary*, CD-ROM.

5. Aside from the anecdotes about our own children and ourselves, none of the names we use in the stories are real. To further guard the privacy of the individuals involved, certain identifying details have also been changed. Additionally, some of the anecdotes are based on composites of several different people. The basic facts and applications, however, are all true.

6. Daystar is a nonprofit counseling ministry established in 1985 to serve the needs of children, adolescents, young adults, and families. Learn more at www.daystarcounselingministries.org.

Part 1: The Way of a Boy

1. John Eldredge, *The Way of the Wild Heart: A Map for the Masculine Journey* (Nashville: Nelson, 2006), 11.

Chapter 1: The Explorer

1. Garrison Keillor, *The Book of Guys: Stories* (New York: Penguin, 1993), 12.

2. If you don't remember from high school health class, a blastocyst is the thin-walled, hollow structure in the earliest stages of the embryo. The outer layer gives rise to the

placenta and other supporting tissues within the uterus, while the inner cells are the basis of the developing fetus.

3. Marianne J. Legato, ed., *Principles of Gender-Specific Medicine* (San Diego: Elsevier, 2004), 1.

4. Ibid., 5.

5. Ibid., 8.

6. Barbara Curtis, "The Truth about Boys (and Girls)," *Christian Parenting Today,* January/February 2001, 26.

7. Anne Moir and David Jessel, *Brain Sex: The Real Difference between Men and Women* (New York: Delta, 1991), 55.

8. Ibid., 56.

9. Ibid., 58.

Chapter 2: The Lover

1. Arnold Gesell and others, *The Child from Five to Ten* (New York: HarperCollins, 1977).

2. Michael Gurian, *The Good Son: Shaping the Moral Development of Our Boys and Young Men* (New York: Tarcher/Putnam, 1999), 126.

3. Andrés Martin, Fred R. Volkmar, and Melvin Lewis, *Lewis's Child and Adolescent Psychiatry: A Comprehensive Textbook* (New York: Lippincott, 2007), 271.

4. Piaget called this "objective morality" or "moral realism." To learn more, see Jean Piaget and Barbel Inhelder, *The Psychology of the Child* (1969; repr., New York: Basic, 2000).

5. Gurian, *The Good Son*, 127.

6. Eleanor E. Maccoby, *The Two Sexes: Growing Up Apart, Coming Together* (Cambridge, MA: Harvard University, 1999), 39.

7. Ibid., 39–40.

8. Eileen Bailey, "Successful People with ADHD," http://www.healthcentral.com/adhd/understanding-adhd-161681-5.html.

9. Ibid.

10. Dan Kindlon and Michael Thompson, *Raising Cain: Protecting the Emotional Life of Boys* (New York: Ballantine, 1999), 49.

11. Gurian, *The Good Son*, 148.

12. Roberto Suro, "Holding Back to Get Ahead," *New York Times,* January 5, 1992, http://query.nytimes.com/gst/fullpage.html?res=9E0CE7DA133BF936A35752C0 A964958260.

13. Jane Nelsen, Cheryl Erwin, and Roslyn Duffy, *Positive Discipline for Preschoolers,* 3rd ed. (New York: Three Rivers, 2007), 15.

14. Gurian, *The Good Son,* 132. Gurian recommends nine affirmations to every one critique.

15. Ibid., 131–132.

Chapter 3: The Individual

1. Kindlon and Thompson, *Raising Cain,* 142.

2. Eric is like hundreds of boys I have encountered who have never had anyone dialogue openly with them about the changes that will take place as they move into stage three of their development. Although Eric had heard of wet dreams, he had absolutely no idea what they were. Instead, when his body was doing exactly what it was designed to do, he was paralyzed with fear that he was dying. We are strong advocates of having an ongoing and open dialogue with boys about their bodies, starting as early as stage one (Explorers). Yes, stage one! If you have a stage-three son and haven't started yet, you're not too late, but you need to play catch-up. We recommend a series of books by Stan and Brenna Jones that describe in words (and pictures) what happens at each stage of a boy's life. The Joneses put everything in a spiritual context and explain God's design for man and woman. The Joneses' books include *How and When to Tell Your Kids about Sex, The Story of Me, Facing the Facts,* and *What's the Big Deal?*

3. Michael Gurian, *The Wonder of Boys: What Parents, Mentors and Educators Can Do to Shape Boys into Exceptional Men* (New York: Tarcher/Putnam, 1997), 10.

4. Office of Applied Studies, Substance Abuse and Mental Health Services Administration (**SAMHSA**), *The NSDUH Report* (October 22, 2004), http://www.oas.samhsa. gov/2k4/ageDependence/ageDependence.htm.

5. Here are some recommendations for boys to read. (Read through them yourself first and then with your son.)

Stan and Brenna Jones, *Facing the Facts: The Truth about Sex and You* (Colorado Springs: NavPress, 2007).

Stan and Brenna Jones, *What's the Big Deal?: Why God Cares about Sex* (Colorado Springs: NavPress, 2007).

Here are some resources for you as a parent or caregiver to read:

Mark Laaser, *Talking to Your Kids about Sex: How to Have a Lifetime of Age-Appropriate Conversations with Your Children about Healthy Sexuality* (Colorado Springs: WaterBrook, 1999).

Stan and Brenna Jones, *How and When to Tell Your Kids about Sex: A Lifelong Approach to Shaping Your Child's Sexual Character*, rev. ed. (Colorado Springs: NavPress, 2007).

Dennis and Barbara Rainey, *Passport to Purity* (FamilyLife, 1999).

6. William Pollack, *Real Boys: Rescuing Our Sons from the Myths of Boyhood* (New York: Henry Holt, 1999), 56.

7. Ibid., 57.

8. Eldredge, *The Way of the Wild Heart*, 102.

Chapter 4: The Wanderer

1. Dan B. Allender, *How Children Raise Parents: The Art of Listening to Your Family* (Colorado Springs: WaterBrook, 2003), 21.

2. Michael Gurian, *A Fine Young Man* (New York: Tarcher/Putnam, 1998), 125.

3. http://xxxchurch.com/gethelp/parents/intro.html

4. Gurian, *The Good Son*, 305. Gurian points out that, during this time, if a boy has experienced "significant abuse or other trauma before puberty, he may very well manifest the trauma stress now."

5. Anne Lamott, *Plan B: Further Thoughts on Faith* (New York: Riverhead, 2006), 96.

6. Ibid., 197–198.

7. U.S. Centers for Disease Control and Prevention, "Teenagers in the United States: Sexual Activity, Contraceptive Use, and Childbearing, 2002. A Fact Sheet for Series 23, Number 24," www.cdc.gov/NCHS/data/series/sr_23/sr23_024FactSheet.pdf.

Chapter 5: The Warrior

1. Homer Hickam, *Rocket Boys* (New York: Random House, 1998).

2. Ibid., 1.

3. Gurian, *A Fine Young Man*, 155.

4. John Eldredge speaks to this paradigm extensively in his book *The Way of the Wild Heart*, 193–195.

5. *L'Abri* is a French word that means "shelter." The first L'Abri community was founded in Switzerland in 1955 by Dr. Francis Schaeffer and his wife, Edith. Dr. Schaeffer was a Christian theologian and philosopher who also authored a number of books on theology, philosophy, general culture, and the arts. The L'Abri communities are study centers in Europe, Asia, and America, where individuals have the opportunity

to seek answers to honest questions about God and the significance of human life. L'Abri believes that Christianity speaks to all aspects of life. You can learn more at www.labri.org.

6. Outward Bound is a nonprofit educational organization with five core programs that change lives, build teams, and transform schools. They deliver adventure in the wilderness, urban centers, workrooms, and classrooms to help mostly young adults achieve their possibilities and to inspire them to serve others and the world around them. Visit their Web site to find out more: www.outwardbound.org.

7. AmeriCorps is an opportunity to make a big difference in your life and in the lives of those around you, by helping others and meeting critical needs in the community. Each year, AmeriCorps offers 75,000 opportunities for adults of all ages and backgrounds to serve through a network of partnerships with local and national nonprofit groups. Find out more at www.americorps.org.

8. Tracing its roots to the 1960s, the Peace Corps is a federal agency that sends volunteers to developing countries to work on issues ranging from AIDS education to information technology and environmental preservation. For more information, visit www.peacecorps.gov.

9. See Luke 15:11-32.

10. Gurian, *The Good Son*, 161–163.

Chapter 6: A Boy's Brain

1. Much of this research comes from the work by Ruben C. Gur, Ph.D., director of the brain behavior program at the University of Pennsylvania. For more in-depth reading on his studies, check out his Web page and his list of published articles: www.med.upenn.edu/bbl/staff/ruben_gur.shtml.

2. Raul G. Paredes and Michael J. Baum, *Annual Review of Sex Research* VIII (1997).

3. Susan C. Levine and others, "Early Sex Differences in Spatial Skill," *Developmental Psychology* 35, no. 4 (1999): 940–949.

4. Simon Baron-Cohen, *The Essential Difference: The Truth about the Male and Female Brain* (New York: Basic, 2003), 1.

5. A. Nehlig, J. L. Daval, and G. Debry, "Caffeine and the central nervous system: mechanisms of action, biochemical and psychostimulant effects," *Brain Research Reviews* 17 (May–August 1992): 139–170.

6. R. N. Elkins, J. L. Rapoport, and T. P. Zahn, "Acute effects of caffeine in normal prepubertal boys," *American Journal of Psychiatry* 138 (February 1981): 178–183; and J. L. Rapoport, M. Jensvold, and R. Elkins, "Behavioral and cognitive effects of caffeine in boys and adult males," *Journal of Nervous and Mental Disease* 169 (November 1981): 726–732.

7. Markus Dworak and others, "Impact of singular excessive computer game and television exposure on sleep patterns and memory performance of school-aged children," *Pediatrics* 120, no. 5 (2007): 978–985.

8. Ronald D. Chervin and others, "Inattention, Hyperactivity, and Symptoms of Sleep-Disordered Breathing," *Pediatrics* 109, no. 3 (2002): 449–456.

9. Russell A. Barkley, *Attention-Deficit Hyperactivity Disorder: A Handbook for Diagnosis and Treatment* (New York: Guilford, 1990).

10. Alan J. Zametkin and Monique Ernst, "Problems in the management of attention-deficit-hyperactivity disorder," *New England Journal of Medicine* 340 (January 1999): 40–46; Ronald D. Chervin, "Attention-deficit–hyperactivity disorder" [letter], *New England Journal of Medicine* 340 (January 1999): 1766.

Chapter 7: Different Learning Styles

1. American Academy of Pediatrics, "New AAP Report Stresses Play for Healthy Development," American Academy of Pediatrics, http://www.aap.org/pressroom/play-public.htm. The article cited in the AAP report, "The Importance of Play in Promoting Healthy Child Development and Maintaining Strong Parent-Child Bonds" by Kenneth R. Ginsburg, can be read online at http://www.aap.org/pressroom/playFINAL.pdf.

2. Ginsburg, "Importance of Play."

3. Frances A. Campbell and Craig T. Ramey, "Effects of early intervention on intellectual and academic achievement: A follow-up study of children from low-income families," *Child Development* 65, no. 2 (1994): 684–689.

4. "Pulling sticks" is a behavior-modification game in which students are given five sticks at the beginning of the week with the goal to still have five sticks at the end of the week. Students can lose sticks (hence the name "pulling sticks") for not following expectations or for other disapproved behavior, but they can also earn them back the next day. Kids who have five sticks at the end of the week earn a reward, such as Friday Fun (in which they can choose candy or a prize from a treasure box or time for drawing or working on the computer). An even more effective form of "sticks" is to have the kids start with no sticks and earn sticks for good behavior (following directions, staying on task, behaving in the hallway, being good for a substitute, etc.). They have to earn five sticks to have Friday Fun. In this version of the game, they can still lose sticks, but they get more positive attention from the teacher.

5. Committee on the Support for the Thinking Spatially, *Learning to Think Spatially* (Washington, D.C.: National Academies, 2006).

6. These ideas are adapted from "Are you a creator?" by Linda Kreger Silverman in *Gifted Education Communicator* 34, no. 1 (2003): 12–13. See also "Are You a Creator? An Essay for Kids!" by Linda Kreger Silverman, which can be read online at http://

www.visualspatial.com/Articles/creator.pdf. For more information on visual-spatial learning, see the Visual-Spatial Resource Web site: http://www.visualspatial.org.

7. Cyril Houle, *Continuing Learning in the Professions* (San Francisco: Jossey-Bass, 1980), 221.

Chapter 8: "Sit Still! Pay Attention!"

1. Martha J. Countinho and Donald P. Oswald, "State variation in gender disproportional in special education: Finding and recommendations," *Remedial and Special Education* 26, no. 1 (2005): 7–15.

2. Nathlie A. Badian, "Reading disability defined as a discrepancy between listening and reading comprehension: A longitudinal study of stability, gender differences, and prevalence," *Journal of Learning Disabilities* 32, no. 2 (1999): 138–148.

3. It's also interesting that females account for the majority of undergraduate enrollment and the majority of bachelor's and master's degree recipients.

4. Peg Tyre, "The Trouble With Boys," *Newsweek*, January 30, 2006, http://www.newsweek.com/id/47522.

5. First Lady Laura Bush led the Helping America's Youth initiative to get adults involved in the lives of students. This was a nationwide effort to raise awareness about the challenges facing youth in America, particularly at-risk boys, and to motivate caring adults to connect with youth in three key areas: family, school, and community. See http://www.helpingamericasyouth.gov/facts.cfm.

6. Dr. Sheppard Kellam, quoted in Gurian, *The Good Son*, 148.

7. Phil Brennan, "Pupils at Single-Sex Schools Excel, Research Shows," *NewsMax.com*, May 3, 2002, http://archive.newsmax.com/archives/articles/2002/5/2/155112.shtml.

8. Some of these ideas are adapted from Michael Gurian and Kathy Stevens, *The Minds of Boys: Saving Our Sons from Falling Behind in School and Life* (San Francisco: Jossey-Bass, 2005).

9. Adapted from Carolyn Y. Johnson, "Parents get look at teens' brains," *The Boston Globe*, November 10, 2005, http://www.boston.com/news/local/articles/2005/11/10/parents_get_look_at_teens_brains.

Chapter 9: Deficits and Disappointments

1. Jim Fay, "Three Types of Parents," Love and Logic Institute, Inc., http://www.loveandlogic.com/pages/threetypes.html.

2. Shannon Colavecchio-Van Sickler, "Mommy, tell my professor he's not nice!: (Over)involved baby boomer parents—and cell phones—redefine adulthood,"

St. Petersburg Times, June 19, 2006, http://www.sptimes.com/2006/06/19/State/
Mommy__tell_my_profes.shtml.

3. *Remember the Titans*, DVD, written by Gregory Allen Howard (Walt Disney Pictures, 2000).

4. Terrence Real, *I Don't Want to Talk about It: Overcoming the Secret Legacy of Male Depression* (New York: Simon & Schuster, 2000).

Part 3: The Heart of a Boy

1. It's also helpful to think of a boy's journey toward being a man in terms of the Israelites' Exodus from Egypt.

2. Henry David Thoreau, *Walden* (Stilwell, KS: Digireads Publishing, 2005), 7.

3. This idea of "heart" was adapted from the work of Dr. Chip Dodd, and his book *The Voice of the Heart: A Call to Full Living* (Sage Hill, 2001).

Chapter 10: Noble Creatures: Nurturing a Boy's Heart

1. "Although the rhyme cannot be absolutely verified as Southey's, it is generally thought to be by him and dated at about 1820." Excerpted from Gloria T. Delamar, *Mother Goose: From Nursery to Literature* (Lincoln, NE: iUniverse, 2001), 177.

2. H. W. F. Gesenius, *Gesenius' Hebrew-Chaldee Lexicon to the Old Testament* (Grand Rapids: Baker, 1979).

3. Ibid.

4. *kardia*, in *The NAS New Testament Greek Lexicon*, http://www.biblestudytools.net/Lexicons/Greek/grk.cgi?number=2588&version=nas

5. One of the most beautiful verses of the Bible speaks to the power of naming: "He who has an ear, let him hear what the Spirit says to the churches. To the one who conquers I will give some of the hidden manna, and I will give him a white stone, with a new name written on the stone that no one knows except the one who receives it" (Revelation 2:17, ESV). What is so beautiful is that God has a name for each of his children that is specific to each person and is secret between the person and God.

6. Institute for Propaganda Analysis, *Propaganda Analysis* (New York: Columbia University, 1938); cited in "Name Calling," Propaganda, http://www.propagandacritic.com/articles/ct.wg.name.html.

7. Stephen James and David Thomas, *How to Hit a Curveball, Grill the Perfect Steak, and Become a Real Man: Learning What Our Fathers Never Taught Us* (Carol Stream, IL: Tyndale, 2008), xiv–xv.

8. Erwin Raphael McManus, *Soul Cravings* (Nashville: Nelson, 2006), 3.

9. Full living has to occur within the framework of relationships. We're all relational beings made to experience life through the context of relationships. This part is a little heady but really quite important. We cannot be known outside of relationship. Philosopher Martin Buber called this "dialogical relationship." To describe it rather crudely, Buber said that we are always interacting in a relationship of sorts with either objects ("I/It," which he called monologues) or in conversation with other beings ("I/You," or dialogue). Dialogue is a shared, holistic relationship between two beings (either person/person or person/God.) Dialogue lacks structure and content. It just is what it is—being together. It's a concrete, authentic encounter without any qualification or objectification of one another. One of Buber's examples of this concept is a person and a cat. Neither can communicate but they can have an encounter. "I/It" monologues are almost the opposite of "I/You" dialogues. Unlike I/You relationships, in which two beings encounter each other, in I/It relationships the beings do not actually interact. Instead, the "I" confronts, qualifies, and justifies ideas or information to the other being in its presence, treating the other as an object. In this way, the "I/It" relationship is actually only a relationship with oneself. For further information, see Martin Buber, *I and Thou* (New York: Hesperides, 2006).

10. Adapted from Michael Arndt, *Little Miss Sunshine: The Shooting Script* (New York: Newmarket, 2006).

11. Kindlon and Thompson, *Raising Cain*, 241.

12. Ibid. For a great summary of some strategies for raising emotionally strong boys, see "PBS Parents Guide to . . . Understanding and Raising Boys," http://www.pbs.org/parents/raisingboys/emotion.html.

13. Ibid., 257.

14. Ibid., 249.

15. Ibid., 249–250.

16. Larry Crabb, Don Hudson, and Al Andrews, *The Silence of Adam: Becoming Men of Courage in a World of Chaos* (Grand Rapids: Zondervan, 1998), 91, 95.

17. Proverbs 22:6, NLT.

Chapter 11: A Boy and His Mother

1. Pollack, *Real Boys*, 81.

2. The Bible says it this way: "For this reason a man will leave his father and mother and be united to his wife, and they will become one flesh" (Genesis 2:24, NIV).

3. In *Real Boys*, William Pollack discusses a Rutgers University study that shows how mothers of young boys and young girls treat them differently in terms of soothing

negative emotions, and how these differences instigate a shame-based process that discounts the volatile emotions of boys. "In general, the researchers found, mothers were far less likely to mirror their infants' unhappy feelings; but when mothers were interacting with infant boys, the mothers were particularly resistant to recognizing their sons' negative emotional states." In fact, the mothers ignored their sons' unhappy emotions altogether (compared to mimicking their daughters' negative emotions 22 percent of the time). *Real Boys*, 41.

4. Pollack, *Real Boys*, 41.

Chapter 12: A Boy and His Father

1. U.S. Census Bureau, "Children's Living Arrangements and Characteristics: March 2002, P200-547, Table C8." (Washington, D.C.: GPO, 2003).

2. Kristin Harknett, "Children's Elevated Risk of Asthma in Unmarried Families: Underlying Structural and Behavioral Mechanisms" (working paper #2005-01-FF, Princeton, NJ: Center for Research on Child Well-being, 2005), 19–27.

3. "America's Children: Key National Indicators of Well-Being," Table Special 1, Washington, D.C.: Federal Interagency Forum on Child and Family Statistics, 1997.

4. National Center for Education Statistics (NCES), "Fathers' Involvement in Their Children's Schools," September 1997, http://nces.ed.gov/pubs98/fathers/. See also http://nces.ed.gov/Pressrelease/father.asp (accessed March 14, 2008).

5. This statistic is widely quoted on the Internet, and is most often attributed to the U.S. Department of Health and Human Services or the U.S. Bureau of the Census.

6. This statistic is widely quoted on the Internet, and is most often attributed to the U.S. Centers for Disease Control and Prevention.

7. Frank Pittman, "Fathers and Sons," *Psychology Today*, September/October 1993.

8. Ibid.

9. Ibid.

10. Ibid. Pittman points out that boys' being raised by women would not have been as detrimental if there were "uncles and cousins and grandfathers and older brothers around to model masculinity for boys." But when the status is that every family have its own home, "families trim themselves down to the size of a married couple and their children."

11. Ken Canfield, "Five Needs of Sons," National Center for Fathering, April 30, 2007, http://www.fathers.com/content/index.php?option=com_content&task=view&id=273& Itemid=63.

12. Ibid.

Chapter 13: Rituals, Ceremonies, and Rites of Passage

1. The Old Testament tells us that when the Israelites had defeated the Philistines, the prophet Samuel built a memorial to commemorate the victory. He named it Ebenezer, which means "stone of help." It was to remind everyone that God was Israel's help (see 1 Samuel 7:12). Similarly, Joshua set up stones as a memorial of what the Lord had done for Israel when God parted the Jordan River (see Joshua 4:20-24).

2. Richard Rohr, "Boys to Men: Rediscovering Rites of Passage for Our Time," John Mark Ministries, http://jmm.aaa.net.au/articles/5358.htm.

3. Ibid.

4. Henri J. M. Nouwen, *The Wounded Healer: Ministry in a Contemporary Society* (New York: Doubleday, 1979), 1, 4.

5. Rohr, "Boys to Men."

6. Ibid.

7. Ibid. Rohr writes, "Perhaps no world religion deals so directly and effectively with the issue of human suffering as healthy Christianity. The crucified and raised-up Jesus is an ultimate transformation-initiation symbol."

8. Ibid.

9. Ibid.

10. Arnold Van Gennep, *The Rites of Passage*, trans. Monika B. Vizedom and Garielle L. Caffee (Chicago: University of Chicago, 1960), 11.

11. Ibid., 18.

12. Brad Griffin, "Through the Zone: Creating Rites of Passage in Your Church," Fuller Youth Institute, June 13, 2006, http://fulleryouthinstitute.org/2006/06/through-the-zone/.

13. John Eldredge, *Wild at Heart* (Nashville: Nelson, 2001), 9.

Conclusion: Sailing for Home

1. Zephaniah 3:17, NIV.

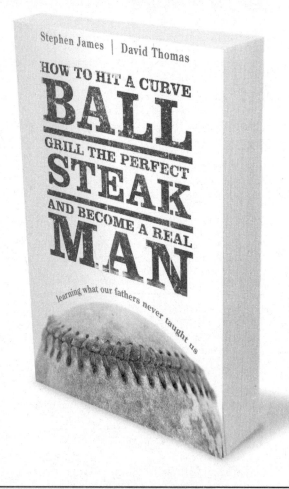
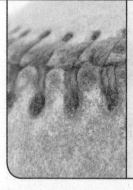